Harvard English Studies 7

Shakespeare: Aspects of Influence

HARVARD ENGLISH STUDIES 7

Shakespeare: Aspects of Influence

Edited by

G. B. Evans

Harvard University Press
Cambridge, Massachusetts
London, England
1976

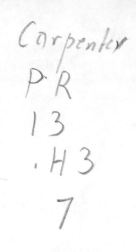
Library of Congress Cataloging in Publication Data
Main entry under title:

Shakespeare: aspects of influence.

(Harvard English studies ; 7)
1. Shakespeare, William, 1564-1616 — Influence.   2. English
literature — History and criticism — Addresses, essays, lectures.
3. American literature — History and criticism — Addresses, essays, lectures.   I.   Evans, Gwynne Blakemore.   II.   Series.
PR2965.S4   822.3'3   76-7077
ISBN 0-674-80330-2
ISBN 0-674-80331-0 pbk.

To the memory of
Alfred Bennett Harbage
(1901–1976)
this book is dedicated by his
colleagues and friends at Harvard

Preface

The central focus of this collection of essays is on some aspects of Shakespeare's influence on English and American letters from the beginning of the seventeenth century to the present day. The concept of "influence" is multifaceted, ranging from the practice of wholesale plagiarism (as when a hack like William Heminges, son of Shakespeare's close colleague John Heminges, pillaged unassimilated chunks of Shakespeare's plays to construct his unspeakably bad revenge tragedy *The Fatal Contract*) to a kind of spiritual discipleship, through which (as with Keats) Shakespeare becomes an informing vision that permeates and enriches, while it complements, a major writer's personal voice (such, at least, is the most commonly accepted view of Keat's relation to Shakespeare, but for a more tempered comment see Douglas Bush's essay in the present collection). Between such extremes many other kinds and degrees of influence may usefully be distinguished, some weighty, some comparatively trivial, but together bearing strong witness to the extraordinary generative power that Shakespeare, as poet and dramatist, has continued to wield over the course and growth of literature, language, and criticism in the western world for over three hundred and fifty years. Shakespeare is, indeed, and to a degree that even the astutely critical Ben Jonson could not have envisioned, "not of an age, but for all time."

As the title suggests, the present collection of essays attempts no systematic or chronological survey of Shakespeare's influence. To do so would require volumes, some of them already written. The accent, therefore, falls elsewhere: not on the already acknowledged scope or importance of his influence, but on a few of the many different ways that influence, as catalyst, has manifested itself in shaping, modifying, even twisting the individual talent or the popular consciousness.

G. B. E.

Contents

Shakespeare: Aspects of Influence

MORTON W. BLOOMFIELD

Quoting and Alluding:
Shakespeare in the English Language

Not marble, nor the gilded monuments
Of princes, shall outlive this powerful rhyme.

Sonnet 55

Like most aspects of his genius, Shakespeare's English has not
been neglected by scholars, although until we have a proper dictionary of Tudor English there are limits to what we can know.
The *Oxford English Dictionary* is, however, helpful if not complete or always exact,[1] and we have had and will no doubt continue to have scholarly surveys of his language from different
angles.[2] Recently, for instance, in keeping with present-day

1. "It is clear that the student of Shakespeare's vocabulary must not
place too much reliance on the *N. E. D.*, and must bear in mind that
many words and meanings of words that would appear from the columns
to be Elizabethan in origin may have entered the language at least a century earlier." (W. S. Mackie, "Shakespeare's English: And How Far It
Can Be Investigated with the Help of the *New English Dictionary*," *MLR*,
XXXI [1936], 1–10.) Among other lists, Mackie provides a list of Shakespearean words not recorded in the *NED*. Mackie's list is, as he himself
acknowledges, by no means complete.
2. On Shakespeare's English, see Helge Kökeritz, "Shakespeare's Language" in *Shakespeare: Of an Age and for All Time*, ed. C. T. Prouty
(New Haven: Shoestring Press, 1954), pp. 35–51 (stresses vocabulary);

1

tastes, Shakespeare's bawdy has had some special attention. On the whole, however, little has been done.

Shakespeare's impact on the English language has also not been completely neglected, but it is even less a favorite topic of scholars. Those studies that do exist such as Henry Bradley's brief comments in *The Making of English* and Jespersen's in *The Growth and Structure of the English Language* consist largely of lists of words and above all phrases with which Shake-

---

George Gordon, *Shakespeare's English*, SPE Tract XXIX (Oxford: Clarendon Press, 1928) (mainly interested in words); John Crowe Ransom, "On Shakespeare's Language," *Sewanee Review*, LV (1947), 181–198 (especially interested in Shakespeare's use of Latinate words); Paul A. Jorgenson, *Redeeming Shakespeare's Words* (Berkeley and Los Angeles: University of California Press, 1962) (a study of some key words); Alfred Hart, "The Growth of Shakespeare's Vocabulary," *RES*, XIX (1943), 242–254 (a chronological study of Shakespeare's vocabulary, its growth and frequency); F. P. Wilson, "Shakespeare and the Diction of Common Life," reprinted in *Shakespeare Criticism 1935–60*, ed. Anne Ridler, The World's Classics (London: Oxford University Press, 1963), pp. 90–116 (original: British Academy Shakespeare Lecture 1941, printed in *Proceedings of the British Academy* 27) (discusses Shakespeare's use of popular idiom, paronomasia, imagery, and proverbs); Hilda M. Hulme, *Explorations in Shakespeare's Language: Some Problems of Lexical Meaning in the Dramatic Text* (London: Longmans, 1962); B. Ifor Evans, *The Language of Shakespeare's Plays* (London: Methuen, 1952) (not very significant); Gladys Willcock, "Shakespeare and Elizabethan English," *Shakespeare Survey*, VII (1954), 12–24 (too general and vague): Kenneth Hudson, "Shakespeare's Use of Colloquial Language," *Shakespeare Survey*, XXIII (1970), 39–48; Vivian Salmon, "Sentence Structures in Colloquial Shakespearean English," *TPS* (1965), pp. 105–140 (rather technical, but important); Vivian Salmon, "Some Functions of Shakespearean Word-Formation," *Shakespeare Survey*, XXIII (1970), 13–26 (important): Dolores M. Burton, *Shakespeare's Grammatical Style: A Computer-Assisted Analysis of "Richard II" and "Antony and Cleopatra,"* The Don Danciger Publications Series (Austin and London: University of Texas Press, 1973) (mainly on word order and collocations); Muriel St. Clare Byrne, "The Foundations of Elizabethan Language," *Shakespeare Survey*, XVII (1964), 223–239 (rather general); M. M. Mahood, *Shakespeare's Wordplay* (London: Methuen, 1957); and Jürgen Schäfer, *Shakespeare's Stil: Germanisches and romanisches Vokabular* (Frankfurt on the Main: Athenäum, 1973) (concentrates on different functions of Germanic and Romance elements in Shakespeare's language); Randolph Quirk, "Shakespeare and the English Language," in the *The Linguist and the English Language* (London: Edward Arnold, 1974), pp. 46–64 (attempts to "establish the kind of language study that is most significant for students of Shakespeare" and is very perceptive and helpful in emphasizing Shakespeare's use of language).

speare "enriched" the English language. I should like to pursue yet another aspect of this subject, more closely related to the second than to the first subject: the impact of Shakespeare on English as representative of a common linguistic situation: what a world-shaking artistic figure can bring to his language, what the impact of a figure of such stature can be on the later history of his own language. What does the presence of a Shakespeare in the past mean to present-day users of English? I am interested in short in what one may call the internal point of view: Shakespeare *in* the English language as it evolves and changes through time. Why and how is such a figure referred to and "quoted" is my concern rather than what in particular in Shakespeare's writings is referred to and quoted. How does his impact make itself felt? What does he give in general to modern-day English?

To study the impact of a great writer on his own language and tradition is to study both an aspect of what the Germans call the *Nachleben* (post-life) of an author and the changes in the language effected by his *Nachleben*. The study of a great writer is like scanning a palimpsest in which the first text is still largely visible. The purely historical scholar attempts as far as possible to erase the traces of the interpretations and glosses superimposed on the original text, but the student of the *Nachleben* is more interested in the overwriting the original text has experienced during its existence. An important part of that *Nachleben* (though not the only part) is the use to which the author's writings have been put in language. Shakespeare lives not only because of the performing and reading of his plays and poetry but also because of his language and the special role it plays in the history of the English language. Quoting from and alluding to Shakespeare creates continually a new audience for him and adds more on to the palimpsest. If we were to undertake a quantitative study of Shakespeare's *Nachleben*[3] we would find, I'm sure, that he is resuscitated much more through the use of his language than through his plays as plays or reading experiences. Furthermore, it is only his language that makes Shakespeare

---

3. A comparison of the extent of the use of quotation and allusion by different famous writers would be most helpful in evaluating Shakespeare's influence. A good candidate for the winner could be Byron, whose letters are continuously interrupted by Shakespearean quotations (this habit of his was brought to my attention by Steven Marcus).

part of the English tradition. His plays as plays belong to the ✓
whole world, but his language alone makes him uniquely part of
the Anglo-Saxon tradition.

There are two major requirements (besides genius) necessary
if a writer is to occupy a towering position in his own tradition:
what may be called canonicity and monumentality. If Shakespeare did not occupy the place he has in the affections and beliefs of the Anglo-Saxon tradition, his usefulness as a source of
strength to our language would be much impaired. More quot-
able clichés may be taken by users of English from Pope than
from Shakespeare, yet Pope does not have the aura of genius
and established power Shakespeare has and hence cannot be
used for new purposes the way Shakespeare is or has been used.
Shakespeare is a living repository of allusions, quotations, and
language usage; Pope is not. In the English-speaking tradition,
only Shakespeare and the King James version of the Bible pos- ✓
sess this quality of linguistic potential combined with respect-
ability and basic authority. By themselves almost they create a
willing acceptability in speakers and writers of English that no
one else in English does.

The two qualities we have alluded to — canonicity and monumentality — are linked to each other, but the first primarily refers to the authoritative quality of writings and the second to the
extensive charismatic quality of text and person. By canonicity
I do not mean classicism as T. S. Eliot defines it. His *What is a
Classic*[4] defines a classic in such strict terms that perhaps only
Virgil's and Dante's masterpieces would qualify. Shakespeare
certainly does not. I have no objections to calling Shakespeare a
classic, but I am not referring to the qualities that make him so
when I speak of his canonicity. By canonicity I mean possessing
a certain authority which arises from a text or group of related
texts which is generally accepted by a culture so that it may be
appealed to for support as a final court of authority.

Did the canonicity come because of the innate power of

4. *Delivered before the Virgil Society on the 16th of October 1944*
(London: Faber and Faber, 1945). To Eliot the literature of Europe
from Homer on "has a simultaneous existence and composes a simultaneous order." (*The Sacred Wood*, London: Methuen, 1934, p. 42).
Shakespeare, however, does not occupy a very prominent place in that
order.

Shakespeare's thought, ingenuity, and language or did the innate power come from the canonicity? For the Bible, the issue of the origin of its canonicity creates no problem. The Bible claims to be the word of God Himself and carries its own authentication so to speak. The formal establishment of a Biblical canon by rabbinic or episcopal authority only gave a human seal to what claimed to be divine authority.

With Shakespeare the problem is more complicated. However, as with most questions of this kind, each contributed to the other. The innate ability created the fame and the fame fed his reputation. Each continued to spur and explain the other as the various facets of Shakespeare's genius gradually unfolded themselves in time.

His power, his "honey tongue," as many of his contemporaries and close successors testify, was almost immediately recognized. In 1595 John Weever speaks of "honie-tong'd Shakespeare" and Thomas Edwardes of "his bewitching pen." Richard Barnfield in 1598 writes of Shakespeare's "honey-flowing vaine." Somewhat later Thomas Heywood in *The Hierarchie of the Blessed Angells* (1635), book IV (p. 206), praises "Mellifluous Shakespeare, whose inchanting Quill / Commanded Mirth or Passion, was but Will." As Gladys D. Willcock writes "there can be no doubt that the impact of Shakespeare on those who could see his plays while his own fellow-actors were still on the boards left the impression of Nature herself at work, and . . . it is interesting to note the predominating extent to which this impression is translated into terms of language: 'gentle expression,' 'easie numbers,' 'woodnotes,' etc." [5]

Monumentality is a more difficult concept to define. A monument is overwhelming. It is a sign detached from its designation. It serves the pride of a nation as a flag does. It does not exude authority, but it concretizes in itself all the pride one takes in one's own people. It can lift the heart and it symbolizes durability. It is the materialization of that gratitude and pride which are

5. "Shakespeare and Elizabethan English," p. 13. The quotations in this paragraph are taken from volume I of *The Shakespeare Allusion-Book: A Collection of Allusions to Shakespeare from 1591–1700*, 2 vols., originally compiled by C. M. Ingleby and others, reedited, revised, and rearranged by John Munro (1909), and reissued with a preface by Sir Edmund Chambers (London: Oxford University Press, 1932).

extremely evanescent though real feelings. All texts which persist in a nation's consciousness (not just scholarly consciousness) have monumentality to some extent. Shakespeare is the monument par excellence in the Anglo-Saxon's consciousness of his own culture. The work itself gets separated from its creator and assumes new dimensions.[6]

By the early seventeenth century, English badly needed a canonical and monumental literary figure. Chaucer was hard to read and unpoetical in meter to Elizabethan ears. Lydgate's and Gower's defects were pretty clear. Speakers of English spoke, in Elizabethan and Jacobean times, a minor language on the outskirts of Europe, with an impact something like that of Icelandic today. Like all speakers of minor languages, the English felt a sense of inferiority about their language in spite of their boasting comments. Besides Englishmen and some Scots and Irish, who would want to learn it? True there were Englishmen of international reputation, but they could be read in Latin or occasionally in French. One did not need to learn English to read Bede, Duns Scotus, Ockham, Bradwardine, Sir Thomas More, William Harvey, nor later even Newton. As Edmund Waller writes:

> But who can hope his lines should long
> Last in a daily changing tongue?
> Poets that lasting marble seek,
> Must carve in Latin, or in Greek;
> We write in sand, our language grows,
> And, like the tide, our work o'erflows.[7]

We see in various comments on English by Englishmen in the sixteenth, seventeenth, and even early eighteenth centuries that feeling of inferiority towards, combined with a love of, their own language that was not to disappear until the mid- and late eighteenth century when it became clear to Europe that Englishmen

6. See Edward Said's "An Ethics of Language," *Diacritics*, Summer 1974, which is mainly devoted to explicating and interpreting Foucault, during the course of which he discusses the notion of monumentality in Valéry and Foucault. I am indebted to Said for some of my notions of monumentality.

7. "Of English Verse," *Poems*, ed. G. Thorn Drury (London, 1893), pp. 197–198.

wrote things well worth reading in their own language. Shakespeare was a godsend. When Germany discovered him in the eighteenth century and, soon after, the rest of Europe, he became the king of English as well as of modern dramatic literature. Political expansion did the rest.

Canonicity and monumentality in the senses in which I am using the words imply acceptance by the general public in a special way. The writer or book must be considered in a class by itself and must bear a kind of authenticity and power that can be invoked and that needs no proof or justification. Pope and Donne are great poets, but they are not well known outside of literary and humanistic circles in the non-student world. They do not have canonicity and monumentality as Shakespeare does. A good example of how Shakespeare (and practically nothing else in English except the Bible) can be used for his canonicity and monumentality and which beautifully illustrates his unique place may be found in the *New York Times* of September 13, 1975, where an article by Edward F. Murphy entitled "The Bard; Losing that Pound of Flesh" may be found. It consists wholly of quotations from Shakespeare such as the following: "I have gained" (*Antony and Cleopatra*, II.vi); "O that this too solid flesh would melt" (*Hamlet*, I.ii); "My bosom is full" (*Tewlfth Night*, II.i); "A dish of skim milk" (*Henry IV*, II.iii); "O Bottom, thou art changed" (*A Midsummer Night's Dream*, III.i) and ending with "All losses are restored" (*Sonnet* 30). Even the Bible can't be used in this fashion.

Shakespeare is more satisfactory as a canonical and monumental text than the Bible because he is uniquely English and because he is *not* the word of God. As we shall shortly see, one of the pleasures of having a Shakespeare in one's language lineage is that one can use him both to give allegiance to the past and at the same time to suggest one's superiority to it by placing and using him as one wishes. Even if Shakespeare is hated by rebels against authority for his "dead hand," they will need him, just as we need dirty words to be available when necessary even if they are never or rarely used.

Shakespeare's value for one's language and tradition also lies in his pastness. Canonicity and monumentality demand pastness, and the longer the better. As Shakespeare recedes in time, he becomes even more valuable as a canonical and monumental figure. It is important to come after Shakespeare so that he can be properly pillaged. The past is both real and unreal and both aspects can be used. The past is there to be translated into the present and Shakespeare guarantees its worth.

Shakespeare, then, filled a need in various ways. He helped to give Englishmen a sense of security and pride in their own language. He was their canonical and monumental figure; and as time went on, much to their pleasure, the rest of the world gradually agreed with them, even if there were some recalcitrants like Voltaire and Shaw.

In some ways Shakespeare's English functions as the secular equivalent of what Christine Mohrmann calls a sacred and hieratic language, applying these terms to liturgical Latin. Since she has written (in 1957),[8] Latin itself has all but disappeared from the Mass so that the secrets of the Eucharist can be more open to all men even at the cost of less mystery.

With the increasing disappearance of the hieratic and sacred in life and language, great vernacular writers who are sufficiently removed in time from us so as to give us a sense of distance and dignity take on some of their functions. They are not perfect substitutes as they lack the divine imperatives and a sense of the numinous, but they can do in a pinch. Like hieratic languages, Shakespeare's text can provide fresh but powerful ways of saying new and exciting things, or if necessary, another synonymous way of saying things already said. Liturgical Latin tried to preserve the sacredness of ecclesiastical Greek by keeping some difficult Greek words in its missal and breviary. These served as a "vinculum unitatis," as Professor Mohrmann puts it, to the sacred past. So quotations of canonical and monumental writers in modern times help in some contexts to give a sense of the hieratic so missing in modern life.

Furthermore, like hieratic languages, Shakespearean English can be parodied to relieve the sense of tension too much monumentality and canonicity generate. Parody is the important other side of the sacred coin, and Shakespeare's language can be and is constantly parodied.

8. See her *Liturgical Latin: Its Origins and Character, Three Lectures* (Washington: Catholic University of America, 1957).

Shakespeare lives to the world as a purveyor of profound entertainment in dramatic form, in scenes and characters which are memorable, presenting to those who seek them exempla and stories. Shakespeare lives to the Anglo-Saxon world in these ways, of course, but also in another way — as a linguistic resource of extraordinary power. He does not live to that world merely as a writer of plays sometimes read and even more rarely seen. He also lives as an authoritative language figure. He gives us an almost endless collection of allusion and quotation on which we can draw. And he provides us with a syntax bank, a store of new and exciting ways to put words together. The supply of syntax and vocabulary he provides us with is a rich gift which only English speakers can use with any frequency. He is available as background for anyone who wishes to use him and even to those who use him unconsciously.

It may seem that Shakespeare's greatest role here is not to provide the clichés which again and again recur, but rather to be a linguistic resource on which one can draw in original fashion. To some extent this summation is true, but also his clichés, his "to be or not to be," "ripeness is all," "lend me your ears," "all the world's a stage," provide a certain unique advantage. The less familiar phrases may delight a few literati (not too many these days) even if they are "caviar to the general." It is a pleasure to the decoder to recognize that "wailful sonnets," for instance, comes from Shakespeare's *The Two Gentlemen of Verona*, or that "indistinct as water is in water" from *Antony and Cleopatra*, and to admire or envy the users of those phrases. However, the well-worn phrases also provide occasions for creative use when one discovers a new side to them or uses them in an original and satisfying way. They may be like much used words which may also be given new and unexpected meanings. They can be barely hinted at and get some response. As Baudelaire writes (though with some irony), "Existe-t-il . . . quelque chose de plus charmant, de plus fertile et d'une nature plus postivement excitante que 'le lieu commun?' " [9] Commonplaces and trite phrases have their uses too.

9. *"Salon de 1859"*, *Curiosités esthètiques* in *Oeuvres complètes*, ed. Jacques Crepet (Paris: 1923), p. 25. The suggestive element in the use of the cliché allusion is discussed perceptively by Vladimir Jankéle-

However, even more, in order for Shakespeare to exercise a large part of his role, it is necessary that he be recognized as Shakespeare. To draw on him linguistically from not generally recognized lines defeats in part his public function. To the German bourgeois who used to quote Goethe and Schiller to his family around the Sunday table, it is important not only that they understand the quotation but that they recognize it as Goethe's or Schiller's. So too with Shakespeare for the general. The allusion of the speaker or writer must be recognized fairly quickly as Shakespeare or fall flat or make no difference. Canonicity and monumentality must not be wasted. Even prefixing the remark with "As Shakespeare's says" is not as satisfactory as instantaneous recognition in the decoder. But it will do in a pinch.

However, the situation is even more complex, for it is often the case that the cliché is not recognized as from Shakespeare. Many popular sayings from Shakespeare are so widely known that they are not recognized as from the master. We all know about the old lady who on seeing *Hamlet* complained it was all made up of quotations. Certain Shakespearean quotations even if not recognized as Shakespeare's have acquired a canonicity and monumentality themselves as anonymous sayings.

When Shakespeare is quoted or alluded to in a written context, then, the desire that the phrase be recognized becomes less important. Allusion in journalism and literature is part of what Kristeva[10] calls "intertextuality." A literary work not only presents ideas and form, but also suggests or alludes to those of other writers and literary traditions. Between the lines of a piece of writing, other writers and works are suggested by its genre, language, ideas, characters, and plot (if they are present). It drags its literary past with it. Shakespeare functions heavily in English intertextuality. If one prefers, one can avoid such a

---

vitch in *L'Ironie* (Paris: Alcan, 1936), pp. 84ff. ("Quant à l'allusion proprement dite, elle n' est autre chose que la réticence . . . une évocation ou conduction spirituelle," p. 87.)

10. See her Σημειωτική: *Recherches pour une sémanalyse* (Paris: Seuil, 1969), p. 255, where she writes, "le signifié poétique renvoie à des signifiés discursifs autres, de sorte que dans l'énoncé poétique plusieurs autres discours sont lisibles. Il se crée ainsi autour du signifié poétique, un espace textuel multiple dont les elements sont susceptibles d'être appliqués dans le texte poétique concret."

intertextualidad
es más fuerte

phrase and say he is suggested in more varied ways and more
frequently in English writings than any other writer.

In any case, Shakespeare's language, as well as his ideas,
characters, and plots, is a major part of his *Nachleben* and is
heavily drawn on by English speakers both in oral and written
contexts. He is a major linguistic resource to users of English.
We are born into a language; we do not choose it. Our language
is largely an anonymous gift of the past. But we do have a few
figures who rise out of this anonymous mass, and these are
mainly our major (and occasionally our minor) writers. Shakespeare is certainly the greatest of these and has as his only com-
petitors the translators of the Bible whom King James brought together and the Hebrew writers who inspired them.

Quotations and allusions are words and concepts wrenched
from their natal context and put into a new and later context. To
this extent, then, quotations and allusions are original. When we
use "absent thee from felicity awhile" in a new verbal and life
situation, we not only support or characterize our comment or
interpretation, we bring Shakespeare again to life in another
context and extend his power. When a quotation or allusion is
used creatively it lives again and brings a new dimension to an
old phrase or situation. This process, as we have stated, goes on
continually even when we use ordinary words. "Broadcast" provides a good example. It was a beautiful old English word which
was moribund until the invention of the radio when it took on a
new life and a new extension of meaning.

Michael Walzer in a recent lecture said that in the humanities
we do not have an authoritative method but we do have authorities. We live on authorities in different ways, and one way is to
quote them in different contexts and spread their power abroad.
We need Shakespeare and others like him to help give an historical dimension to our arguments, expositions, and descriptions,
linking ourselves with the past to recreate it for present use. The
creative use of older quotations and allusions serves to link us,
or to make us think we are linked, with the ancient wisdom of
tradition and make it usable for today and tmorrow. It is a raid
on the past to capture part of it with its aura of authenticity and
authority and bring it back alive. Even those who claim to despise the past will make use of it for support if it can be so used.

There are revolutionaries who look backward as well as those who look forward or look backward so that they may recreate a mythical future.

We have so far assumed that quoting and alluding are basically the same activity from our point of view and in general this assumption is true. The use of allusions parallels in large measure the use of quotations. They need not, however, be verbal allusions, although many are. They can be used to recall a scene or character or historical event or foreign words or phrases or even a well-known quotation. Usually more is required of a listener with an allusion than with a quotation. If he misses the fact that he is being quoted at, he will still or often get the point. However, the essence of the allusion is that it be recognized.

There are in writing typographical signs, quotation marks, to indicate quotations. Allusions bear no such indication. When quotations are used orally, however, they may easily be missed unless they are accompanied by phrases like "As X says."

A style is called allusive if it is filled with allusions and often such styles require much knowledge to appreciate or even to understand. It flatters more if an allusion is understood than if a quotation is. Allusions are mainly used for the same reasons quotations are and may, as we have done above, be considered together. However, the one basic difference, to stress the point again, is that an allusion is not necessarily tied to one text nor to a verbal construct but may range freely over various texts and various concepts.

I think we may say that quoting and alluding have at least six functions: (1) Self-gratifying and self-aggrandizing and even more self-healing, (2) archaizing, (3) gaining authority, (4) distancing, (5) bringing aesthetic pleasure and being witty, and (6) bridging the past to the present and the present to the future.

(1) Traditionally, we use quotations as Carl van Doren puts it in his introduction to the *Oxford Book of Quotations* (1941) to "derive authority from masters who appear to have found the right words once and for all. A sudden apt quotation may raise a laugh, end a debate, or give the quoter a new standing as a wit. A writer who quotes can enrich his actual matter and his apparent style." This statement sums up the simple and practical

view of quoting. You quote to shine in company. It will help you make good and be a success. Carl van Doren also recognizes that quoting provides one with an escape from the prison of one's own language customs. Needless to say, quoting and alluding can be misused and if so, succeed in vulgarizing the whole procedure. One can gain disdain rather than glory.

No doubt these reasons often prevail acknowledged or unacknowledged, but quoting does more for the psyche than feed dreams of social glory. It may heal or move to heal. Such a habit can be satisfying on a more profound level about which little can perhaps be said. Herbert Leibowitz comes close to it when speaking of Edward Dahlberg; he writes, "The quotations from his favorite authors, his authoritative geographers of the spirit, are his lost father giving voice to, and glossing, the text of his torn life." [11]

(2) The second function needs little comment. Frequently, archaisms create a conscious poetic or artistic foregrounding. Ancient quotation, like archaic diction, not only helps the self-referential function of verbal art but also suggests tradition, wisdom, and age, which may help the dignity of the work and suggest sublimity and measured judgment when needed. Not all quotations are from ancient sources, but a quotation or allusion must always come from another source. With Shakespeare we do have the advantage of seriously archaizing, but not every source of quotations or allusions gives us the advantage or illusion of raiding the distant past.

Jespersen makes the point of the use of archaisms for foregrounding when he writes "Words that are too well-known and too often used do not call up such vivid images as words less familiar. This is one of the reasons that impel poets to use archaic words; they are 'new' just on account of their being old, and yet they are not so utterly unknown as to be unintelligible." [12]

We can also use quotations and allusions anachronistically when we put into the mouths of figures of the past sayings or

11. "Stoking the Oedipal Furnace: Edward Dahlberg's *Because I Was Flesh*," *The American Scholar*, XLIV (1975), p. 483.
12. "Shakespeare and the Language of Poetry," *Growth and Structure of the English Language*, 9th ed. (Oxford: Blackwell, 1958), p. 214.

events which were only uttered or which only occurred later. If we have Julius Caesar quoting "Take physic, pomp," we are using quotations anachronistically; or an event can be anachronistically used as when Shakespeare has a chiming clock in *Julius Caesar*. Anachronisms need a future to become anachronistic and hence we must move into the past to use them from a more recent past. Archaisims only need the simple past. They are hence much more common than anachronisms.

(3 & 4) Authority and distancing are also gained by judicious use of quotation and allusion. Authority is particularly linked with the notion of canonicity, which I believe lies behind much of Shakespeare's appeal as a quotation and allusion resource. Few if anyone else (excepting always the English Bible) can give the sense of authority that Shakespeare affords. However, it must be remembered that any recognizable or denoted quotation or allusion gives some kind of authority. Among other things, the straightforward use of quotations for support or strengthening says that at least one other person in the universe agrees with me, that this is not just my opinion. The more status or canonicity the source has, the more authority the reference brings.

Distancing also benefits from the use of authority and canonicity. The distinguished support removes the quoter or alluder from the argument to some extent. What he says involves not only the arguer or observer but also someone else of great authority. It is not only I who am involved in writing this, the writer seems to say, but someone else who is not immediately involved. This sense helps to forward the argument. The speaker or writer is removed from the heat of battle, if only for the moment.

But as with almost all things, the overuse of quotation and allusion can increase an awareness of the weakness of an argument or case. By appealing to authority too much, authority itself becomes less authoritative and its own position is undermined.

(5) The goal of the use of quotations and allusions is often aesthetic pleasure and wit. They can and often do contribute to the elegance of a speech or piece of writing. Slight shifts and puns can be witty and pleasing, like Max Beerbohm's statement that "he sold his birthright for a pot of message." The creative

use of quotations gives a kind of pleasure for its own sake. Walter Benjamin is supposed to have longed to write a work made up completely of quotations, like the Virgilian centos of the late classical period. Or much more recently, like Norman O. Brown's *Closing Time*, made up in large measure of quotations from Vico and Joyce's *Finnegans Wake*.[13] The writer of a cento creates at secondhand his work. If it is successful, his achievement is somewhat like that of an electronic engineer who puts together from many recorded performances of the same work the perfect recording of a piece of music, or the editor who puts together the perfect Shakespearean folio out of many extant folios by selective reproduction. The director of a play may make a greater play out of his direction than the text itself seems to offer. So at second level, a cento writer creates, or hopes to create, something greater and beyond the great writing he uses. Ezra Pound's *Cantos* are not strictly speaking centos, but they often come close to being so.

The romantic dream of complete self-expression and the complete sovereignty of a self who is forced to use a public language can get its revenge on the world by using the language of others to create one's own language. These dreams free the dreamers from the "domination" of culture and tradition by using them (which alas you must) completely in the dreamer's own way. You force the past to obey you by using once used phrases or sentences in a completely new way and break the bonds of tradition. By perpetual quotation, you are changing the fixity of the past and revealing one of its numerous faces which has until now remained hidden. The use of the past by modern writers such as Eliot, Joyce, and Pound may well be somewhat motivated by these wishes.

(6) Finally, by using quotation and allusion, one bridges the

13. (New York: Random House, 1973). Other sources used by Brown include George Steiner, Emerson, Shakespeare, Owen Barfield, Foucault, as well as the author himself. The popularity of the epigram, sentential, proverb, aphorism, and quotation as a method of writing and expressing oneself and as a method of teaching has never been properly studied. It begins for the West with the Book of Proverbs and continues with collections of proverbs in the Middle Ages, with La Rochefoucault, Brunetière, Lichtenberg, Schopenhauer, Nietzsche, and down to Benjamin and Horkheimer to mention only a few names.

distance between past and present and to some extent between present and future. All quoting or alluding draws on the past, often the deep past. By using quotation in a normal manner, we are both bowing to the past and at the same time surpassing it in some way. In yet another sense, past and present come together in using, and quoting from, the great literature, above all the canonical and monumental literature of the past whereby the union of a man with a great man in the past is acheved. Thoreau puts this point very well: "The oldest Egyptian or Hindoo philosopher raised a corner of the veil from the statue of the divinity; and still the trembling robe remains raised, and I gaze upon as fresh a glory as he did, since it was I in him that was then so bold, and it is he in me that now reviews the vision." [14] The past is thus eternally relevant or seems to be.

When Shakespeare used an apt phrase to sum up or characterize a situation or person, like "our little life is rounded with a sleep," he created it for that particular purpose. By taking it out of context in a Shakespearean play and using it in another, a contemporary context, we are both bringing the past into the present and the present into the past. We cross a boundary in time though not in language. Time is being ignored and to some extent annihilated. The use of the past in the present enables us to redo or even undo to some extent that past. We both archaize and contemporize at the same time. We are claiming the past for ourselves, contributing to the imperialism of the present.

A whole method of bringing the past into the present and the present into the past is what we might call the exegetical or hermeneutical method. Here quotations and allusions are used interpretatively or reinterpretatively, not just for descriptive or argumentative purposes. The classic example of this procedure is to be found in law treatises and legal debate. The continuous use of earlier decisions or law in the application to new situations evokes continuity and change. We should do things today thus, because they were done this way in the past, we are saying as we argue or write a law brief. Legal, scriptural, and even scholarly exegesis is the ideal pattern of all uses of quotation to bridge past and present and becomes an exemplar of what can be done

14. *Walden,* chap. 3.

in this way. The law, the scripture, and Shakespeare (or any Shakespeare) are each being extended and being kept relevant by continuous contemporary use. By quoting we are not only making the old modern, but we are also making the modern old.[15]

Louis Milic[16] traces learnedly the use and reuse of an allusion (or topos) in the notion of "violets" springing from a grave in Tennyson's "And his ashes may be made / The violet of his native land" (from *In Memoriam*) which picks up Shakespeare's "And from her fair and unpolluted flesh / May violets spring" (*Hamlet*, V.i.263–264). This idea may go back to Persius' *First Satire*. If we wish to go further or not limit the flowers to violets, many more allusions besides this sample may be brought in.

Allusions and quotations may also be played with. James Joyce's *Finnegans Wake* is a monument of both activities and indeed of allusions in allusions and quotations on quotations. Slight deformation of both can give much delight and amusement. Much, however, is lost, since the more arcane the reference the fewer the people who can enjoy it even if the writer himself can enjoy his own wit and learning. An audience helps, though.

15. See the interesting recent book by Roland Posner, *Theorie des Kommentierens: Eine Grundlagenstudie zur Semantik und Pragmatik*, Linguistische Forschungen IV (Frankfurt on the Main: Athenäum, 1972). Many of these functions of quotations are summed up by Jean Weisgerber in "The Use of Quotations in Recent Literature," *CL*, XXII (1970), 45, when he writes: "Quotations constitute the epitome of a perennial and inexhaustible heritage, a way of making oneself understood or of arresting attention, an exhortation to learn and to create, and the irrefutable evidence of our concern with a tradition, which we try not so much to imitate as to reshape and reinterpret." Weisgerber attempts to complement and broaden Hermann Meyer, *Das Zitat in der Erzählkunst, zur Geschichte und Poetik des europaischen Romans* (Stuttgart: Metzler, 1961; 2nd ed., 1967). Both of these works though interesting on the subject of the use of quotations in general are primarily concerned with the use and role of quotations in narrative and stress the difference between borrowings and adaptations. Weisgerber is interested, furthermore, in the psychological reasons for quoting in a literary context.

16. See his delightful little essay on "Allusion: Using Other Men's Flowers" in *The Unicorn*, 5 (Newsletter of the Department of English, The Cleveland State University) of May 1974. I am indebted to this essay for several of the following ideas.

A canon of authorities or even authorities can help in tracking down an allusion or quotation. An established culture usually has its canonical resources, not all of whom are necessarily in that culture's language. Latin and Greek writers served for the learned in that capacity in Western culture down almost to our time. Traditions like the Hungarian, whose canonical figures, Petöfi and Madach, can hardly have world acclaim, made much of Latin as a hieratic and monumental language to supplement its own. The passing of Latin as an international language has affected Hungarian culture. French too served traditions such as the Russian and Levantine in this capacity until their own literary and linguistic traditions became more widely accepted.

In studying a tradition or culture the network of allusions and quotations is enormously complex. In a major sense, the topoi Ernst Curtius drew our attention to in the forties are common allusions embedded in language and used again and again, often in the same metaphors and syntax. In fact, one might say that if we define allusions broadly enough, one of the major functions of humanistic scholarship is to trace and track down allusions, thereby building a network through time.[17]

There are some remarkable similarities between using quotations and allusions, and translation. Both attempt to bring the past into the present, one by crossing a language and time barrier, the other by crossing only the time barrier.[18] Both are also exegetical and renewing activities. Both rest upon reinterpretation and contribute to the *Nachleben* of their source text.

In one sense, the original author may be thought of as quoting himself as he writes (or speaks). There are those who have argued that thinking is internal dialogue.[19] If this is so, one is in some sense continually quoting oneself in writing or speaking. One is reminded of the old Irish lady who, on being asked what she thought, said "How do I know what I think until I hear what I say."

17. See George Steiner, *After Babel: Aspects of Language and Translation* (New York: Oxford University Press, 1975), pp. 424 ff.

18. "Every act of translation except simultaneous translation as between earphones, is a transfer from a past to a present" (George Steiner, *After Babel*, p. 334). I am indebted to this stimulating book for some of my ideas in this section.

19. See for instance Plato, *Theaetetus*, 189E–190A and *Sophist*, 263E.

Although in some ways, as Steiner suggests,[20] Shakespeare by his dominating presence may have been and still is a possible weakness to the English tradition because he has by his work determined what is the "proper" way in our tradition to express the sublime and elevated, he is, as far as the English language is concerned, basically a source of strength, a fountain of language.[21] His poetry, his words, his syntax are there for all to use, but he also affected English in ways not recognized — he stretched creatively the range of meaning of many English words. When we "cudgel our brains," "fall to blows," or "breathe our last," we are indebted to Shakespeare. When we use certain words in other parts of speech (conversion it is called), when we use certain compounds, he is again on our lips. Like all great poets of one's own language he is a resource. But he is a special resource, the resource par excellence because he is Shakespeare. He is part of an English speaker's grammatical and lexical competence. Although our use of him is often unconscious, it is nonetheless there. He can be used to delight and to strengthen, to gain distance or intimacy, to subject oneself to authority and at the same time to master authority, and to participate in the on-going linguistic tradition to which we belong.

Vivian Salmon makes the interesting point that Elizabethan English is a dead language, in some ways even deader than classical languages. She writes, "When analyzing Elizabethan English, we may profit by the fact that we are dealing with a language which although dead in the sense that it has no living speakers (and not even, like Latin and Greek, living writers) is alive in the sense that it is still partially encodable in terms of our own language; and since our grammatical systems overlap, we may use native intuition to deduce forms where evidence in the corpus is totally lacking." [22] As an investigator of Shake-

20. See *After Babel*, pp. 366–367. Among other things, Steiner there writes, "A Shakespearean presence seems to consume certain energies of form and perception through its own finality." One can argue, as some have argued, that the English Bible has also had its limiting effect on English prose style.

21. "Let us regard Shakespeare as a fountain of language, from which was to flow and is yet to flow our peculiar English literature" (John Crowe Ransom, "On Shakespeare's Language," p. 181).

22. Vivian Salmon, "Sentence Structures in Colloquial Shakespearean English," *TPS* (1965), 109.

speare's English, Salmon must be concerned with this problem. But from the point of view of a student of Shakespeare's impact on our language, it is clear that his language is still very much alive. His monumentality and canonicity give him a continuing presence in our midst. He keeps Elizabethan English alive and enables it to operate still on our language — to control, to extend, and to fascinate. He is in short a treasure as long as English is spoken.[23]

23. I wish to acknowledge with thanks suggestions, some of which have proved very helpful, from Siegfried Wenzel and Robert Roy Edwards.

CYRUS HOY

Shakespeare and the Drama of His Time

To consider Shakespeare's influence on the dramatists who were contemporary with him and who succeeded him in the Jacobean and Caroline theater is to encounter a critical paradox. Traces of his influence can be found almost anywhere one looks in the drama of the first half of the seventeenth century, but because his influence resides in imitation of language or character types or plot details and never genuinely informs the spirit of a play, it is not finally important. The result is that Shakespeare has no really determining effect on the direction drama takes before 1642, and yet the drama of the period is inconceivable without him. The critical anomaly that is here will be the subject of this essay.

As amply demonstrated in a number of critical assessments and scholarly compilations,[1] virtually every dramatist from the 1590s to the closing of the theaters borrows a phrase or imitates details of situation or characterization from Shakespeare at one time or another. One of the earliest to take notice of his work and to be affected by it was Marston. The very striking parallels between Marston's *Antonio's Revenge* and *Hamlet* can probably never be satisfactorily accounted for, given the uncer-

1. A recent study is David L. Frost's *The School of Shakespeare* (Cambridge: Cambridge University Press, 1968), which contains a useful bibliography.

tainty that surrounds the dates of both plays. Such evidence as
exists seems to suggest that *Antonio's Revenge* (c. 1599–1600)
predates Shakespeare's *Hamlet* (c. 1600–1601) by a year or so.
The most recent editor of *Antonio's Revenge* has noted that, for
all the very prominent structural similarities between the two
plays, there is an "astonishing lack of verbal correspondence"
between them.[2] The most likely explanation is that *Antonio's
Revenge* draws its similarities to the Shakespearean *Hamlet* from
its imitation of a pre-Shakespearean *Hamlet*. The relation of
Hamlet to Marston's *Malcontent* (which most probably dates
from c. 1602–1603) is a good deal clearer.

Given Marston's preoccupation in his nondramatic satires
with the personna of the humane spirit made malcontent by the
spectacle of human folly and vice, it must have seemed only a
step from Hamlet's antic disposition to Malevole's bitter railing.
Each protagonist occupies a comparable position in the design of
his play: the royal figure whose state has been usurped and who
lingers on at court biding his time for revenge. Toward the
usurper, Malevole displays a Hamlet-like ferocity in his de-
termination that his revenge will extend not only to his victim's
body but will also involve his soul:

> The heart's disquiet is revenge most deep:
> He that gets blood, the life of flesh but spills,
> But he that breaks heart's peace, the dear soul kills.
> (*The Malcontent,* I.iii.155–157)[3]

And the usurper, Pietro, is plagued even as Claudius is by a
guilty conscience. In the corrupt court, Malevole has one confi-
dant whom he can trust, Celso, whom he addresses in the accents of Hamlet to Horatio ("I tell thee, Celso, I have ever
found / Thy breast most far from shifting cowardice / And fear-
ful baseness" — III.iii.13–15; cf. *Hamlet*, III.ii.54–55).[4] At the

2. G. K. Hunter, ed., *Antonio's Revenge* (Lincoln: University of
Nebraska Press, 1965), p. xix.
3. Quotations from *The Malcontent* are from the text edited by
Martin Wine in the Regents Renaissance Drama Series (Lincoln: Uni-
versity of Nebraska Press, 1965).
4. All quotations from Shakespeare are from the text of the *Riverside
Shakespeare*, ed. G. Blakemore Evans and others (Boston: Houghton
Mifflin Co., 1974).

other extreme of trust is the old, time-serving courtier Bilioso whom Malevole taunts with a shrillness reminiscent of Hamlet's scenes with Polonius. In the course of a confidential exchange between Malevole and Celso, Bilioso enters and, according to the stage direction, "Malevole shifteth his speech" (I.iv.43.1), even as Hamlet does when he tells Horatio "I must be idle" as the members of the court enter to attend the play (*Hamlet*, III. ii.90). Bilioso comes on announcing "I can tell you strange news" (I.iv.50), and Polonius interrupts Hamlet's meeting with Rosencrantz and Guildenstern to report "My lord, I have news to tell you" (*Hamlet*, II.ii.389). The language of Shakespeare's play comes in for a certain amount of parody.[5] Hamlet's famous passage beginning "What a piece of work is a man" and ending "Man delights not me — nor women neither" (II.ii.303–309) is burlesqued in the soliloquy in which *The Malcontent*'s Machiavellian villain, Mendoza, gives vent specifically to his delight in women:

> Sweet women, most sweet ladies, nay, angels! By heaven, he is more accursed than a devil that hates you, or is hated by you, and happier than a god that loves you, or is beloved by you. . . . How imperiously chaste is your most modest face! But, O, how full of ravishing attraction is your pretty, petulant, languishing, lasciviously composed countenance! . . . In body how delicate, in soul how witty, in discourse how pregnant, in life how wary, in favors how judicious, in day how sociable, and in night how — O pleasure unutterable!
>
> (I.v.33–47)

Later in the play, Malevole greets Mendoza with words drawn from the scene following Hamlet's interview with the Ghost: "Illo, ho, ho, ho! art there, old truepenny?" (III.iii.37; cf. *Hamlet*, I.v.115–116, 150). Yet, for all the fact that Marston clearly had his eye on Shakespeare's tragedy while composing his tragicomedy, it is equally clear that the moral and metaphysical profundities of *Hamlet* either escaped him or failed to interest him.

5. In fact, Marston seems to have had a fondness for parodying *Hamlet*. He does so again in his share of *Eastward Ho* (written in collaboration with Jonson and Chapman); see the Herford and Simpson edition of Ben Jonson, ix, 641 and 643 (where Marston's parody of a famous line from *Richard III* is also noted).

The protagonist of each play exhibits a notable disenchantment
with his world, but since in the case of Malevole the disenchantment is but an aspect of his role of railing malcontent —
assumed for a purpose (getting back his dukedom) and set aside
when the purpose is accomplished — such pronouncements on
the corruption of the world and the deceit of man as *The Malcontent* issues are bound to seem facile and tendentious. Marston's practice of developing hints from Shakespeare in most
un-Shakespearean contexts is typical of succeeding dramatists
throughout the Jacobean and Caroline periods.

Nothing in *Hamlet* seems to have made a deeper impression
on contemporary dramatists than the protagonist's musings over
the skulls which the grave-digger so casually disinters: "That
skull had a tongue in it, and could sing once . . . This might be
the pate of a politician . . . Why may not that be the skull of a
lawyer? . . . This fellow might be in 's time a great buyer of land,
with his statutes, his recognizances, his fines . . . Is this the fine
of his fines, and the recovery of his recoveries, to have his fine
pate full of fine dirt?" (V.i.75–108). In Dekker and Middleton's
Honest Whore (1604), the protagonist, plunged in melancholy
at the death (as he believes) of his beloved, contemplates first
her picture and then turns to look upon a skull which has been
placed beside it:

> Whats here?
> Perhaps this shrewd pate was mine enimies:
> Las! say it were: I need not feare him now:
> For all his braues, his contumelious breath,
> His frownes (tho dagger-pointed) all his plot,
> (Tho 'nere so mischieuous) his Italian pilles,
> His quarrels, and (that common fence) his law,
> See, see, they're all eaten out; here's not left one;
> How cleane they're pickt away! to the bare bone!
>   (*The Honest Whore*, part I, IV.i.55–63)[6]

Hamlet's grim comment on the vanity of painted faces ("Now
get you to my lady's chamber, and tell her, let her paint an inch
thick, to this favor she must come") is developed. Hippolito in

    6. Quotations from *The Honest Whore*, part I, are from the text edited
by Fredson Bowers for volume II of his edition of *The Dramatic Works
of Thomas Dekker* (Cambridge: Cambridge University Press, 1964).

The Honest Whore addresses first the painted picture of his beloved: "these coulours / In time kissing but ayre, will be kist off"; then turning to the skull, he continues:

> But heres a fellow; that which he layes on,
> Till doomes day, alters not complexion.
> Death's the best Painter then:
>
> (IV.i.81–83)

The scene is probably the work of Middleton, who may also be responsible for the echo of the passage in *The Revenger's Tragedy*, where Vendice contemplates the skull of his murdered mistress: "Here's a cheek keeps her color, let the wind go whistle" (III.v.60).[7] In Tourneur's *Atheist's Tragedy*, Charlemont speculates in the manner of Hamlet on the worldly condition of the inhabitants of sundry graves: "This graue. — Perhappes th' inhabitant was in his life time the possessour of his owne desires . . . And there. — / In that graue lies another. He (perhaps) / Was in his life as full of miserie / As this of happinesse. And here's an end / Of both. Now both their states are equall" (IV.iii).[8]

There is no more impressive tribute to Shakespeare's genius than the speed with which his contemporaries and successors writing for the stage turned to his work for examples of felicitous verbal expression and striking dramatic portraiture. But there is nothing systematic about their borrowings, and the random nature of the details which they choose to imitate suggests just how superficial their response to Shakespeare's plays generally was. The part and not the whole is what attracted them: the elegant sentence, the poetic description, the telling dramatic gesture, the lively stage situation. For example, Hotspur's description of the river Severn's fright at the furious combat of Mortimer and Glendower taking place on its banks seems particularly to have impressed Fletcher:

7. Quotations from *The Revenger's Tragedy* are from the text edited by Lawrence Ross in the Regents Renaissance Drama Series (Lincoln: University of Nebraska Press, 1966).
8. Quotations from *The Atheist's Tragedy* are from *The Works of Cyril Tourneur*, ed. Allardyce Nicoll (London, The Franfrolico Press, n.d.), pp. 229–230.

> Three times they breath'd and three times did they drink,
> Upon agreement, of swift Severn's flood,
> Who then affrighted with their bloody looks,
> Ran fearfully among the trembling reeds,
> And hid his crisp head in the hollow bank,
> Blood-stained with these valiant combatants.
>
> (*1 Henry IV*, I.iii.102–107)

Fletcher reworks this passage twice in his tragicomedy, *The Loyal Subject* (1618):

> I yet remember when the Volga curl'd,
> The aged Volga, when he heaved his head up,
> And raised his waters high, to see the ruins,
> The ruins our swords made, the bloody ruins;
>
> (I.iii.26–29)[9]

and later:

> Then, when the Volga trembled at his terror,
> And hid his seven curl'd heads, afraid of bruising
> By his arm'd horses' hoofs . . .
>
> (IV.v. 69–71)[10]

The association of martial fury and the crisp or curling heads of waves obviously pleased Fletcher, for he uses it again in *The Humorous Lieutenant* (c. 1619):

> when your angers,
> Like so many brother-billows, rose together,
> And, curling up your foaming crests, defied
> Even mighty kings, and in their falls entomb'd 'em . . .
>
> (I.i.127–130)[11]

9. Quotations from *The Loyal Subject* are from the text edited by John Masefield for volume III of A. H. Bullen's Variorum Edition of *The Works of Beaumont and Fletcher* (London, 1908).

10. Fletcher is perhaps also remembering the King's description (in *2 Henry IV*, III.i.21–23) "of the winds, / Who take the ruffian billows by the top, / Curling their monstrous heads." Behind the image of the river hiding its head is Ovid's account of one of the consequences to earth caused by Phaethon's disastrous effort to drive the chariot of the sun: "The Nile fled in terror to the ends of the earth, and hid its head" (*Metamorphoses* II.254–255, the Loeb Classical Library).

11. Quotations from *The Humorous Lieutenant* are from the text edited by R. Warwick Bond for volume II of Bullen's Variorum (London, 1905).

In *The Double Marriage* (a collaboration with Massinger, c. 1620), Fletcher applies the image to a ship:

> Let her bestride the billows till they rore,
> And curle their wanton heads.
>
> (II.i; Folio 1647, p. 25b)[12]

And it is typical of the casual way in which Fletcher employs what he borrows that — as the adjective "wanton" in the preceding quotation suggests — the image of curling waves can be put to gentler uses. In *The Island Princess* (c. 1621), it has a part in depicting an idyllic landscape:

> The very rivers as we floate along,
> Throw up their pearles, and curle their heads to court us;
>
> (I.iii; Folio 1647, p. 97a)

and in *The Maid in the Mill* (a collaboration with William Rowley, 1623), we are a long way from the bloody violence in the context of which we first encountered the image, both in Shakespeare and in Fletcher:

> Every thing smiles abroad: me thinks the River
> (As he steals by) curles up his head, to view ye:
> Every thing is in Love.
>
> (I.i; Folio 1647, p. 1a)

In the Beaumont and Fletcher plays, the influence of Shakespeare has often been claimed to be of an especial prominence, and much has been written concerning the relation of the dramatic romances which Shakespeare wrote at the end of his career and the romantic tragicomedies which won success for Beaumont and Fletcher at the beginning of theirs. But the similarities that have been noted between plays like Shakespeare's *Cymbeline* and Beaumont and Fletcher's *Philaster* — a heroine falsely accused by a jealous husband/lover, who attempts to kill

---

12. Quotations from *The Double Marriage, The Island Princess,* and *The Maid in the Mill* are from the 1647 folio edition of Beaumont and Fletcher's *Comedies and Tragedies.* The designations *a* and *b* with page numbers refer respectively to left and right folio columns.

her; the heroine's father who would marry his daughter to a princely braggart whom she despises; a maiden who takes on male disguise through the duress of injured or unrequited love — are less impressive than the absence of any trace of the vision of human destiny that informs all of Shakespeare's last plays. Of the vision of human error and loss, of patience under sufferings and an ultimately happy issue out of all afflictions, which informs *Pericles* and *Cymbeline, The Winter's Tale* and *The Tempest,* there is nothing at all in *Philaster* or *A King and No King.* Here again one is struck by the superficiality of the response of contemporary dramatists to Shakespeare's achievement; the total conception which gives coherence and shape to a Shakespearean play as a whole seems to have been lost on them (at least they learned nothing from it), and their attention was satisfied instead by the dramatically effective part, the histrionic detail. What seems to have impressed Fletcher most about Shakespeare's *Pericles* was not the poignant scene in which the protagonist recognizes the daughter he has believed dead, nor the vision of the goddess Diana, nor the joyous finale in which the protagonist is reunited with his wife whom he has also believed dead, but rather the scenes of Marina in the brothel. In *Valentinian* (c. 1614), Fletcher imitates the dismay of the Bawd, the Pander, and Boult concerning the unassailable virtue of Marina (*Pericles,* IV.vi) in the persons of the two palace bawds, Ardelia and Phorba, whose job it is to work the chaste Lucina to the Emperor's lustful will, and who fail in their efforts.

> PHORBA.   Worms take her!
> She has almost spoil'd our trade.
> ARDELIA.   So godly?
> This is ill breeding, Phorba.
> PHORBA.   If the women
> Should have a longing now to see this monster,
> And she convert 'em all!
> ARDELIA.   That may be Phorba;
> But if it be, I'll have the young men gelded.
>   (*Valentinian,* I.ii.169–174)[13]

13. Quotations from *Valentinian* are from the text edited by Robert Grant Martin for volume IV of Bullen's Variorum (London, 1912).

And in *The Humorous Lieutenant*, Fletcher devotes a whole
scene (II.iii) to depicting the court bawd at work dispatching
orders to agents throughout the kingdom for fresh supplies of
maidens to replenish the court's exhausted stock ("we are out
of beauty, / Utterly out, and rub the time away here / With
such blown stuff, I am ashamed to vend it" — II.iii.46–48), a
scene that seems to have been inspired by *Pericles*, IV.ii. The
ultimate Fletcherian treatment of this sort of material is in *The
Custom of the Country* (a collaboration with Massinger, c.
1620), where a bawd's efforts to secure fresh recuits are made
piquant for being directed at a male, not a female brothel.

How the example of Shakespeare's dramatic practice might
serve a pair of young playwrights seeking a start in the theater
is well illustrated by Beaumont and Fletcher's *Cupid's Revenge*
(c. 1608). The incident which opens their play is derived from
the *Arcadia* (book II, chapter 13) and concerns the beauteous
daughter of the King of Lycia. Here is the way Sidney begins
her story:

> This Princesse *Erona*, being 19. yeres of age, seeing the countrie
> of *Lycia* so much devoted to *Cupid*, as that in every place his
> naked pictures & images were superstitiously adored (ether moved
> therunto, by the esteeming that could be no Godhead, which could
> breed wickedness, or the shamefast consideration of such naked-
> nes) procured so much of her father, as utterly to pull downe,
> and deface all those statues and pictures.[14]

In transforming this state of affairs into the action of the play's
first scene, Beaumont and Fletcher availed themselves of the
model which Shakespeare had recently provided in *King Lear*
for setting a tragic plot in motion. *Cupid's Revenge*, like *King
Lear*, opens with a trio of courtiers awaiting the formal enact-
ment of their monarch's oath in behalf of his offspring, in this
case, his promise "to graunt his Daughter any thing she shall
aske on her byrth day" (I.i.8–9).[15] Following a brief prose ex-

14. *The Prose Works of Sir Philip Sidney*, ed. Albert Feuillerat
(Cambridge: Cambridge University Press, 1969), I, 232.

15. Quotations from *Cupid's Revenge* are from the text edited by
Fredson Bowers for volume II of *The Dramatic Works in the Beaumont
and Fletcher Canon* (Cambridge: Cambridge University Press, 1970).

change between the courtiers, the Duke Leontius enters with his daughter Hidaspes and other members of the court and proceeds at once to the ritual that will permit Hidaspes to ask whatever she desires. "Are you prepard? then speake," he says to her (I.i.38), and she responds with the fatal request that all the "erected obsceane Images [of Cupid] / May be pluckt downe and burnt: and every man / That offers to 'em any sacrifice, / May lose his life" (I.i.74–77). The Duke repines only briefly at her request before decreeing that it be performed; then he exits with his entourage, leaving the stage to the three lords, whereupon the scene shifts into a new gear as it takes on the accents of another recent Shakespearean play, *Measure for Measure*. In a closing prose exchange, the lords comment on the rigors of the new morality to which they must now conform, and they wonder how human nature will be satisfied; plucking down the images of Cupid is to this play what plucking down the bawdy houses in the suburbs of Vienna is to *Measure for Measure* (cf. I.ii.95–96 of Shakespeare's play). According to a stage direction, "one" enters "with an Image" that is bound for destruction, thereby demonstrating the fact that the new decree is already in force, even as Claudio's appearance en route to prison in *Measure for Measure* (I.ii) bears witness to the same effect. Claudio says that his restraint comes "from too much liberty" (I.ii.125), and one of the lords in *Cupid's Revenge* says that the new continence that is going to be forced upon them all "comes of fulnes, a sin too frequent with us" (I.i.146). Earlier, one of the lords has wryly acknowledged the appropriateness of the rigorous new law: "Yet to say truth, we have deserv'd it, we have liv'd so wickedly" (I.i.119–120).

The analogy with *Measure for Measure* is enforced in this opening scene of *Cupid's Revenge* by the character of the brother, Leucippus, with whom Beaumont and Fletcher provide Hidaspes (the corresponding character in Sidney is an only child). He is as puritanical as she is, and as zealous in the campaign against Cupid, and for a moment it seems as if the dramatists were going to give us a study of male chastity yielding to the erotic in the manner of Angelo. But nothing comes of this, and when next seen (in II.ii) Leucippus has been assimilated into another story from the *Arcadia*, which in fact provides the rest of the plot of *Cupid's Revenge.* In Sidney, the punishment Cupid inflicts on the Princess Erona for her impiety is to cause her to be "stricken with most obstinate Love, to a yong man but of mean parentage, in her fathers court, named *Antiphilus*: so meane, as that he was but the sonne of her Nurse." [16] Beaumont and Fletcher turn the young man of mean parentage into a deformed dwarf, thereby heightening the grotesquerie of Hidaspes' passion; and whereas in Sidney, Erona's story continues for some time as she steadfastly persists in her ruinous dotage, Beaumont and Fletcher cut short Hidaspes' anguish when her father, outraged at her unseemly affection, causes the dwarf who is the object of it to be executed, whereupon the unfortunate girl quickly sickens and dies. The rest of the play, from act II on, is concerned with Cupid's revenge on the father and the son, and to this end Beaumont and Fletcher adapted the story of Plangus, son of the King of Iberia, from the *Arcadia* (book II, chapter 15). Sidney's story, which the dramatists follow closely, tells how the prince has an affair with a common woman, how his father learns of it, and how the prince to protect himself and her tells his father that the woman is chaste despite his own attempts upon her virtue. The father believes his son's lies, and is so smitten with the woman's beauty and apparent chastity that he marries her himself; when she attempts to resume her liaison with the son, he refuses her, whereupon she works his ruin with his father (at which point Sidney's story takes on overtones of the tragic fate of Hippolytus).

Both *Measure for Measure* and *Cupid's Revenge* deal with efforts to repress human sexuality. Shakespeare, in the course of his play, deals with a good deal more than that, specifically in his appraisal of the conflicting claims of justice and mercy. Beaumont and Fletcher deal only with the sexual, and this is altogether typical of the manner in which, in their theater, dramatic interest inheres exclusively in erotic passion, which in their plays becomes indeed the only power capable of generating dramatic action. If a comparison of the two plays makes evident a fatal narrowing of the Shakespearean breadth and range of vision, it also makes evident a fatal superficiality on the part

16. *Prose Works of Sidney*, I, 232.

of the younger dramatists. In *Measure for Measure*, the power of sex is made vivid in the near tragic scenes in which Angelo watches the idealized image of his own purity collapse. In *Cupid's Revenge*, the power of sex is shown by having a beautiful princess caress a dwarf (shades of Titania stroking Bottom in the ass's head, but without the innocence of the scenes in *A Midsummer Night's Dream*), or having an elderly ruler curl his hair and ape the fashions and behavior of a sprightly youth in order to woo a woman half his age. This last is, in fact, a typical figure in the Beaumont and Fletcher canon; Fletcher represents it again in the character of the elderly king in *The Humorous Lieutenant*. Whatever hints from *Measure for Measure* the playwrights may have acted on in their dramatization of Sidney's story material, the spirit of Shakespeare's play eluded them. When later Fletcher drew on it in *Valentinian*, it was, typically, Angelo's perversity in lusting after Isabella precisely because she was good that he remembered. And so he has his hero declare of the virtuous Lucina:

> But she is such a pleasure, being good,
> That, though I were a god, she'd fire my blood.
>
> (*Valentinian*, I.iii.245–246)

And after she has been raped, her ravisher addresses her in terms that must have been prompted by Angelo's "The tempter, or the tempted, who sins most?"

> If I have done a sin, curse her that drew me,
> Curse the first cause, the witchcraft that abus'd me,
> Curse those fair eyes, and curse that heavenly beauty,
> And curse your being good too.
>
> (*Valentinian*, III.i.54–57)

Measure for Measure was the most effective demonstration that the English stage had yet seen of how a potentially tragic situation may be resolved by nontragic means, and in that respect it seems to have been of particular interest to contemporary dramatists. Dekker, for example, imitates a number of its features in the finale of the second part of his *Honest Whore* (c. 1605): the Duke of Milan's directive for rounding up whores and thus purging his city and its suburbs (IV.ii.90ff);[17] the dramatic moment in which Orlando Friscobaldo, who like the Duke in *Measure for Measure* has been controlling the action in disguise, discovers himself (V.ii.179); the punishment which the Duke pronounces upon Bots for his whoremongering and which is reminiscent of the sentence pronounced upon Lucio in *Measure for Measure* (V.ii.459ff); the manner in which Bellafront, like Marianna in *Measure for Measure*, asks pardon for a faithless husband who has been trying to seduce another woman (V.ii.462ff).

The importance of *Measure for Measure* to Shakespeare's career cannot be overestimated, because while he was not to continue his experiment with tragicomedy at the time, he would return to it some two years later in *Pericles*, and proceed with his refinements on the form through the three further romances which end his career. When, in the preface to *The Faithful Shepherdess* (c. 1608), Fletcher defined tragicomedy by stating that "it wants deaths, which is enough to make it no tragedy, yet brings some near it, which is enough to make it no comedy," [18] he was describing the kind of play that courtly audiences had witnessed on December 26, 1604, when *Measure for Measure* was acted at Whitehall. The manner in which tragicomedy established itself on the Jacobean stage through the plays comprising the Beaumont and Fletcher canon is a well-known chapter in the history of English drama. What is not always adequately recognized, however, is the extent to which the impulse to tragicomedy on the Jacobean stage clearly came from Shakespeare. Throughout his career, he was ever drawn to dramatic situations that brought some near to death but eventually allowed for a surprising deliverance. The characters in the early plays who are snatched from the fatal reach of outrageous laws, like Egeon in *The Comedy of Errors* or Antonio in *The Merchant of Venice* or Claudio in *Measure for Measure*, are pre-

17. Parenthetical references to act, scene, and line numbers of *The Honest Whore*, part II, throughout this paragraph are based on the text of the play edited by Fredson Bowers for volume II of his edition of *The Dramatic Works of Thomas Dekker* (Cambridge: Cambridge University Press, 1964).
18. *The Faithful Shepherdess*, ed. by W. W. Greg, in the Bullen Variorum, vol. III, p. 18.

cursors of those figures in the late plays who manage to endure the worst that nature — human or elemental — can inflict on them: Pericles, Belarius in *Cymbeline*, Prospero in *The Tempest*; and the early heroines whom the malice of the world has apparently destroyed but who survive to win their lovers — Hero in *Much Ado About Nothing*, Helena in *All's Well That Ends Well* — are prototypes of all those female figures in the last plays whom death has threatened to claim, has even seemed to claim, but who elude its grasp: Thaisa, Imogen, Perdita, Hermione. These are the eternal figures of romance, falling prey to sudden evils only to be rescued when it appears that the worst must happen. As Shakespeare develops them and their circumstances in the course of his career, they become ever more human and at the same time more mysterious. This is especially true of the three great figures who create the dominant impression in each of the three last plays: Imogen, Hermione, Prospero. The human trials through which they pass have the effect of transfiguring them.

Tragicomedy, with its dual tendency toward realistic representation and idealization, provided Shakespeare with the perfect means for projecting into a single dramatic image both the misery and the sublimity of experience. But whereas in the case of Shakespeare the form can serve admirably for conveying the dramatist's ultimately comedic vision which, at the end of a rich creative life, has penetrated to a vision beyond tragedy, tragicomedy of the profound kind (the kind, that is, of *Cymbeline* and *The Winter's Tale* and *The Tempest*) is the least imitable of dramatic forms, as the history of English drama in the decades after Shakespeare's retirement from the stage was to prove. What in fact was imitated by dramatists in the years to come was the form without the vision: the shifts of plot with their sudden rescues or surprising changes of purpose or unexpected revelations which allow for a happy ending in spite of everything. Plays like Beaumont and Fletcher's *Philaster*, or *A King and No King*, have little enough in common with Shakespeare's last tragicomic romances, as has already been noted, but the Beaumont and Fletcher plays gave currency to the tragicomic form, which carried all before it in the three decades that preceded the closing of the theaters.

Shakespeare's last plays are, in fact, a dead end so far as the history of the theater is concerned. The vision they project, and the art which enshrines it, are too intimately involved in the playwright's profound sense that life is a dream which imagination keeps from turning into a nightmare, for either the vision or the art to be useful to succeeding dramatists. Thus it is not surprising to find Jacobean and Caroline tragicomedy stemming not from Shakespeare but from Beaumont and (especially) Fletcher, who translated the form into more accessible terms. Dramatists of Shakespeare's generation, accustomed to take a more problematic view of things than Fletcherian tragicomedy ever permits, are never at ease with the form as it develops in its new and voguish aspect. Plays like Webster's *Devil's Law-Case* (c. 1617) or Middleton's *More Dissemblers besides Women* (c. 1615) are failures not because they are bad imitations of Fletcher but because they treat of subjects of a Shakespearean complexity with a Fletcherian inconsequence. The younger dramatists (Massinger, Shirley, Brome, for example) handled the form more gracefully, though tragicomedy in their hands never ceases to be inconsequential; with them and their Caroline contemporaries, English drama is in full retreat from seriousness.

Echoes of Shakespeare are everywhere in the plays written during the twenty-five years between his death and the closing of the theaters, but all that these bear witness to is the familiarity of later dramatists with his work and the ease with which they turned to it for a phrase, a plot design, a character type which might be used to embellish works of an essentially different — because essentially trivial — kind. For example, *The Tempest* is often said to have influenced other seventeenth-century plays. Dryden, in his preface to his and Davenant's adaptation of it (*The Tempest, or the Enchanted Island*, 1670), names two of them:

> our excellent *Fletcher* had so great a value for [*The Tempest*], that he thought fit to make use of the same Design, not much varied, a second time. Those who have seen his *Sea-Voyage*, may easily discern that it was a Copy of *Shakespear's Tempest*: the Storm, the desart Island, and the Woman who had never

seen a Man, are all sufficient testimonies of it. But *Fletcher* was
not the only Poet who made use of *Shakespear's* Plot: Sir *John
Suckling*, a profess'd admirer of our Author, has follow'd his
footsteps in his *Goblins*; his Regmella [*sic*] being an open imitation of *Shakespear's Miranda*; and his Spirits, though counterfeit,
yet are copied from *Ariel*.[19]

Both plays — Fletcher and Massinger's *Sea Voyage* (1622) and
Suckling's *Goblins* (c. 1637) — witness the simplification of the
ambiguous and often disturbing resonances of Shakespeare's
final tragicomic romances into the excitements and surprises of
romance pure and simple.

A more interesting example of how a contemporary dramatist
made use of a Shakespearean structural design in the creation of
his own work is provided by Webster, whose *White Devil* (c.
1612) is modeled on the example of *Antony and Cleopatra*. The
fate of Webster's near contemporary pair of lovers must have
been intended as a modern instance of the famous romantic
tragedy from the antique world; *The White Devil* is set against
a claustrophobic background of papal Rome that seems meant
to function to as dangerous and glamorous an end as the background of the Roman world on the eve of empire had done in
Shakespeare's play. Webster's Antony is Paulo Giordano Orsini,
Duke of Brachiano, whose public and political life is made
turbulent by his adulterous affair with Vittoria Corombona. Just
as Antony is married to Octavia, sister to Octavius Caesar who
is more powerful than he and who will eventually destroy him,
so Brachiano is married to Isabella, sister to Francisco de
Medici who will design his ruin. The episode in which Octavius
dispatches Thidias to try his cunning with Cleopatra and win
her to a separate peace (*Antony and Cleopatra*, III.xii–xiii)
seems to have provided Webster with the hint for the letter
which Francisco sends to Vittoria declaring his love for her and
promising to deliver her from the house of convertites (*The
White Devil*, IV.i–ii). In each case the messenger is intercepted,
and the lover, suspecting that his mistress looks with favor on
his enemy, denounces her in a furious scene which ends, none-

19. *Dryden: The Dramatic Works*, ed. Montague Summers (London,
1931), II, 152.

theless, on a note of reconciliation between the pair, who find themselves in each case increasingly embattled by the opposing forces in the world around them.

But it is in the tempo of the action of act V of *The White Devil* that Webster can be seen most clearly attempting to emulate Shakespeare's daring example. Antony dies at the end of act IV of Shakespeare's play, and Cleopatra is left alone to deal with the rush of events until, at the end, she dies and the double tragedy is complete. In *The White Devil*, Brachiano is murdered in V.iii and Webster attempts a similar suspension of his catastrophe, until the murder of Vittoria (and of her brother Flamineo) at the end of V.vi. But while he was sufficiently struck by Shakespeare's suspended catastrophe in *Antony and Cleopatra* to imitate it in *The White Devil*, Webster did not apparently see the point of it: to follow the death of the tragic hero with a closing movement which would depict the agony and death of the tragic heroine. Given the title of Webster's play, and given the form which he seems to have taken pains to impose on its finale, it does not seem unreasonable to assume that, with Brachiano dead, attention will focus on Vittoria. In a way it does, but the way is typical of this cluttered play. Between the two deaths, the dramatist makes us harken to the sexual ambitions of Zanche the moor; to the mad scene of Vittoria's mother, Cornelia, with its Ophelia-like bestowal of flowers; to the plottings of Lodovico and Francisco; and most of all to the grim self-interest of Flamineo, whose game of playing at death with his sister is cut short only when Lodovico and his fellow revengers break in on him and Vittoria and her maid, rather in the manner in which the Romans break in on Cleopatra and her women. Vittoria is absent from much of the finale that ought rightly to be hers, and when at last she is brought on the scene, she is made to share it with Flamineo, whose role here as elsewhere overshadows hers.

Still, whatever fault one may find with Webster's management of the finale to *The White Devil*, he seems to have been sufficiently pleased with it to design the finale to his next tragedy, *The Duchess of Malfi* (c. 1614), along similar lines. There again he employs the same double catastrophe with its two parts extended over an entire act — from the death of the Duchess at

the end of act IV to the death of her husband Antonio in V.iv
and of the brothers who have been her tormentors in V.v — that
he had admired in *Antony and Cleopatra*. It is interesting to
watch Webster adapt the Shakespearean design to his own purposes in each of his tragedies. In each, he begins his finale long
before the actual end of the play: between the death which
launches the catastrophe and the death (or deaths) which close
it, he is at pains to show the workings of evil, destroying itself
and others. For reasons that have already been suggested concerning the earlier play, this is less effectively managed in *The
White Devil* than in *The Duchess of Malfi*; in the later play, the
suspended period that intervenes between the catastrophe's in-
ception and its culmination enables the dramatist to demonstrate
with the utmost clarity the full corruption of the forces that have
just destroyed the Duchess and are now in process of destroying
themselves (the Cardinal and Ferdinand). In both plays, Webster can be seen adapting the Shakespearean design to accommodate a typically Websterian figure: the eternal outsider who has
nonetheless been insidiously inside the workings of the tragedy,
the figure who in the first play is named Flamineo and in the
second Bosola, and whose role as agent to the passions of others
involves him at last among the victims of passion.

What *Antony and Cleopatra* was to Webster, *Macbeth* seems
to have been to Middleton. David L. Frost, whose comparison
of Shakespeare's tragedy with Webster's efforts to emulate it re-
dounds at every point to Webster's discredit, finds more to ap-
prove in Middleton's closest approach to the manner of Shakespearean tragedy in *The Changeling*. Of this play, Frost writes:
"The moral order is that of *Macbeth* . . . The guilty couple become more and more enmeshed in deceit and intrigue of their
own making, until their crimes become apparent to all. Middleton presents a Shakespearean universe, one that is fundamentally, if harshly, moral, purging itself of its own diseases." [20] *The*

20. Frost, *The School of Shakespeare*, pp. 74–75. In his discussion of
Webster and Shakespeare, Frost contrasts "the clarity of *Antony and
Cleopatra*" with the ambiguity of both *The White Devil* and *The Duchess
of Malfi*: "while in Webster's plays a sensitive response must resolve
in cloud and contradiction, to be satisfied with ambiguity in *Antony
and Cleopatra* is to balk Shakespeare's intention" (p. 136). But a more
recent study, Janet Adelman's *The Common Liar: An Essay on "Antony*

Changeling is an uncompromising study in moral deterioration, dramatized by means of a tragic plot that exhibits a truly classic simplicity and shape;[21] Beatrice's efforts to win Alsemero and rid herself of De Flores cause her to lose Alsemero and win De Flores, thereby comprising a peripeteia worthy of Sophocles. And the peripeteia is combined with a recognition, in the manner of the best tragedy,[22] as Beatrice comes to see that for all her loathing of De Flores, her fate has been darkly tied to his all along. *The Changeling* has few explicit links with Shakespeare, but no play of the period approaches more nearly the vision of Shakespearean tragedy.

In assessing the influence of any great artist on the work of his contemporaries and immediate successors, one finds oneself viewing in isolation what is never separate in the reality of creative achievement: on the one hand, the artist's technical command of his medium; on the other, the range and depth of the vision which he embodies by means of his technical resources. The latter is, of course, the rarer quality, one that is not really communicable. Contemporaries and successors could readily enough imitate details of Shakespeare's language and of his dramatic action; what eluded them was the sense of spaciousness, of tectonic harmony, of moral order that informs all his finest work. What happened to seventeenth-century English drama after Shakespeare is rather like what happened to sixteenth-century Italian painting after Raphael. In their respective media, both artists had created figures that quickly became classic exemplars of their kind, be their kind a dramatic mood or gesture, a personal or social type; they thereby established a repertoire of forms on which their successors would freely draw. In doing so, the successors (both painters and dramatists) would display both a high degree of bold inventiveness and a depressing capacity for slavish imitation, a startling genius for juxta-

and Cleopatra" (New Haven: Yale University Press, 1973), makes it clear that Shakespeare's play is not so unambiguous as Frost imagines.

21. Critical attention to the relation of the play's two plots — of which enough has been made — has tended to overlook the formal perfection of the main, tragic one.

22. Aristotle, *Poetics*, chap. 11, in *Literary Criticism: Plato to Dryden*, ed. Allan H. Gilbert (New York: American Book, 1940), p. 84.

posing the received forms in unfamiliar and often grotesque
combinations as well as for reducing them to vapidness through
oversimplification. The most impressive of the successors possessed a dazzling technical command of their art. Fletcher, for
example, who may be said to have come out of the workshop of
Shakespeare (at any rate, he completed Shakespeare's last two
post-*Tempest* plays[23]), is as dazzling a technician as a painter
like Giulio Romano, who emerged from the workshop of Raphael. What the successors never managed was to recreate the
vision that was able to invest with beauty and moral design the
crowded scenes that cover the walls of the Stanza della Segna-
tura and the Stanza d'Eliodoro, that take the stage in *King Lear*
and *The Tempest* and a score of other Shakespearean comedies,
histories, tragedies, and romances.

What the successors lacked in profundity of vision they made
up for in sophistication. Beaumont and Fletcher, Webster, Middleton, Ford, and the host of Caroline playwrights who succeeded them (Shirley, Brome, Randolph, Davenant, Cartwright,
Suckling, for example), like Rosso Fiorentino, Pontormo, Bec-
cafumi, Salviati, Pellegrino Tibaldi, Parmigianino, Bronzino, or
Vasari, are immensely sophisticated artists, which means among
other things that their plays or pictures are based as much on
their observation of other plays or pictures as they are on life.
Their art implies the creative achievement of one or two predecessors whose genius far exceeded any of theirs: Raphael and
Michelangelo in the one case, Shakespeare and Jonson in the
other. This was what was meant when, at the outset of this paper, it was said with regard to Shakespeare's successors that the
drama of the later Jacobean and Caroline periods is inconceivable without him, even though his influence on it is not of the
profoundly informing kind.

To a remarkable degree, Shakespeare's younger contemporaries and successors managed to assert distinctly individual and
original dramatic styles even while freely borrowing from the
repertoire of forms he had provided. Whatever later generations
of scholars may think of them, the plays of Beaumont and
Fletcher, of Webster, Middleton, and Ford are no servile imita-

23. *Henry VIII* and *The Two Noble Kinsmen*; and perhaps a third,
the lost *Cardenio*.

tions of Shakespeare, but are products of very distinct dramatic talents. That may be the problem: where the universally acknowledged genius of Shakespeare is the measure, any departure from it is bound to seem a sign of decadence. It is almost too easy to derogate contemporary dramatists like Webster, Beaumont and Fletcher, Ford, and Massinger; measured by the standard of Shakespeare they are bound to seem even thinner than they are. Since their work as dramatists is inconceivable without Shakespeare, it is impossible to measure their achievement without reference to his, and to say this is to acknowledge the artistic plight which conditions their stature as artists: the plight of a generation whose complex fate it is to follow a figure who has brought their artistic medium to a pitch of perfection and in the process imposed on it for all time the definitive stamp of his genius. Beaumont and Fletcher, Webster, Middleton, and Ford, however, have this to be said for them: overshadowed by Shakespeare though they be, they had sufficient boldness to appropriate from him what took their fancy and to use it to their own ends. Trimmed out in Shakespeare's feathers though their work might be, the Shakespearean borrowings were always essentially decoration; but while the plays they wrote may often have been poor things, they were their own. The day when a dramatist would solemnly announce his intention "to imitate the Divine Shakespeare" was still in the future, though not the very distant future. With Dryden's *All for Love*, the influence of Shakespeare is summoned to the aid of English drama, and for the next two centuries the shadow that it casts will shed its pall on the efforts of every playwright who attempts to write tragedy, from modest hacks like Rowe and Lillo to the best poets in the land like Coleridge, Keats, Byron, and Tennyson. Shakespeare's contemporaries in the drama had what seems on balance a happier response to the bard. They somehow sensed that Shakespeare was to be lightly pilfered from, not gravely imitated.

The Nondramatic Poems

The influence of Shakespeare's nondramatic poems, including the sonnets, from the 1590s to the present day is of course much less, both in volume and importance, than that of the plays. And while the effect of his poems on the work of other poets was either nil or very minor, when it is noticeable it is usually downright bad. Hugh Kenner was probably not exaggerating when he said that Keats was the only imitator whom Shakespeare did not ruin.[1] This essay will attempt to outline, with many omissions, the influence and reputation of Shakespeare's nondramatic poems in four parts: *Venus and Adonis*, *Lucrece*, the Sonnets, and *The Phoenix and Turtle*. But first it is worth recalling that Titania's wooing of a human and somewhat reluctant lover has perhaps an association with *Venus and Adonis*, and, more significantly, that scenes of murder in *Macbeth*, such as II.i.49–56, specifically evoke *Lucrece*:

> Now o'er the one half world
> Nature seems dead, and wicked dreams abuse
> The curtain'd sleep; witchcraft celebrates
> Pale Hecat's off'rings; and wither'd Murther,

---

1. "Words in the Dark," *Essays by Divers Hands*, n.s., XXIX (1958), 117.

Alarum'd by his sentinel, the wolf,
Whose howl's his watch, thus with his stealthy pace,
With Tarquin's ravishing strides, towards his design
Moves like a ghost.

In *Cymbeline*, II.ii.11–14, there is a kind of symbolic rape when
Jachimo emerges from the trunk in Imogen's bedroom where she
lies asleep after reading the tale of Philomele and Tereus:

The crickets sing, and man's o'erlabor'd sense
Repairs itself by rest. Our Tarquin thus
Did softly press the rushes ere he waken'd
The chastity he wounded.

The most powerful influence Shakespeare's nondramatic poems
have had, in short, is upon Shakespeare himself.

Venus and Adonis was extremely popular in the 1590s. Our
own decade, which is awash with pornography, may find it easy
to understand why. The poem exploits erotic Ovidian material,
naturalizes it, and, to use an old-fashioned expression, "sweet-
ens" it. Contemporaries were in no doubt about the import and
effect of the poem. Gabriel Harvey said it pleased "the younger
sort," whose main interest was of course love, and this is reflected
in several references in the university Parnassus plays performed
at Cambridge. Hyder Rollins, in his monumental Variorum edition of the *Poems*, traces the various poets and poetasters who
imitated Shakespeare's successful poem. His conclusion cannot, I
think, be overthrown, despite many references to the sweetness
of the versification, that "Shakespeare's poems [I would prefer
to say *Venus and Adonis*, since *Lucrece* belongs to a different
genre and appealed to a different taste] were the favorite reading of loose and degenerate people, and that, as a consequence,
they led to looseness and degeneracy."

Contemporary evidence may well be summarized by the prolific Richard Brathwait, who wrote in his *A Spiritual Spicerie*
(1638) a retraction, which, however conventional, involves
others beside himself:

For alas! how many chaste eares have I offended; how many light
eares have I corrupted with those *unhappie workes* which I have

published? What wanton measures have I writ for the nonc't, to move a light Curtezan to hugge my conceit, and next her *Venus and Adonis*, or some other immodest toy, to lodge me in her bosome?[2]

Rollins does ample justice to the vogue of the poem up to 1938. Anyone who wishes to follow the eccentricities of more recent criticism of *Venus and Adonis* may do it best in the edition of J. C. Maxwell in *The New Shakespeare*. Here he may find summarized the bizarre interpretations that the poem is an allegory, that it is hugely and infinitely comic, that it is a poem on the nature of evil (that is, the boar), or that it is really more about the nature of horses than anything else. Among the great critics it seems that Coleridge alone has looked on beauty bare and found in *Venus and Adonis* some clues to the presence of genius in a beginning poet and some illustrations of his celebrated distinction between fancy and the imagination.[3]

When Gabriel Harvey noted, sometime before 1603, that Shakespeare's *Lucrece* and his *Hamlet* "have it in them to please the wiser sort," he was making a distinction which perhaps the poet himself had hinted at when he promised, in the dedication to *Venus and Adonis*, to offer his patron some "graver labor." As early as the year of its publication, *Lucrece* naturally sprang to the mind of those who dealt with the popular subject of chastity. In 1594, in *Willobie His Avisa*, a commendatory versifier wrote that Collatine contrived

> To have a fair and constant wife,
> Yet Tarquin plucked his glistering grape,
> And Shakespeare paints poor Lucrece' rape.

2. Quoted by Roland Mushat Frye, "Three Seventeenth Century Shakespeare Allusions," *Shakespeare Quarterly*, XIII (1962), 361. David O. Frantz, " 'Leud Priapians' and Renaissance Pornography," *SEL*, XII (1972), 157–172, very usefully connects English and Italian pornography and gives a judicious introduction to the whole subject.

3. In addition to Rollins for the earlier period, one should consult Douglas Bush's two volumes, *Mythology and the Renaissance Tradition in English Poetry*, rev. ed. (New York: W. W. Norton & Co., 1963) and *Mythology and the Romantic Tradition in English Poetry*, rev. ed. (Cambridge: Harvard University Press, 1967). A more recent survey of the critical vogue of *Venus and Adonis* is by A. C. Hamilton in *SEL*, I (1961), 1–15.

Though *Lucrece* was somewhat less popular than the sala-
cious *Venus and Adonis*, judging by the number of editions in
the sixteenth and early seventeenth centuries, yet the antholo-
gizers found more extracts to print from *Lucrece* than from the
earlier poem. Robert Allot in his *England's Parnassus* (1600)
chooses thirty-nine passages from *Lucrece* (more than from all
the plays known to him) against twenty-six from *Venus and
Adonis*. John Bodenham's *Bel-vedere, or the Garden of the
Muses* (1600) favors *Lucrece* even more, with ninety-one se-
lections compared to thirty-four from *Venus*.

The direct influence of Shakespeare's graver labor is most
prominent in Thomas Middleton's *Ghost of Lucrece*. It was published in 1600, probably several years after its composition.
Middleton's poem is a stilted and grotesque sequel to Shakespeare's. It takes the form of the complaint of an unfortunate
female, deriving from Churchyard's complaint of Jane Shore in
the *Mirror for Magistrates* in the 1560s and revived into popularity by Samuel Daniel in his *Complaint of Rosamund* in 1592.
Several minor poets wrote imitations, and a more significant one,
Michael Drayton, changed his style in imitation of Shakespeare
when he wrote *Matilda, the Fair and Chaste Daughter of the
Lord Robert Fitzwater* (1594).

Shakespeare's poem, together with some of its source material, was dramatized by Thomas Heywood. It has come down
to us in an edition of 1608 as a Red Bull play featuring the
songs of Valerius, "the merrie Lord amongst the Roman
Peeres." Its modern editor, Alan Holaday, has offered reasons to
believe that the 1608 version is a revival and that the original,
now lost, was produced soon after the poem's publication in
1594. Since Heywood had imitated *Venus and Adonis* in his
Oenone and Paris, the suggestion seems plausible.

The vogue and influence of the sonnets is almost the opposite
of that of the early narrative poems. *Venus and Adonis* and *Lucrece* had an almost exclusively late sixteenth- and early seventeenth-century popularity; they dropped out of attention for two
centuries or so. The high prestige of the sonnets, on the other
hand, is almost entirely modern.

The sonnets were published in 1609, though some of them

were in circulation among the poet's private friends in 1598 and
two of them (138 and 144) were included in a miscellany in
1599. By 1609 the Elizabethan sonnet vogue was over, although
poets like Drayton and Daniel continued to include their sonnet
cycles in collections of their works, with the poems frequently
amended and changed. It is, however, not strange that no further
editions of Shakespeare's sonnets were called for, and the assumption that there must have been some kind of suppression is
entirely without supporting evidence. In 1640 John Benson, a
publisher with some queer habits, published all but eight of the
sonnets in an edition called *Poems: Written by Wil. Shake-speare.*
They are jumbled together with other matter, given titles, and
sometimes altered in such a way as to conceal the original meaning. For nearly 150 years this served as the principal source of
men's knowledge of Shakespeare's sonnets. In 1780 Edmond
Malone published the first scholarly edition, but at that time
sonnets were still thought to be trivial. George Steevens, another
important Shakespeare scholar, said of the sonnets in 1793 that
"the strongest act of Parliament that could be framed would fail
to compel readers into their service." Steevens was, admittedly,
something of a joker, but appreciation of the poetic qualities of
the sonnets had to wait for the Romantics.

An early serious student of the sonnets was Charles Armitage
Brown, remembered principally nowadays as the friend of Keats,
but described by Sidney Lee in the *Dictionary of National Biography* as a "writer on Shakespeare's sonnets and friend of
Keats." After Keats's death Brown became a friend of Walter
Savage Landor and about 1828 began discussing the sonnets
with him. Ten years later he published, and dedicated to Landor, *Shakespeare's Autobiographical Poems: Being His Sonnets
Clearly Developed; with His Character Drawn Chiefly from His
Works.* So began in 1838 an approach to the poems that continues down to the present time, as may be seen in a recent
declaration: "In the first 126 sonnets Shakespeare has set up a
system, a vindication of love and poetry that is as self-sufficient
and self-contained in its way as *Adonis*, only to expose it to a
tougher, more sensual and threatening realism." [4]

4. Michael Goldman, *Shakespeare and the Energies of Drama* (Princeton: Princeton University Press, 1972), p. 31.

Up to about 1830 Milton's sonnets were preferred to Shakespeare's, but about that time a reversal of opinion began to set in. Elizabeth Barrett Browning and Edward Fitzgerald among the Victorians saw their merit, as did some of the anthologists, but there were still dissenters. "Thomas Campbell, Landor, and [Henry] Hallam made adverse criticism of the poems, yet Hallam admitted that 'No one ever entered more fully than Shakespeare into the character of this species of poetry.' " [5]

There are, however, a number of elements in the sonnets that disturbed the Victorians. One of them is the expression of feelings of love (not necessarily homosexual) of a man for a man. It happened that Arthur Hallam was devoted to Shakespeare's sonnets, and some critics find themselves able to trace the influence of the sonnets in Tennyson's celebration of his friend Arthur called *In Memoriam A.H.H.* One of these critics was Arthur's father Henry, who said, "It is impossible not to wish that Shakespeare had never written them." Tennyson was not swayed; he said bluntly, "Henry Hallam made a great mistake about them; they are noble." [6]

Arlene Goldin points out that there are a number of love sonnet cycles by well-known Victorians which are in part at least autobiographical and which have homosexual overtones. John Addington Symonds' *Stella Maris*, privately printed in 1884, is based upon a homosexual affair. Swinburne, perhaps more for practice than anything else, wrote a series of sonnets with Shakespearean echoes at Oxford c. 1858–1860. After 1870, Goldin maintains, the sonnet cycle usually evoked associations of illicit love. "All this suggests that an author who wished to treat sexual subjects could do so with less restraint in the sonnet sequence in which sex was expected than in any other genre . . . Most Victorian love sequences are deeply autobiographical, many are extremely erotic or unusually frank in dealing with sexual themes, and almost all employ sequence conventions to ally

5. George Sanderlin, "The Repute of Shakespeare's Sonnets in the Early Nineteenth Century," *MLN*, LIV (1939), 254.
6. Christopher Ricks, *Tennyson* (New York: Macmillan, 1972), p. 215.

themselves with the amorous tradition, even when calling attention to their contemporaneity." [7]

A most explicit acknowledgment of Shakespeare's sonnets as a model for poetry expressing homosexual love is in the words of G. Lowes Dickinson, addressing Ferdinand Schiller:

> Could I but sing, my love, as I can feel,
> I would not turn to Shakespeare for a tongue,
> Nor to an alien music make appeal
> To sing the love that never yet was sung.

Dickinson wrote twenty-seven such sonnets in 1893–1894.[8]

This influence did not cease with the end of the nineteenth century. W. H. Auden published in *New Verse* in 1933 a series of five sonnets which he never included in his collected works. They are "Sleep on beside me though I wake for you"; "I see it often since you've been away"; "At the far end of the enormous room"; "The latest ferrule now has tapped the curb"; and "Love had him fast: but though he caught his breath." According to Cyril Connolly, Shakespeare's sonnets proved "extremely stimulating to the younger poet seeking to revive a convention in which it was possible to celebrate homosexual love." [9]

The critical vogue of the sonnets is far more significant than their appropriation — or misappropriation — by other poets as models. Since Rollins' monumental Variorum Edition there has been a veritable explosion of interest. Leaving aside the puzzle-solvers who vie with each other in attempts to identify the Fair Youth, the Dark Lady, or the Rival Poet, serious studies of the sonnets as poetry have poured from the press in a steady stream during the decades of the fifties and sixties and half way through the seventies.

Some of the most sensitive criticism of the sonnets has come from critics who rearrange the order of the 1609 quarto. Most

---

7. Arline Golden, "Victorian Renascence: The Revival of the Amatory Sonnet Sequence, 1850–1900," *Genre*, VII (1974), 133–147.

8. G. Lowes Dickinson, *Autobiography*, ed. Dennis Proctor (London: Duckworth, 1973), pp. 19, 109, 111, 249–263.

9. *Encounter*, March 1975, p. 92.

notable among these are Tucker Brooke (1936), J. W. Lever
(1956), and Brents Stirling (1968). The difficulty with rear-
rangements is that each one may seem plausible but does not
agree with the others. Despite this fact, it would be a mistake to
toss aside these efforts along with the distracting and generally
useless attempts to date the sonnets with precision and to identify the characters referred to in them.

Studies of formal, logical, and syntactical patterns in the sonnets continue to proliferate, and even linguistic scholars of the
eminence of Roman Jakobson have been drawn into the game.[10]
One might draw the conclusion that Shakespeare has, in his
sonnets, become a complex modern poet in the view of the
commentators. One critic, indeed, concludes that "Shakespeare is
dealing with great complexities of the mind and the heart, on to
which is added the driving need of the poet to use his art, with
all its complexities, to make sense of his condition . . ." He finds
appropriate Wallace Stevens' remark, "Poetry is a response to
the daily necessity of getting the world right." [11]

Finally, just as *Venus and Adonis* and *Lucrece* exerted their
most profound influence on Shakespeare himself, significant
recent commentary is insisting upon the close relationship between the sonnets and the plays. A good example is Cyrus Hoy:
"The sonnets are the direct expression of Shakespeare's most
intimate feelings; the plays are the oblique expression of these
. . . The result is quite remarkable: real feeling consciously applied to an unreal object . . . Sonnets and plays are bound together by an emotional continuum, and to ignore it, or treat one
body of poetry in isolation from another, is to impose a discon-
tinuity on the emotional and psychological experience from
which Shakespeare's art takes its being and which is all very
much of a piece." [12]

10. Roman Jakobson and Lawrence G. Jones, *Shakespeare's Verbal
Art in Th' Expence of Spirit* (New Jersey: Humanities Press, 1970);
but see Helen Vendler, "Jakobson, Richards, and Shakespeare's Sonnet
CXXIX" in *I. A. Richards: Essays in his Honor*, ed. R. Brower and
others (New York: Oxford University Press, 1973), pp. 179–198.
11. Philip Edwards, *Shakespeare and the Confines of Art* (New
York: Barnes & Noble, 1968), p. 31.
12. "Shakespeare and the Revenge of Art," *Rice University Studies*,
LX (1974), 74–76.

Rollins was able to find no significant comment on *The Phoenix and Turtle* before the twentieth century except for that of Emerson, who admired it himself but thought it was a poem for poets, not for the general public. In surveying criticism up to 1938 Rollins reached the conclusion that "Editors and other more or less professional scholars seldom indulge in praise of the *P. & T.*" Accordingly he found Middleton Murry's rhapsodic praise in 1922 "the apex of Shakespeare idolatry." It is worth remarking, however, that Quiller-Couch, professing to range over all poetry in English from the thirteenth century to the closing year of the nineteenth in search of "quite simply, the best," included *The Phoenix and Turtle* in *The Oxford Book of English Verse* (1900). Even granting the point, however, scholarly and critical opinion seems to have shifted since 1938. J. W. Lever reviewed twentieth-century studies of this poem, as well as Shakespeare's other nondramatic works, in *Shakespeare Survey*, XV (1962) and reached the conclusion that "above all else, it is 'a brave poem.'" (I assume he uses "brave" in the Elizabethan sense.)

Even more than with the sonnets, several difficulties stand in the way of an undistorted appreciation of the poem. There is the problem of its relationship to the other poems in the volume in which it was published, Robert Chester's *Love's Martyr* (1601). There is the problem of the identity of the phoenix, conventionally a symbol of uniqueness and rebirth, and the turtledove, conventionally representative of connubial fidelity — if, indeed, "these dead birds," as they are called in the last line, refer to real people at all. Finally, one must face the question as to just what kind of poem this is.

Helen Gardner includes it in her anthology called *The Metaphysical Poets* (1957, revised edition 1966), but then, as she says, "What we call metaphysical poetry was referred to by contemporaries as 'strong lines,' a term which calls attention to other elements in metaphysical poetry than its fondness for indulging in 'nice speculations of philosophy' in unusual contexts." She concludes that *The Phoenix and Turtle* is "the most 'strong-lined' of all poems, if 'strong lines' are riddles."

The riddles involve not only the matter of bird symbolism, but also some themes relating to the Platonic tradition and the pres-

ence in the poem of language ordinarily used in scholastic discussions of the three Persons of the Trinity. Lacking conclusive
answers to these riddles, some critics have closely examined the
structure. A. Alvarez pointed out in 1955 that the poem with-
draws into itself: "The anthem is sung by the invoked birds,
themselves part of a literary tradition; the Threnos, in turn, is
composed by Reason, an abstract quality within the song sung
by these characters . . . we are still left with a song within a song
within a literary setting." [13]

The Platonic riddle has been tackled by Robert Ellrodt, who
says: "The poet's theme is not the rational intuition of Plato-
nism: it is the triumph of Love over Reason . . . Shakespeare is
not arguing. He flies in the face of Reason with the blind confidence of sheer faith, by-passes her in a flashing intuition of
utter transcendence. On these heights the 'two-in-one' paradox
has specifically Christian connotations. Indeed, some of Shakespeare's statements would apply correctly only to the relationship between persons of the Trinity . . . The scholastic echoes
have been recognized, but no theological construction should be
forced upon the poem . . . [Shakespeare] nowhere suggests an
allegory of religious mysteries or even of divine love." [14]

Ellrodt goes on to emphasize the final negation in the Threnos:
"Beauty, truth and rarity here enclosed in cinders lie, and
any assurance, any hint of survival in a world beyond, is with-
held. The rest is silence, and the finality of death is consciously
emphasized . . . How shall we reconcile with this claim the final
call to those that are either 'true or fair'? In this apparent contradiction lies the deeper meaning of the poem. Shakespeare has
not been celebrating true lovers and beautiful creatures. He has
been dreaming of Love and Constancy, Truth and Beauty,
straining after the highest intensity, in which lies 'the excellence
of every art' (Keats)."

The best of the modern editors of Shakespeare's *Poems*, J. C.
Maxwell, remarks that *The Phoenix and Turtle* is utterly unlike anything else he ever wrote, a statement with which most

13. *Interpretations*, ed. John Wain (Philadelphia: Richard West,
1955), p. 6.
14. "An Anatomy of *The Phoenix and the Turtle*," *Shakespeare Survey, XV* (1962), 99–110.

people would agree. That is what makes it, Maxwell concludes, "now that we have it, such a rare and irreplaceable possession." [15]

Shakespeare's output of nondramatic verse was comparatively small. The total, including *Venus and Adonis*, *Lucrece*, the Sonnets, *A Lover's Complaint* (which was published with them), and *The Phoenix and Turtle*, amounts to only 5600 lines of verse. For comparison, three plays written in the mid-1590s, sometimes called "the lyrical group," *Richard II*, *Romeo and Juliet*, and *A Midsummer Night's Dream*, contain over seven thousand lines of verse. But some readers would say that not all the poetry in the plays is really *dramatic* poetry—that any account of Shakespeare's nondramatic poetry ought to take into account Mercutio's Queen Mab speech, for example. Such "beauties" of Shakespeare, as they have been called ever since Nicholas Rowe's edition of 1709, have been constantly popular down to the present time. These passages are anthologized and enjoyed by readers, though directors of stage productions often muffle or suppress them entirely. Theater people recognize nondramatic verse when they see it in a play.

Of the poetry which is professedly and admittedly nondramatic, we have seen that the reputation and influence varied considerably. The narrative poems enjoyed a vogue in the late sixteenth and early seventeenth century, but have seldom been appreciated for their own sake in recent periods. The sonnets and *The Phoenix and Turtle*, on the contrary, were neglected for centuries but now have come into their own because they can serve the interests of the present time in obliquity, ambiguity, and structural subtlety.

15. The New Shakespeare (Cambridge: Cambridge University Press, 1966), p. xxxiii. Mention should be made of the New Arden edition of the Poems by F. T. Prince (New York: Barnes & Noble, 1960) and of William H. Matchett, *The Phoenix and the Turtle: Shakespeare's Poem and Chester's Loue's Martyr* (New Jersey: Humanities Press, 1965). Matchett revives Grosart's idea that the poem refers to Elizabeth and Essex. The most recent, and, I think, very judicious treatment of the context of Shakespeare's poem is Walter Oakeshott, *"Love's Martyr,"* *HLQ*, XXXIX (1975), 29–49.

ARTHUR SHERBO

Johnson's *Shakespeare* and the Dramatic
Criticism in the *Lives of the English Poets*

Except for a few essays and even fewer reviews Samuel Johnson's reputation and worth as a literary critic reside in his edition of the plays — he chose not to include the poems — of
Shakespeare and in his *Lives of the English Poets*. Most, if not
all, of what he had to say about English dramatic literature in
the essays written before 1765, the date of publication of the
Shakespeare edition, found its way into that edition, the first
great gathering place and testing ground for his critical ideas,
and then was resurrected some fourteen years later for the *Lives*.
Indeed, while the fact is generally either not widely realized or
simply ignored, the major part of Johnson's literary criticism is
criticism of English drama, not only of the greatest English
dramatist but also of those lesser dramatists who qualified, by
virtue of their nondramatic poetic efforts, for inclusion in the
Lives. Even Milton can be included, for Johnson tries his *Samson Agonistes*, closet drama though it is, by the Aristotelian
rules of drama: *Comus*, too, is considered as drama and found
wanting. In any event, the necessity to frame a critical statement
about Shakespeare, i.e., the Preface to the edition, and to provide
a commentary for the plays, including those summing-up final

notes to most of the plays which we term the General Observations, forced Johnson over a period of almost nine years to
put his thoughts about drama and poetry into order. Hence,
when he came to render critical judgment on the plays of those
English poets who also wrote one or more plays — or those
English dramatists like Otway and Rowe, who also wrote poetry
— he had his own ready-made body of opinion as well as a
critical vocabulary upon which to rely.

Johnson devoted more of his time to Shakespeare's plays than
to the works of any other writer. He was deeply affected by
some scenes in the plays as a boy. He evidently had decided very
early to edit Shakespeare, and there is evidence that he had done
some work toward such a project around or before 1745 when
he issued his first proposals and offered *Miscellaneous Observations on the Tragedy of Macbeth* as a specimen of his editorial
and critical abilities, for there is a small body of work — nine-
teen notes on fourteen plays — which are contemporary with or
antedate the *Observations*.[1] Johnson also culled thousands of
passages from the plays as illustrations for words in his *Dictionary*, 1755. Between 1745 and 1765 there were other pieces
dealing solely or partly with Shakespeare's plays, and it was not
long after 1765 that Johnson, at the urging of George Steevens,
agreed to collaborate with him in a revision of his, Johnson's,
edition. I have recently studied some of the back-and-forth influence of the revision of the Shakespeare edition and Johnson's
revision of his *Dictionary*, both published in 1773, further evidence of the life-long interest in Shakespeare.[2] The 1773 *Shakespeare* underwent further revision in 1778, and Johnson even
contributed three corrections of passages in his edition to Edmond Malone's *Supplement to the Edition of Shakespeare's
Plays Published in 1778*, itself published in 1780. Now, it must
be remembered that on March 29, 1777, three London booksellers, delegated by their colleagues, visited Johnson to ask him
to write short lives or those English poets whose works were to
be included in a new and extensive edition. Johnson accepted

1. See my "Johnson's *Shakespeare*: Sanguine Expectations," *SQ*,
IX (1958), 426–428.
2. "1773: The Year of Revision," *Eighteenth-Century Studies*, VII
(1973), 18–39.

and immediately set to work on those biographical-critical essays that we know as *The Lives of the Poets*, a task that took him about four years to complete. A number of people helped him in one way or another, but "he was principally indebted to my [Boswell's] steady friend Mr. Isaac Reed of Staple-inn, whose extensive and accurate knowledge of English literary History I do not express with exaggeration, when I say it is wonderful." [3] It was to Reed that Johnson and Steevens had entrusted a further revision of their *Shakespeare*, a revision that was published in 1785, shortly after Johnson's death. Thus it can be seen that from 1765 to 1777, when he agreed to do the *Lives*, and from 1777 to his death at the end of 1784, Johnson was almost continuously occupied with successive editions of his *Shakespeare* and, with the help of Reed, himself the next editor of the so-called Johnson-Steevens *Shakespeare*, with the *Lives* of the poets. Inevitably, the early preoccupation left its marks on the later work.

The principal English dramatists in the *Lives* are Dryden, Congreve, Otway, and Rowe. Milton, as has been already stated, is considered a dramatist by virtue of *Samson Agonistes* and *Comus*. Stars of lesser magnitude are Addison, whose *Cato* Johnson admired for some things and criticized for others, Young, Gay, and Thomson, the last of whom Johnson had suggested for inclusion in the *Lives*. All the other poets, with the exception of Sir Richard Blackmore, John Pomfret, Thomas Yalden, and Isaac Watts, none of them playwrights, had been chosen by the booksellers. In addition to the nine already named, English drama in the *Lives* was represented by the less than impressive efforts of George Granville, Baron Lansdowne, principally remembered for his *Jew of Venice*; John Hughes, whose *Siege of Damascus* began a vogue of "Siege" plays; Ambrose Philips who wrote three tragedies, one virtually a translation of Racine's *Andromaque*; Richard Savage, friend of Johnson's early London days and the author of a play on Sir Thomas Overbury; and Edmund ("Rags") Smith whose *Phaedra and Hippolitus*, despite Addison's praise, is known only to close students of the drama. The number of plays critically considered is

3. James Boswell, *Life of Johnson*, ed. George B. Hill and L. F. Powell (Oxford: Oxford University Press, 1934–1950), IV, 37.

not small, twenty-eight by Dryden (the figure is Johnson's);
four by Congreve (nothing on *The Way of the World*); Otway's *Orphan* and *Venice Preserved*; six by Rowe; Milton's
two; three each by Thomson and Young; and nine more,
divided among the others — a total of fifty-seven. Actually,
Johnson did not devote a major share of any of the *Lives* of
these poet-dramatists to their dramatic works, his task being to
concentrate primarily on their nondramatic poetry.

It will come as no surprise to those familiar with Johnson's
literary criticism that he should praise or condemn a work because of its moral or immoral bias. His chief criticism of Shakespeare is that "he sacrifices virtue to convenience, and is so
much more careful to please than to instruct, that he seems to
write without any moral purpose" (Preface, p. 71).[4] Coupled
with this emphasis upon morality is Johnson's constant search
for moral lessons, a search which finds expression in his General
Observations on the two *Henry IV* plays (p. 523), *As You
Like It* (p. 265), *King Lear* (p. 704), *Timon of Athens* (p.
745), and *Macbeth* (p. 795). Otway's *Venice Preserved* is cen-
sured for its "want of morality in the original design, and the
despicable scenes of vile comedy" (I, 245).[5] Granville's *Once
a Lover and Always a Lover* "is said to be in a great degree in-
decent and gross" (II, 290). And John Gay is linked with
Shakespeare by the exact repetition of a phrase in the Preface
(quoted a few sentences above), for his *Beggar's Opera* "was
plainly written only to divert, *without any moral purpose* [my
italics], and is therefore not likely to do good" (II, 278). The
criticism of Rowe's Lothario in *The Fair Penitent* looks back to
Rambler 4 and, nearer in time, to Johnson's remarks on Falstaff
and on Iago. For just as Johnson could say that the moral to be
drawn from the two *Henry IV* plays is that "no man is more
dangerous than he that with a will to corrupt, hath the power
to please; and that neither wit nor honesty ought to think themselves safe with such a companion when they see Henry se-

4. All references to Johnson's *Shakespeare* are to my edition of
Johnson on Shakespeare (New Haven: Yale University Press, 1968),
vols. VII and VIII (continuously paged) of the *Yale Edition of the
Works of Samuel Johnson.*
5. All references to the *Lives* are to the *Lives of the English Poets*,
ed. G. B. Hill (Oxford: Oxford University Press, 1905).

duced by Falstaff" (pp. 523–524) and of Iago that "there is always the danger lest wickedness conjoined with abilities should steal upon esteem, though it misses of approbation" (p. 1047), he could also say that "Lothario, with gaiety which cannot be hated, and bravery which cannot be despised, retains too much of the spectator's kindness" (II, 67). Whatever one thinks of this as a critical stance, it is obvious that it was early arrived at and long cherished.

Perhaps it may be well to analyze Johnson's critical reaction to Dryden's plays in the light of his criticism of Shakespeare, if only because Dryden wrote so many plays and because more of Johnson's critical preoccupations are present there than in any other of the *Lives* of the poet-dramatists. And perhaps, too, one might start with Johnson's remark on Dryden's genius, imbedded in the General Observation on *Romeo and Juliet*, for there he says it was "not very fertile of merriment, nor ductile to humour, but acute, argumentative, comprehensive, and sublime" (p. 957). Compare the life of Dryden, noting the verbal similarities: "he appears to have had a mind very comprehensive," "the favourite exercise of his mind was ratiocination," "what he had of humorous or passionate, he seems to have had not from mature, but from other poets," and "next to argument, his delight was in wild and daring sallies of sentiment" (I, 457, 459–460). From this general assessment of Dryden's genius one may turn to matters that have to do more strictly with the drama. One of the most forward-looking of Johnson's pronouncements in the Preface to Shakespeare is his defense of tragicomedy. He states that the "mingled drama" can "convey all the instruction of tragedy or comedy" because "it includes both in its alternations of exhibition" (p. 67), a slight echo of *Rambler* 156 and an anticipation of the discussion in the life of Dryden who, according to Johnson, maintains "that the drama required an alternation of comick and tragick scenes, and that it is necessary to mitigate by alleviations of merriment the pressure of ponderous events and the fatigue of toilsome passions" (I, 357). Dryden, however, had actually written in the dedication to his *Spanish Friar*, "I dare venture to prophesy that few tragedies except those in verse shall succeed in this age, if they are not lightened with a course of mirth."

Johnson's position on poetic justice is curious; he accuses Shakespeare of neglecting poetic justice (Preface, p. 71); he objects to Angelo's going unpunished in *Measure for Measure* (p. 213); he gives his reasons for championing poetic justice in the general observation on *King Lear*: "A play in which the wicked prosper, and the virtuous miscarry, may doubtless be good, because it is a just representation of the common events of human life: but," and he goes on to justify the doctrine (p. 704), invoking it again in the general observation on *Hamlet* (p. 1011). In the life of Milton he seems partially to reverse himself, berating Dryden, who "petulantly and indecently, denies the heroism of Adam because he was overcome; but there is no reason why the hero should not be unfortunate except established practice, since success and virtue do not necessarily go together" (I, 76). He applauds Rowe's observance of poetic justice in *The Royal Convert* (II, 69–70), only to take issue with John Dennis' attack on Addison's *Cato* for the neglect of the doctrine in that play. "Whatever pleasure there may be in seeing crimes punished and virtue rewarded, yet, since wickedness often prospers [note the echo of the phrase in the endnote on *King Lear*] in real life, the poet is certainly at liberty to give it prosperity on the stage" (II, 135). One is not entirely unprepared for these echoes of the *Shakespeare* in the *Lives*.

When Johnson states that *Timon of Athens* is a "domestick tragedy" (p. 745), the statement that the characters of Dryden's *Aureng-Zebe* are "imperial; but the dialogue is often domestick" (I, 360) comes as no surprise, although one may not have thought of either play, wholly or in part, as "domestic." Johnson, to turn elsewhere in the *Lives*, could excuse much in a domestic tragedy. He could thus say of Otway's *Orphan* that it "is a domestick tragedy drawn from middle life" [note the distinction]. Its whole power is upon the affections, for it is not written with much comprehension of thought or elegance of expression. But if the heart is interested, many other beauties may be wanting, yet not be missed" (I, 245). Rowe's *Fair Penitent* was one of Johnson's favorite plays, "for there is scarcely any work of any poet at once so interesting by the fable and so delightful by language. The story is domestick, and therefore easily received by the imagination, and assimilated to common life" (II, 67). Despite its failure to imitate Shakespeare's style, Rowe's *Jane Shore*, "consisting chiefly of domestick scenes and private distresses, lays hold upon the heart" (II, 69). In the *Shakespeare* (p. 416) Johnson conjectured that Rowe had borrowed the first lines of *The Fair Penitent* from King Philip's speech in *King John* (III.i.75–82), and he remembered and quoted a use of "coy" as a verb in *Jane Shore* (p. 966), further, if slight, evidence of an interest that extends at least from the edition to the *Lives*. Incidentally, he sees Otway's speech beginning "When you would bind me, is there need of oaths" in *Venice Preserved* as an imitation of Brutus's "Swear priests, and cowards, and men cautelous" (p. 829).

There are fourteen references to Dryden's plays in the *Shakespeare*. Some anticipate remarks in the life of Dryden, even to the point of verbal similarity. Johnson found the "union of two actions in one event" in *The Merchant of Venice* "eminently happy," and went on to remark that "Dryden was much pleased with his own address in connecting the two plots of his *Spanish Friar*" (p. 241); in the life of Dryden he wrote that "*The Spanish Fryar* is a tragi-comedy eminent for the happy coincidence and coalition of the two plots" (I, 356).[6] Johnson's criticism of *All For Love*, that it admitted "the romantick omnipotence of Love" (I, 361), might be anticipated from the stern paragraph in his Preface on the abuse of the theme of love in modern drama, especially in the remark that love "is only one of many passions, and . . . it has no great influence upon the sum of life" (p. 63). That same paragraph in the Preface foreshadows the equally stern paragraph on the two parts of Dryden's *Conquest of Granada* (I, 348–349) and may even be referring to it and other specimens of heroic drama. Johnson was evidently unpleasantly struck by an image in *Don Sebastian*, citing the passage in *Rambler* 125 and in a note on *Henry V, IV.iii.* 104, where he writes that "perhaps from this putrid valour [of Shakespeare's image] Dryden might borrow the posthumous empire of Don Sebastian, who was to reign wheresoever his atoms should be scattered" (p. 558). The passage, with one from *Tyrannick Love*, is quoted in the life of Dryden where both

6. See also pp. 340 and 351 for the double plots in *The Merry Wives of Windsor* and in *The Taming of the Shrew*.

are termed "tumid." Now Johnson, in that same *Rambler* 125, after animadverting on the passage in *Don Sebastian* and on one from *Aureng-Zebe*, characterizes tragedies "of the last century" as exhibiting a "perpetual tumor of phrase"; in the Preface he accuses Shakespeare of "tumor" in his tragedies and brands the speeches in *Antony and Cleopatra* "tumid." "Tumor" is defined in Johnson's *Dictionary* as "Affected pomp; affected magnificence; puffy grandeur; swelling mien; unsubstantial greatness"; "tumid" is "falsely sublime," as well as "pompous; boastful; puffy." "Tumid" and "tumour," then, take their place in Johnson's critical vocabulary, additional links between the two major critical endeavors.

Johnson commented in his general observation on *King Lear* that

> if we turn our thoughts upon the barbarity and ignorance of the age to which this story is referred, it will appear not so unlikely as while we estimate Lear's manners by our own. Such preference of one daughter to another, or resignation of dominion on such conditions, would be yet credible, if told of a petty prince of Guinea or Madagascar. Shakespeare, indeed, by the mention of his earls and dukes, has given us the idea of times more civilised, and of life regulated by softer manners; and the truth is, that though he so nicely discriminates, and so minutely describes the characters of men, he commonly neglects and confounds the characters of ages, by mingling customs ancient and modern, English and foreign.
>
> (p. 703)

Something the same is true of Dryden's *Aureng-Zebe*, for, although the "tragedy [is] founded on the actions of a great prince then reigning," his "country is at such a distance that the manners might be safely falsified and the incidents feigned" (I, 360). And so, too, is it with Smith's *Phaedra and Hippolitus*, for "the fable is mythological, a story which we are accustomed to reject as false, and the manners are so distant from our own that we know them not from sympathy, but by study" (II, 16). Young's *Busiris* is "too remote from known life to raise either grief, terror, or indignation" whereas the same writer's *The Revenge* "approaches much nearer to human practices and manners" (III, 397). Johnson objected to Thomson's *Agamemnon*, Rowe's *Ulysses*, and Granville's *Heroick Love* (treating of the love of Agamemnon and Chryseis) as "mythological" and thus without merit.[7] Although I find no parallel in the *Shakespeare*, it is worth mentioning that Johnson considered Richard Savage's choice of the subject of Sir Thomas Overbury for tragic treatment unfortunate because it was "perhaps not far enough removed from the present age, to admit properly the fictions necessary to complete the plan" (II, 338).

It may be recalled, to return to the *Lives* as a whole, that what Dryden "had of humorous or passionate, he seems to have had not from nature, but from other poets" (I, 460, quoted above), and thus he is found deficient in the cardinal virtue of writers, nature. Shakespeare is, of course, "above all writers, at least above all modern writers, the poet of nature," and his characters "are the genuine progeny of common humanity" (Preface, p. 62). Johnson praised Otway's *Orphan* highly and objected to the want of morality in *Venice Preserved*, but he wrote of Otway's achievement in the latter play as that of "one who conceived forcibly and drew originally by consulting nature in his own breast" (I, 246). Of Rowe's plays he wrote, "I know not that there can be found in his plays any deep search into nature" (II, 76). Ben in Congreve's *Love for Love* "is not accounted very natural, but he is very pleasant" (II, 218). And it was Congreve's tender age, twenty-one at the acting of his first play, *The Old Batchelor*, which gave Johnson pause. "As the lighter species of dramatick poetry [comedy] professes the imitation of common life, of real manners, and daily incidents, it apparently presupposes a familiar knowledge of many characters and exact observation of the passing world" (II, 216), qualities which, he decided, Congreve did not exhibit in his first comedy. Shakespeare, despite his deep insight into human nature, was similarly at fault in *All's Well That Ends Well*, for while there are "some happy characters," they are "not new, nor produced by any deep knowledge of human nature. Parolles is a boaster and a coward, such as has always been the sport of the stage" (p. 403); Bluff, in *The Old Batchelor*, is one of the "easy and common" characters, "a swaggering coward" (II, 216). Johnson was evidently

7. Respectively III, 291; II, 68; and II, 290.

on the lookout for what we today call stock characters. Indeed, Milton, according to Johnson "would not have excelled in dramatick writing; he knew human nature only in the gross, and had never studied the shades of character" (I, 189). Dryden's mirth does not "arise from any original humour or peculiarity of character nicely distinguished" (I, 459); again and again in the edition of Shakespeare Johnson had laid great stress on the necessity to "discriminate" characters.[8]

One of the best known if somewhat overrated passages in Johnson's Preface is that in which he is incorrectly supposed to have written the dramatic unities out of existence. Despite his defense of Shakespeare's neglect of the unities, Johnson applauds Shakespeare for observing the unities of action and place in *Measure for Measure* (p. 216), is concerned about the possible violation of "the rules of the drama" in *Othello*, and concludes of that same play that "had the scene opened in Cyprus, and the preceding incidents been occasionally related, there had been little wanting to a drama of the most exact and scrupulous regularity" (pp. 1037, 1048). This ambivalence about the unities is resolved in the *Lives*, for there Johnson writes of Rowe that he is not "a nice observer of the Unities. He extends time and varies place as his convenience requires. To vary the place is not, in my opinion, any violation of Nature, if the change be made between the acts, for it is no less easy for the spectator to suppose himself at Athens in the second act, than at Thebes in the first." G. B. Hill, at this juncture, quotes the parallel passage from the Preface in a footnote: "He that can take the stage at one time for the palace of the Ptolemies may take it in half an hour for the promontory of Actium" (II, 76, and n. 2). And Johnson defends Addison's *Cato* against John Dennis' strictures by observing that "Addison has, with a scrupulosity [a faint echo of the note on *Othello*] almost unexampled on the English stage, confined himself in time to a single day, and in place to rigorous unity" (II, 136).

Consideration of the unities leads one to other aspects of the drama. While Johnson had nothing to say in the Preface about Shakespeare's use of a chorus, he objected to its presence in *Henry V* in these words, "The lines given to the chorus have

8. See pp. 64, 341, 523, 703, 795, 875, and 938.

many admirers; but the truth is, that in them a little may be praised, and much must be forgiven; nor can it easily be discovered why the intelligence given by the chorus is more necessary in this play than in many others where it is omitted" (p. 566), words similar to his objection to the second-act chorus in *Romeo and Juliet*, "The use of this chorus is not easily discovered, it conduces nothing to the progress of the play, but relates what is already known, or what the next scenes will shew; and relates it without adding the improvement of any moral sentiment" (p. 944). (Curiously enough, although he devotes four notes to it, Johnson makes no objection to the chorus in *The Winter's Tale*.) So it is with Milton's use of the chorus in *Samson Agonistes*, for "it could only be by long prejudice and the bigotry of learning that Milton could prefer the ancient tragedies with their encumbrance of a chorus to the exhibitions of the French and English stages" (I, 188–189). That Johnson had considered similarities between *Samson Agonistes* and Shakespeare's plays is evident from two notes in the edition. In one he compares the introduction of Dallilah to that of Lady Fauconbridge in *King John* (p. 408); in the second, commenting upon Mortimer's speech beginning "Let dying Mortimer here rest himself" (*1 Henry VI*), he writes, "I know not whether Milton did not take from this hint the lines with which he opens his tragedy" (p. 571). Johnson's life of Milton, we know, was begun in January 1779 and finished in six weeks; the second Johnson-Steevens *Shakespeare*, with some fifty revisions by Johnson, was published in 1778, and it is not merely fanciful to imagine that the necessity for Johnson to look over the edition influenced his life of Milton, written so close in time.

Johnson set great store upon a writer's invention and originality. "Perhaps," he wrote in the Preface, "it would not be easy to find any authour, except Homer, who invented so much as Shakespeare, who so much advanced the studies which he cultivated, or effused so much novelty upon his age or country" (p. 90), and he commended the two parts of *Henry IV*, among other things, because "the incidents are multiplied with wonderful fertility of invention" (p. 523). He was constantly on the alert for this literary virtue, praising those plays in which it appeared, castigating those from which it was absent. Congreve is an original writer, as far as his plots and dialogue are concerned (II, 228), but he borrows his characters from others (II, 216, 218). The "first design" of Young's *The Revenge* "seems suggested by *Othello*, but the reflections, the incidents, and the diction are original. The moral observations are so introduced and so expressed as to have all the novelty that can be required" (III, 397). Gay's *The What D'Ye Call It* "was one of the lucky trifles that gave pleasure by novelty" (II, 271). It may be recalled also that Johnson accorded high praise to Otway because "he drew originally by consulting nature in his own breast" in *Venice Preserved* (I, 246), though he could not credit Dryden with any originality in his comedies.

There are some interesting verbal similarities in the discussions of Shakespeare and of Congreve as dramatists and especially as writers of comedy. Rowe had written in his life of Shakespeare that perhaps Shakespeare's first plays were the best. Johnson protested,

> But the power of nature is only the power of using to any certain purpose the materials which diligence procures, or opportunity supplies. Nature gives no man knowledge, and when images are collected by study and experience, can only assist in combining or applying them. Shakespeare, however favoured by nature, could impart only what he had learned; and as he must increase his ideas, like other mortals, by gradual acquisition, he, like them, grew wiser as he grew older, could display life better, as he knew it more, and instruct with more efficacy, as he was himself more amply instructed.
>
> (pp. 87–88)

Much the same is said of Congreve's *Old Batchelor*, produced when he was twenty-one: "Such a comedy written at such an age requires some consideration. As the lighter species of dramatick poetry professes the imitation of common life, of real manners, and daily incidents, it apparently presupposes a familiar knowledge of many characters and exact observation of the passing world; the difficulty therefore is to conceive how this knowledge can be obtained by a boy" (II, 216). In Shakespeare's "comick scenes he is seldom very successful, when he engages his characters in *reciprocations* of *smartness* and *contests* of sarcasm" (p.

72). The dialogue in *The Old Batchelor* "is one constant *re-ciprocation* of conceits, or clash of wit, in which nothing flows necessarily from the occasion, or is dictated by nature" (II, 216). Congreve, Johnson stated in his summing up, peoples his comedies with "a kind of intellectual gladiators; every sentence is to ward or strike; the *contest* of *smartness* is never inter-mitted" (II, 228; my italics in this paragraph). Johnson recalls a plot element of *The Old Batchelor* in the *Shakespeare* (p. 335) and, here as elsewhere, sees later dramatists imitating Shake-speare, stating that Bluff of Congreve's play "is a character taken from this of Ancient Pistol" (p. 501). In his Preface Johnson had linked Shakespeare and Congreve, accusing the former of making "no scruple to repeat the same jests in many dialogues, or to entangle different plots by the same knot of per-plexity, which may be at least forgiven him, by those who recol-lect, that of Congreve's four comedies, two are concluded by a marriage in a mask, by a deception, which perhaps never hap-pened, and which, whether likely or not, he did not invent" (p. 92). He did not forget this clumsy deception when he came to the life of Congreve, for there he wrote, of *The Old Batchelor*, that "the catastrophe arises from a mistake not very probably produced, by marrying a woman in a mask" (II, 216). George Steevens reminded Johnson that Young's tragedies "seemed to have one favourite catastrophe, as his three plays, all concluded with lavish suicide" — the words are Johnson's, not Steevens's, and this too acts as a link between the Preface and the *Lives*. Finally, as another slight link between Shakespeare and Congreve, and as a possible addition to Johnson's critical vocabu-lary, one may note that Johnson finds "show and bustle" abounding in Shakespeare's plays (Preface, p. 83), singling out the "bustle" in *2 Henry IV* (p. 522) and commenting, of *Corio-lanus*, that "there is, perhaps, too much bustle in the first act, and too little in the last" (p. 823). In Congreve's *Mourning Bride* there is "more bustle than sentiment" (II, 218–219). For what light it may afford on these uses, "bustle" is defined in Johnson's *Dictionary* as "a tumult; a hurry; a combustion."

In quick summary of other similarities, one can point to John-son's objection that Rowe's *Fair Penitent* has a weak fifth act (II, 68), a fault he found with Shakespeare's plays as a whole

(Preface, pp. 71–72) and which he remarked particularly of *All's Well That Ends Well* (p. 400), of *Henry V* (p. 566), and of *Hamlet* (p. 1011). He disliked writers mixing their mythologies, remarking that the "loves of Theseus and Hippolyta" in *A Midsummer Night's Dream* are "combined with the Gothick mythology of fairies" (p. 72) and that Shakespeare "by negligence gives his heathens [the characters in *King Lear*] the sentiments and practices of Christianity" (p. 702). The same critical objection comes to the fore in the account of Rowe's *Tamerlane*, for in it "there is some ridiculous mention of the God of Love; and Rhodogune, a savage Saxon, talks of Venus, and the eagle that bears the thunder of Jove" (II, 68). Johnson's contention that "length of duration and continuance of esteem" (Preface, p. 60) justify looking favorably upon a work surfaces in the *Lives* as part of his remarks on Otway's *The Orphan* (I, 245) and on John Hughes's *Siege of Damascus* (II, 163). Of the latter, hardly remembered today, he wrote that it "still continues on the Stage, and . . . it is unnecessary to add a private voice to such continuance of approbation." Johnson's statement that Shakespeare's "plan has commonly what Aristotle requires, a beginning, a middle, and an end; one event is concatenated with another, and the conclusion follows by easy consequence" (p. 75) looks back to *Rambler* 139 on *Samson Agonistes* and forward to the life of Milton where Johnson marvels that "a drama can be praised in which the intermediate parts have neither cause nor consequence, neither hasten nor retard the catastrophe" (I, 189).[9]

Johnson, it is abundantly clear, was in a favorable position to undertake the body of dramatic criticism necessary for his *Lives of the Poets*. He had long considered the problems posed by an edition of Shakespeare, had reflected upon them in a few detached pieces, and had then codified the result of his thinking in the editions of 1765, 1773, and 1778. Although he confessed, in his summing-up in the life of Congreve, that "of his plays I cannot speak distinctly, for since I inspected them many years have passed" (II, 228), it has been seen that the Shakespeare edition

9. See also pp. 126, 206, 227, 228, 341, and 744 in the *Shakespeare*, especially 228 and 341, for further doubts on Shakespeare's handling of plot.

in some part bridged the gap between his inspection of Congreve's plays and his later need to say something about them. In short, by the time he came to write the dramatic criticism in the *Lives* Johnson had a repository of critical remarks and a fully tried critical vocabulary, and thus had no need to rethink his views on the drama in general and on certain dramatists in particular. Both the larger issues and the smaller prejudices carried over from the earlier work to the later.

DOUGLAS BUSH

Keats and Shakespeare

John Middleton Murry's sometimes extravagant but finely penetrating *Keats and Shakespeare* (1925)[1] carried the subtitle *A
Study of Keats' Poetic Life from 1816 to 1820,* a phrase which
implied, rightly, that the special inquiry involved all that is in or
between the lines of all the poet's verse and prose. That enterprise is well beyond the compass of a paper. Since one must
choose among topics, I shall not go into the hazardous matter of
probable or possible, conscious or unconscious imitations and
echoes of Shakespeare in the poetry — a negative qualified in
the next sentence. I shall only try, on a concrete and pedestrian
level, first to outline Keats's deepening response to Shakespeare
and glance at two segments of his verse which belong to the
Shakespearean domain; and, secondly, to follow his several
formulations of "Negative Capability," the kind of imaginative
power he saw as supremely exemplified in Shakespeare. Even
the smallest sketch takes us over very familiar ground, but the
path has hills and hollows, curves and branches — and some
pitfalls.[2]

1. Oxford: Oxford University Press, 1925.
2. I can mention — without in general giving specific references hereafter — only a few of the critics and scholars to whom I am more or
less indebted: W. J. Bate, *Negative Capability: The Intuitive Approach*

71

Although Keats wrote no formal critique of Shakespeare, his private appreciation was at one with the new inwardness of perception inaugurated by Coleridge, Lamb, and Hazlitt. It has long been a commonplace that his response to Shakespeare was profound; the question is whether or in what degree critical intuitions discern Shakespeare's influence on his poetry. Reasons for the seeming contradiction are the nature and depth of Keats's assimilation of Shakespeare; the kinds of poetry he actually wrote (as distinguished from what he might have gone on to write); the various manifest influences, bad and good, contemporary and older, which hindered or advanced his poetic development; and the emergence of his own genius, at once decidedly Romantic and unique, through a process of self-education under such special masters as — along with Shakespeare — Hazlitt, Milton, and Wordsworth, the last two being poles of both strong attraction and strong repulsion.

In Keats's *Poems* of 1817 incidental phrases from Spenser, Milton, and others are woven into a commonly thin, soft, romantic, "poetical" texture, the staple medium of minor versifiers of the period. The one great poem owes its massive strength to Keats's exciting discovery of Chapman's *Homer* (October 1816). We may be surprised that two poems of the latter half

---

in Keats (Cambridge: Harvard University Press, 1939); *The Stylistic Development of Keats* (New York: The Modern Language Association of America, 1945); *John Keats* and *The Burden of the Past and the English Poet* (Cambridge: Harvard University Press, 1963 and 1970); David Perkins, *The Quest for Permanence: The Symbolism of Wordsworth, Shelley, and Keats* (Cambridge: Harvard University Press, 1959); Robert Gittings, *John Keats* (Boston: Little, Brown, 1968); Morris Dickstein, *Keats and His Poetry: A Study in Development* (Chicago: University of Chicago Press, 1971); Stuart M. Sperry, *Keats the Poet* (Princeton: Princeton University Press, 1973). I somehow missed, until my own limited piece was done, the full and able discussion of Keats and Shakespeare and of negative capability by B. Chatterjee in *Essays on Shakespeare*, ed. Chatterjee (1965), which the author reproduced, with changes, in *John Keats: His Mind and Work*, 1971 (both published by Orient Longman, Calcutta, and in London by Longman). I must also cite Miriam Allott's edition of the *Poems* (London: Longman, 1970; New York: Norton, 1972) and Caroline F. E. Spurgeon's *Keats's Shakespeare* (Oxford: Oxford University Press, 1928; rev. ed., 1929). Keats's letters are quoted, with the publishers' permission, from Hyder E. Rollins' edition (Cambridge: Harvard University Press, 1958).

of 1816, *I Stood Tip-toe* and *Sleep and Poetry*, much the best long pieces he had done and both earnestly preoccupied with his high ambitions, seem to have meager traces of Shakespeare: *I Stood*, 71, 207 (Allott); *Sleep*, 9 (Cordelia), 198 ("certain wands": *Merchant of Venice*, I.iii.84). The young poet dwelling happily in the realm "Of Flora, and old Pan" has only begun to feel higher claims; he must look forward to grappling with "the agonies, the strife / Of human hearts" (*Sleep and Poetry*, 102, 123–125). While his devoted and reliable friend Richard Woodhouse understood these phrases to signify an ascent from the pastoral or rural genre to the heroic and epic,[3] we may read into them a deeper meaning supplied by Keats's experience: a conflict between his sensuous and visionary instincts and his also instinctive and compelling ambition to deal with the realities of human nature and life, a conflict which was to dominate his few remaining years.

During 1817 Shakespeare assumed the throne in Keats's mind. Letters of March and April have jocular echoes that indicate his spontaneous use of even casual Shakespearean phrases. With his visit to the Isle of Wight, which might be taken to mark his virtual abandonment of medicine and his full dedication to poetry, his increasingly serious devotion to Shakespeare flowers suddenly into utterance. A letter to Reynolds (April 17–18) tells of a portrait of Shakespeare found in his lodging which Keats has hung up over his books, just unpacked (his landlady was to press it upon him as a parting gift). In the same letter, along with incidental phrases, there is the misquoted question from *King Lear* — "Do you not hear the Sea?" — which has haunted him intensely and has occasioned the sonnet *On the Sea*: "It keeps eternal Whisperings around / Desolate shores." We may feel that Shakespeare as well as the sea has contributed to the imaginative and verbal resonance of the opening lines; these are quite different from the normal texture of his earlier verse and of much of *Endymion*, which he was about to begin. Adding to the letter the next day, Keats urges Reynolds, when-

3. S. M. Sperry, "Richard Woodhouse's Interleaved and Annotated Copy of Keats's *Poems* (1817)," *Literary Monographs*, I, ed. E. Rothstein and T. K. Dunseath (Madison: University of Wisconsin Press, 1967), 124.

ever he writes, to record any fresh idea he has had of a Shakespearean passage; such new insights must happen continually,
even if they have read a play forty times. And he quotes lines
from *The Tempest* which never struck him so forcibly as now
(and which are akin to the opening of *On the Sea*): "Urchins /
Shall, for that vast of Night that they may work" and "In the
dark backward and abysm of time." He goes on: "I find that I
cannot exist without poetry — without eternal poetry — half
the day will not do — the whole of it." Such remarks almost
identify poetry with Shakespeare and suggest growing ardor and
critical sensitivity.

We may pass over most of the quotations and echoes that
multiply in subsequent letters and notice only some comments
which are no less important than familiar. On May 10, 1817,
beginning a letter to Haydon with the first lines of *Love's
Labour's Lost*, on fame, Keats talks of his own ambitions: is it
too daring to fancy Shakespeare as his "Presider"? Continuing
on May 11, he tells Haydon that, in spite of "Money Troubles"
and his chief enemy, "a horrid Morbidity of Temperament," he
never quite despairs and he reads Shakespeare; indeed he thinks
he will never read any other book much; he very nearly agrees
with Hazlitt that "Shakspeare is enough for us." On November
22, when he was at Burford Bridge trying to finish *Endymion*,
Keats wrote to Reynolds that he had never before found so many
beauties in the sonnets, which, he acutely observed, "seem to be
full of fine things said unintentionally — in the intensity of
working out conceits — Is this to be borne? . . . He has left
nothing to say about nothing or any thing"; and he quotes from
several sonnets. But his self-critical faculty remains less acute,
since — with misgivings, to be sure — he offers for his friend's
verdict lines from the very uninspired song on Cynthia's wedding (*Endymion*, iv.581–590).

In *I Stood Tip-toe* and *Sleep and Poetry* Keats's delighted,
luxurious wonder at things of earth had allowed or nourished a
sense of infinity, a desire to "burst our mortal bars" — his youthful version of the "Natural Supernaturalism" of the whole Romantic movement. Going on from *I Stood Tip-toe*, Keats made
the myth of Endymion and Cynthia the vehicle for an "allegory" in which the idea of transcendence, while the goal of the

hero-poet's quest, was much complicated by episodes which bring ecstasies and more authentic disillusionments. Whatever the meaning of such episodes, Endymion finally learns that the way to the visionary ideal lies through earthly actuality — a resolution which may be consciously opposed to Shelley's picture in *Alastor* of a fatally self-centered poet-dreamer. The gradations of happiness summarized in i.777f, Keats emphasized to his publisher (January 30, 1818), constituted "a regular stepping of the Imagination towards a Truth," "a kind of Pleasure Thermometer." But the summary, although made while he was revising the whole poem, is not very clearly helpful in explaining what the diffuse, wayward, uncertainly self-exploratory "Romance" had become. However, Keats added that this "Argument" "is my first Step towards the chief Attempt in the Drama — the playing of different Natures with Joy and Sorrow" — the first revelation of dramatic ambitions which Shakespeare must have chiefly kindled. More or less clear reminiscences of Shakespeare (often single words) have little or no significance for ideas, unless in the prelude to book ii, where heroines are named in proof that love, earthly sexual love, is something "to brood on with more ardency / Than the death-day of empires." Since the final identification of the goddess with the Indian maid is only a contrivance of sincerely wishful theory which is not felt on Keats's — or our — pulses, we can hardly answer the large question whether or how far a sense of Shakespeare's substantial world of men and women was a factor in binding the young poet's visionary imagination to the human realities of joy and sorrow.[4]

In the all-important letter to Benjamin Bailey of November 22, 1817, Keats declared that he was "certain of nothing but of the holiness of the Heart's affections and the truth of Imagination." He went on to speak of his faith in "a Life of Sensations rather than of Thoughts," even of an afterlife repeating such sensations "in a finer tone." Both the convictions and the personal speculation are decidedly more Romantic than Shake-

4. Morris Dickstein, citing *Endymion*, i.747–760, says (pp. 83–84): "This conception of imagination, like much else in *Endymion*, owes a great deal to . . . *The Tempest* and *A Midsummer Night's Dream*, Keats' earliest favorites among the plays"; and he sees a more specific debt to Mercutio (*Romeo and Juliet*, I.iv.95–105).

spearean. In the same letter Keats makes his first reference to the idea of "Negative Capability"; but that topic may be postponed. We may, though, continue to record some of Keats's general observations on Shakespeare and on the relative claims of aesthetic and moral values in poetry. Always, of course, we must remember his changing circumstances and frequently shifting or contradictory moods which are part of the process of rapid growth; exploratory ideas, however often inspired, may also be tentative and not fully thought out.

Our recognition of Keats's deepening response to Shakespeare is confirmed by his discussion of Edmund Kean's acting in late December 1817, when, in place of Reynolds, he wrote a theatrical piece for *The Champion* (Hampstead Edition, V, 227–232). He referred to five performances he had seen, *Richard III, Hamlet, Macbeth, Othello*, and *Timon*. With ardent admiration he described Kean as "a relict of romance," an actor who brings passion into an unimaginative world which has lost "all wonder, uncertainty and fear," who does so through the "indescribable gusto" and beauty of his elocution and his "intense power of anatomizing the passion of every syllable," who "delivers himself up to the instant feeling, without a shadow of a thought about any thing else." This review and other items go along with the comments in Keats's letters. His marginalia in volumes of Shakespeare (Hampstead Edition, V, 268–279; Spurgeon, *Keats's Shakespeare*), which include mockery of some of Dr. Johnson's remarks, stress Shakespeare's innate universality and power: "He could do easily Man's utmost." Further suggestive testimony appears in Keats's markings of passages in Shakespeare (Spurgeon) and in Hazlitt's *Characters of Shakespear's Plays* of 1817 (Hampstead Edition, V, 280–286); A. Lowell, *John Keats*, II, 587f). In his article on Kean Keats had spoken of "Shakespearian hieroglyphics," and he uses the word again when Hazlitt describes parts of *Othello* and *King Lear* as "Shakespear's great master-pieces in the logic of passion" and the "alternate contraction and dilatation of the soul." Hazlitt's comment on the "levity" of the Fool in *Lear* is queried and refined.

In the early months of 1818 Keats (in spite of *Isabella*) left behind the cloudy theorizing of *Endymion* to endeavor, with confusion still but also with mature strength, to reconcile the claims of the idealistic imagination and realistic truth; and Shakespeare was one agent in the process. In the letter to his brothers of December 21, 27(?), 1817, Keats said, apropos of Benjamin West's new painting, that "the excellence of every Art is its intensity, capable of making all disagreeables evaporate, from their being in close relationship with Beauty & Truth," a principle he sees exemplified throughout *King Lear* — one that he does not much elucidate. On January 23, 1818, he told Bailey and his brothers that he had felt the greatness of *King Lear* so strongly that he had composed a sonnet: in this, written while he was copying *Endymion* for the printer, he turned away from "Romance" to "burn through" again "the fierce dispute, / Betwixt Hell torment & impassioned Clay." A partly parallel conflict between the aspiring poetic and philosophic soul and mortal pangs and fears had just found utterance in *On Seeing a Lock of Milton's Hair* (January 21) and broke out again in "God of the Meridian" (January 31). Both poems link themselves with the impromptu verse-epistle to Reynolds (March 25): here a fuller, more direct, and more anguished struggle goes on, and reality includes both an inward "Purgatory blind" and the "eternal fierce destruction" in the world of fish, birds, and beasts. Such conflicting emotions may seem more modern than Shakespearean.

Keats's deep reverence for and large debt to Wordsworth did not preclude intermittent dislike of his egotistical and didactic strain. One prolonged outburst was prompted by his receiving from Reynolds two sonnets on Robin Hood (February 3, 1818). With the several kinds of egotism represented by Wordsworth, Hunt, and Byron he contrasted the spacious, impersonal, imaginative creativity of "the Elizabethans," represented by Milton and Shakespeare. On February 19 he writes to Reynolds about passive receptivity to sensation and includes the sonnet that embodied such counsel from the thrush — which he knows to be a mere excuse for idleness. That brings us to the letter of February 27 in which he tells his publisher of his three axioms for poetry: they all emphasize spontaneous, unforced naturalness of inspiration and effect. If *Endymion* serves as "a Pioneer," he goes on, he should be content. He has great reason to be content, for

— this comes in unexpectedly — "thank God I can read and perhaps understand Shakspeare to his depths"; and, too, he has many friends. In a letter to Bailey (March 13) Keats's division of "Ethereal thing[s]" has as its topmost class "Things real — such as existences of Sun Moon & Stars and passages of Shakspeare." Shakespeare is a kind of celestial absolute, a grand phenomenon of nature.

Thinking of Reynolds' and his own gloomy view of life (May 3, 1818), Keats remarks that "axioms in philosophy are not axioms until they are proved upon our pulses: . . . until we have gone the same steps as the Author"; thus Reynolds will understand his saying "that now I shall relish Hamlet more than I ever have done." Yet this long letter, contrasting Milton and Wordsworth and expounding the parable of life as "a large Mansion of Many Apartments" — all this (except the poetic serenity of the ode to Maia) grows out of Keats's feeling Wordsworth's concern with human suffering and the "burden of the Mystery"; the stages of awakening he describes are the process of any sensitive mind's growth into maturity. Milton, with his clear-cut Reformation Protestantism, "did not think into the human heart" as Wordsworth, with the advantage of the "grand march of intellect," has done — a rather inadequate view of Milton, though we grasp what Keats means.

The Scottish tour of the summer of 1818 did much to toughen and complicate Keats's sense of rugged scenery, of real life, of Burns, and of the poetic imagination. In the autumn, while nursing his dying brother, he found some relief in the writing of *Hyperion*, a mature treatment of the theme of *Endymion*, the problem of the poet. The immense advance over the earlier work, in firm control and grandeur of style and rhythm, was of course mainly due to close study of *Paradise Lost*. The clearest Shakespearean element has been seen in the picture of the realmless, impotent Saturn as a sort of King Lear.[5] Robert Git-

5. Possibly Keats, who had translated the *Aeneid* in earlier years, recalled the picture of Saturn as *regnis exsul ademptis* (*Aen.* viii.320). Stuart Sperry, taking hints from Hazlitt, suggests (pp. 181–182) that Saturn, a being of once "strong identity" but now a victim of forces he cannot understand, is somewhat akin to the "egotistical" Wordsworth of the *Excursion* facing — with strength which lapses into weakness — his shaken or broken world.

tings (p. 255), going on from *Lear* and ignoring the usual association of the fallen Titans' debate with Milton's infernal one, sees in it the strong influence of *Troilus and Cressida* — a position it may be difficult to share. In general, we may be stirred less by sympathy with the woes of the Titans than by the beauty, both massive and minute, of the "material sublime." We may feel that Keats's epic purposes, however grandly carried out, pretty well excluded Shakespearean realism and immediacy — as, indeed, they kept him from getting into his central theme, the experience of Apollo.

In his first letter to the George Keatses after Tom's death (December–January 1818–1819), Keats proposed that he and they establish a special and continuing bond by reading a passage of Shakespeare every Sunday morning at ten o'clock. After observing that he has left far behind the verse of Mrs. Tighe and James Beattie, he wonders — but only for a moment — whether it would be possible for a superior being to look on Shakespeare in the same light. He feels his perceptive power growing; he does not think he "ever had a greater treat out of Shakspeare" than a book of prints of frescoes (from the Campo Santo at Pisa), especially because they "left so much room for Imagination" — a remark which doubtless applies to Shakespeare too.

We may here forsake chronology to glance at two special topics. In his dozens of early sonnets — to follow W. J. Bate — Keats used a more or less Petrarchan pattern, sometimes incorporating features of Shakespearean style. But after January 1818 he shifted largely to the English or Shakespearean form of three quatrains and a couplet. This form of course prescribes a different development of the theme: witness, for example, four sonnets of January–March 1818, *On Sitting Down to Read King Lear Once Again* (which combines a Petrarchan scheme with a final couplet), "When I have fears that I may cease to be," *To a Lady Seen for a Few Moments at Vauxhall*, and "Four seasons fill the measure of the year." These and later sonnets carry a growing seriousness of reflection and embrace such Shakespearean themes as tragic experience, acceptance of life, time, mortality, fame, all of sober concern to Keats himself. And the later sonnets in general show an increase in the use of Shakespearean repetitions, parallels, and antitheses. *To a Lady* is of all Keats's sonnets perhaps the closest to Shakespeare in theme, imagery, style, and tone:

> Time's sea hath been five years at its slow ebb,
>   Long hours have to and fro let creep the sand,
> Since I was tangled in thy beauty's web,
>   And snared by the ungloving of thine hand.

But the famous "Bright star" of 1819 (a few scholars have argued for 1818) is Shakespearean in its rhyme scheme while Petrarchan in its distinct division between the octave on the star and the sestet, which brings the celestial image down to the poet and Fanny Brawne.

Along with a mainly backward glance at the sonnets we may here look ahead to the end of Keats's poetic career, his attempts to begin fulfilling his dramatic ambitions. During the productive summer of 1819 he managed to write *Otho the Great*. While he had no high opinion of that, he hoped in a few years "to make as great a revolution in modern dramatic writing as Kean has done in acting" (August 14). On November 17, in the midst of prolonged efforts to get the play produced, Keats wrote to his publisher about his interest in men and women rather than romance; two or three poems of character and sentiment, with a diffusion of such romantic coloring as that of *The Eve of St. Agnes*, would nerve him up to "the writing of a few fine Plays — my greatest ambition — when I do feel ambitious. I am sorry to say that is very seldom." And he asks for books about the Elizabethan Earl of Leicester; at the moment he is reading Holinshed. Keats's craving to deal with men and women in dramatic poems and dramas obviously must have owed much to his passion for Shakespeare. But *Otho* was doomed from the start. Keats worked up scene by scene as his friend Charles Brown unfolded the plot (though Keats took over the fifth act himself). His serious ambition was goaded by his urgent need of money, especially to make marriage possible, and his writing was distracted by feverish thoughts of Fanny Brawne (August 5–6): the lover in the play, he tells her, "is madder than I am — I am nothing to him — he has a figure like the Statue of Maleager [*sic*] and double distilled fire in his heart." Altogether, the vigorous but stagey *Otho* is a work that lovers of Keats read — if they read it at all—with more compassion than pleasure; it was a gallant attempt, but it was inevitably much nearer to the contemporary tragedies of Drury Lane and Covent Garden than it was to Shakespeare.

In the dialogue of *Otho* what might be called semi-Shakespearean phrases and images are pretty well lost in high-pitched rhetoric (not that Shakespeare himself was guiltless of that). We cannot say what *King Stephen*, if completed, would have been, but the several short scenes Keats wrote (late August–November) were a great advance upon *Otho*. He was not now blindly following Brown's melodramatic contrivances but was writing on his own, with energy, economy, and a controlling consciousness of Shakespeare's most imitable group of plays. The small portion he wrote inaugurates a clear-cut dramatic conflict and dialogue of Shakespearean realism, though the scenes are not mere pastiche.

Keats's doctrine of "Negative Capability" had first appeared, in brief and rather cryptic form, in the important letter to Bailey of November 22, 1817.[6] Contrasting men of genius and men of power, he said that the former "have not any individuality, any determined Character." This declaration, in the light of his later remarks, seems to contain two related meanings: that men of genius do not have a character of logical, limited fixity but have instead an empathic or dramatic imagination which projects itself easily and fully into other people, creatures, and things. Of the second idea Keats's letter elsewhere provides an illustration: "if a Sparrow come before my Window I take part in its existince and pick about the Gravel." This second meaning was a main theme in Hazlitt's account of Shakespeare, in both the *Characters of Shakespear's Plays* (1817) and the lectures on the English poets (January 13–March 3, 1818): he emphasized the infinite creativity of the supreme "ventriloquist," who "was

6. The general topic is of course more or less discussed by Keats's critics, notably W. J. Bate and others cited in note 2. Leon M. Guilhamet, in a discriminating analysis, takes account of various predecessors ("Keats's 'Negative Capability' and 'Disinterestedness': A Confusion of Ideals," *University of Toronto Quarterly*, XL, 1970–1971, pp. 2–14).

nothing in himself; but he was all that others were, or that they could become." (A corrective of this half-truth might have come from Coleridge: "All things and modes of action shape themselves anew in the being of Milton; while Shakespeare becomes all things, yet for ever remaining himself": *Biographia Literaria*, end of chapter 15.)

When, on December 27(?), 1817, Keats named and defined "Negative Capability," a gift which Shakespeare possessed "so enormously," he slighted the second of the two meanings noted above and expanded the first, stressing the positive value of indeterminacy (it had come to Keats in talk with his square-toed friend Dilke). The great gift is the capability of "being in uncertainties, Mysteries, doubts, without any irritable reaching after fact & reason" — the weakness of Coleridge, who is "incapable of remaining content with half knowledge." However acceptable the idea of intuition might have been to Shakespeare, Keats's conclusion may seem much more Romantic than Shakespearean: "with a great poet the sense of Beauty overcomes every other consideration, or rather obliterates all consideration." We do not think of Shakespeare, the playwright at least, as consciously concerned with Beauty alone, though we cannot be sure how broad a meaning the word has here for Keats.

On October 24, 1818, in a journal letter to the George Keatses, apropos of his not contemplating marriage Keats told of his rich enjoyment of solitude: as his imagination has strengthened, he lives in a thousand worlds, with Achilles or Theocritus or the Shakespearean Troilus. Three days later such examples of complete empathy are generalized and enlarged into a restatement of negative capability, a restatement again altered in focus, since he now speaks, not of contentment with intuitive half-knowledge, but of large impersonal creativity. As "distinguished from the wordsworthian or egotistical sublime," the kind of poetical character Keats upholds, he tells Richard Woodhouse,

> has no self — it is every thing and nothing — It has no character —
> it enjoys light and shade; it lives in gusto, be it foul or fair . . . It
> has as much delight in conceiving an Iago as an Imogen. What
> shocks the virtuous philosop[h]er, delights the camelion Poet. It
> does no harm from its relish of the dark side of things any more

than from its taste for the bright one; because they both end in speculation. A Poet is the most unpoetical of any thing in existence; because he has no Identity — he is continually . . . filling some other Body.

Along with the reminder of Shakespeare's disinterested, unfettered creative faculty, the word "gusto" is a reminder of Hazlitt, a main source or support of some critical principles which Keats made his own. But, in reacting against the doctrinaire Wordsworth, Keats (who had pronounced *The Excursion* one of the three things in the age to rejoice at) may seem unjust to him and more so to Shakespeare and himself: what he says here could, so far as it goes, be taken as an aesthete's indifference to (though not at all a denial of) moral values — which of course was not his or Shakespeare's position. Against such a one-sided utterance we might remember his declaring — in spite of his consuming poetic ambitions — that works of genius are not "the first things in this world," that Bailey's kind of probity and disinterestedness "does hold & grasp the tip top of any spiritual honours, that can be paid to any thing in this world" (January 13, 1818). And that is only one expression of the ethical and humanitarian conviction or ideal that persistently conflicts with Keats's literary ideal of the poet's detachment.

As he grows older — and his calendar of growth is a matter of weeks and months — Keats is, as glimpses have told us already, increasingly involved with the moral quality of both experience and poetry. What he feels and thinks and intellectually knows as a man becomes more important to him as a poet. In a journal letter (February 19, 1819) he is more oracular than usual (though the occasion is Bailey's ignoble behavior): "A Man's life of any worth is a continual allegory . . . Lord Byron cuts a figure — but he is not figurative — Shakspeare led a life of Allegory; his works are the comments on it" (an anticipation of Thomas Mann's "Who is a poet? He whose life is symbolic").[7] Keats's remark seems to imply in Shakespeare a more philosophical and hieroglyphical imagination than is suggested by the definition of negative capability.

7. Quoted as an epigraph in Maynard Mack's *The Garden and the City* (Toronto: University of Toronto Press, 1969).

On March 13, 1819, Keats talked of a dictum of Hazlitt's about our enjoying the depiction of the ravages of a beast of prey because we enjoy the sense of power abstracted from the sense of good. There follow reflections on our own and others' troubles, on the rarity, in the predatory world of animals and men, of true disinterestedness, a quality possessed only by Socrates and Jesus. "But then as Wordsworth says, 'we have all one human heart' — there is an ellectric fire in human nature tending to purify — so that among these human creature[s] there is continu[a]lly some birth of new heroism." Coming back to the previous question, Keats affirms that, if the display of sheer energy and power is the stuff of poetry, "it is not so fine a thing as philosophy — For the same reason that an eagle is not so fine a thing as a truth." We remember that for Keats "philosophy" means chiefly the understanding in some degree of the mysteries and trials of life — although he has grown more conscious of the power of intellectual knowledge to fortify and illuminate "sensations."

In the same letter (April 21) Keats expounds at length his conception of life as "The vale of Soul-making," a conception which carries on from the painful process of growth gone through by Endymion and outlined in the "Mansion of Many Apartments" (May 3, 1818) and which holds for men in general, poets apparently not being excluded. People "are not Souls . . . till they acquire identities, till each one is personally itself." And that can be achieved only through experience in "a World of Pains and troubles . . . where the heart must feel and suffer in a thousand diverse ways!" There could hardly be a clearer recognition of the inadequacy of negative capability, and it does not stand alone. It was apparently about this time that Keats wrote the fragmentary third book of *Hyperion*, in which he managed at last to set forth — in summary fashion — the theme he had hitherto failed to express: Apollo, dying into life, becoming a god, a true poet, when his mind is flooded with sympathetic comprehension of the course of mankind's history, its vicissitudes and agonies. Apollo's rebirth is an enlarged exposition of the highest poetic aim Keats had looked forward to in *Sleep and Poetry*, a restatement of his declaration to Reynolds that "Sorrow is Wisdom," expanded in the same letter (May 3, 1818) into the "Mansion of Many Apartments" and the exaltation of Wordsworth as a poet who martyrs himself to the human heart. This humanitarian Apollo does not seem to be modeled on Shakespeare. In any case Keats has moved far beyond what he had written to Woodhouse in 1818 about the ideal of mere open-minded, nonmoral creativity.

On May 31, 1819, in a time of special difficulty and discouragement, Keats told Sarah Jeffrey of his melancholy state of mind, citing not Shakespeare but Wordsworth, and taking as his own the loss of sustaining vision avowed in *Intimations of Immortality*. On June 9, however, writing again to Miss Jeffrey, Keats speaks of Boiardo as "a noble Poet of Romance; not a miserable and mighty Poet of the human Heart. The middle age of Shakspeare was all c[l]ouded over; his days were not more happy than Hamlet's who is perhaps more like Shakspeare himself in his common every day Life than any other of his Characters." Keats hopes that he is "a little more of a Philosopher" than he was, "consequently a little less of a versifying Petlamb."

In spite of his emotional turmoil over Fanny Brawne, which was to grow even more intense during the rest of his life, Keats made good progress with writing in his self-imposed summer exile of 1819. On August 14 he wrote to Bailey that he was "convinced more and more every day that (excepting the human friend Philosopher) a fine writer is the most genuine Being in the World — Shakspeare and the paradise Lost every day become greater wonders to me — I look upon fine Phrases like a Lover." The parenthetical exception recalls the remark of five months earlier about the inferiority of an eagle (poetry) to a truth (philosophy). One asks whether "the most genuine Being in the World" implies only a supremely creative, disinterested imagination or a strong moral identity and a repudiation of negative capability (already tacitly repudiated in "The vale of Soulmaking" and *Hyperion*, iii). One queries too Keats's looking "upon fine Phrases like a Lover": here, as in some earlier utterances, is he thinking only or mainly of the extraordinary verbal expressiveness of Shakespeare and Milton? Yet we have seen him lately glorifying Shakespeare as "a miserable and mighty Poet of the human Heart" — a view in full accord with much other personal testimony.

On August 24, 1819, Keats wrote to Reynolds in the same strain as he had written to Bailey: "I am convinced more and more day by day that fine writing is next to fine doing the top thing in the world; the Paradise Lost becomes a greater wonder." Is the omission of Shakespeare this time significant or is it not? Murry (pp. 166–167) took it as a deliberate, honest, and disastrous admission to himself that he has shut out from his heart Fanny Brawne, the world of men and women, and Shakespeare; that may be an overreaction. But there is the fact that a month after his exaltation of *Paradise Lost* Keats abandoned the *Fall of Hyperion* because Milton's "artful" language is stifling and he wishes to give himself up to other sensations — as he had just done in *To Autumn*. And it may seem odd that in his outbursts against Milton (September 21 and 24: *Letters*, II, 167, 212) he proclaims Chatterton — not Shakespeare — the purest writer in the English language. Whether or not language was a real or main cause of his decision against the *Fall*, the most moving of all Keats's deliverances on the problems of life, art, and the artist was the lesson of hopeless endurance which the poet-narrator reads in the face of the prophetess Moneta (i.256f).

Those significant qualifications of August 14 and 24, "excepting the human friend Philosopher" and "next to fine doing," link themselves with what Keats had said about the superiority of fine character to works of genius (January 13, 1818) and with the harrowing distinctions drawn in the induction to the *Fall* (i.147–210) between dreamers and simple, active benefactors of mankind and between dreamers and true poets — distinctions that touch Keats's recurrent questioning of the value of poetry itself. We think too of *Lamia*, partly written just before the *Fall*, in which self-deluded dreamers are destroyed and their destroyer is the harshly skeptical Apollonius (who is not an ideal example of "the human friend Philosopher"). In the half-despairing, half-stoic *Fall* Keats can hardly resolve the complex, gnawing problems of the poet's nature and function, yet his intensely troubled uncertainties — and some earnest certainties

— have carried him far deeper than the old antithesis between negative capability and a fixed identity.[8]

In a sketchy discussion of a well-worn topic, one may reach conclusions which on one level are largely negative and on another are greatly but vaguely positive. About Shakespeare and Keats's major poems of the great year hardly anything concrete can be said, although critics have seen in them the growth and sharpening of his dramatic instincts. *The Eve of St. Agnes* recalls *Romeo and Juliet* and details in other plays, but we do not think of Shakespearean influence as a prime factor even in that poem, much less in the narratives that followed. Of the odes of the spring the two finest owe much of their strength to being half-involuntary attempts at escape which are defeated by the poet's inescapable sense of painful reality. *To Autumn* is — like the ode to Maia of May 1, 1818 — a quiet, almost serene acceptance of the cycle of time and change in which the complexities of human experience are not directly touched; this poem Murry (p. 189) called "deeply Shakespearean," on his general assumption that Shakespeare is behind every utterance in which Keats is accepting life as it is. For Shakespeare Keats's poetry yields very little of the various kinds of evidence that clearly show the influence of Spenser and Milton and Wordsworth and Dryden and Dante. Whatever the themes and whatever incidental echoes, audible or possible, there may be, Keats is going his own way, and it is not Shakespeare's way, except in some of the mature sonnets and the late efforts in drama.

On the higher levels of art, outlook, and personality it is safer to speak of qualities and attitudes which reveal degrees of affinity and which Shakespeare would quicken — such as Keats's power of empathy, his instinct for palpable imagery, and,

8. On September 24, 1819, Keats reverted to his early idea in complaining that Dilke "cannot feel he has a personal identity unless he has made up his Mind about every thing," whereas "The only means of strengthening one's intellect is to make up ones mind about nothing — to let the mind be a thoroughfare for all thoughts." But this presumably has to do with everyday attitudes rather than with writing, since Keats had just been desperately trying to attain unifying and satisfying truth about poetry and life.

in David Perkins' words, his "sense of process in the natural world" and his simultaneous grasp of "a variety of human feelings." Or, knowing that Shakespeare was the one bright star that remained steadfast in Keats's poetic heaven, we may see him as sustaining his worshiper's usually unshakeable faith in poetry, as strengthening the resolute acceptance of human limitations, the realistic and tragic view of life, which overcame or disciplined his early visionary idealism. In letters of February 14 and November 1, 1820, an actual and a probable recollection of the dying Falstaff are poignant reminders of how deeply Shakespeare had entered into Keats's being. We may well share the belief which, as W. J. Bate says, has long been held (in fact since Richard Woodhouse), that Keats was "the most Shakespearean in character of all poets since Shakespeare himself." It is no contradiction of that to remember that he learned much of life and art on his own pulses, that our total view of him is based at least as much on his letters as on his poems.

Shakespeare's personality remains elusive and almost inscrutable to us. He wrote plays in the established genres of history, comedy, and tragedy (and made unique mixtures of these elements); the framework or background of his political, social, ethical, and religious ideas was apparently the normal Christian humanism of his age, however much his imaginative insight might transcend orthodoxy. Keats was a young, skeptical liberal of the Romantic age, of a generation which felt compelled to find its own individual philosophy of life as well as of poetry; and, more than any of his poetic elders or contemporaries, Keats carried the burden of a distinctively modern consciousness of the human and the poetic situation — "straining at particles of light in the midst of a great darkness" (March 19, 1819). "Keats followed Wordsworth by internalizing the quest toward finding a world that answered the poet's desires, and he hoped to follow Shakespeare by making that world more than a sublime projection of his own ego." [9] Yet, for all his Shakespearean devotion, his dramatic aspirations, and growing dramatic power, and his theory of negative capability (so long as that held),

9. Harold Bloom, "Keats and the Embarrassments of Poetic Tradition," in *From Sensibility to Romanticism*, ed. F. W. Hilles and H. Bloom (New York: Oxford University Press, 1965), p. 519.

Keats was, like other Romantics, a deeply subjective poet, even in the first *Hyperion*, and as yet he was by no means ready to create a Shakespearean world; what he might have proved able to do we can hardly begin to guess. We may remember that Matthew Arnold's fervent tribute was strongly qualified: Keats was "with Shakespeare" in his gift of "natural magic," "the faculty of naturalistic interpretation," but not in the higher "faculty of moral interpretation." We, with our understanding of Keats enriched and deepened by twentieth-century criticism, may be moved to strongly qualify Arnold's distinction, though we cannot altogether dismiss it. However, even if Keats's modern stature is much higher than Arnold's high claim, we may or must be content to acknowledge that a demonstration of Shakespeare's influence is impossible.

PAUL A. CANTOR

"A Distorting Mirror":
Shelley's *The Cenci* and Shakespearean Tragedy

Few writers since the Renaissance have been as bold as Percy Bysshe Shelley in inviting comparison with Shakespeare. Shelley's *The Cenci*, the one genuinely dramatic composition he ever finished, contains many echoes of individual lines in Shakespeare, and in some cases seems to be recreating whole passages and indeed whole scenes from Shakespeare's plays. To be sure, the one literary debt Shelley acknowledged in his preface is to Calderon's *El Purgatorio de San Patricio*, but the fact that he speaks of the "only plagiarism" which he "intentionally committed in the whole piece" [1] suggests that he was aware that other plagiarisms had crept into his work unconsciously.[2] Whatever Shelley's own view of the sources of *The Cenci* may have been, critics have by and large refused the bait offered by his footnote, ignoring Calderon's influence on the play to concentrate on the more disturbing problem of Shakespeare's. Ever

1. I have used the Library of Liberal Arts edition of *The Cenci*, ed. Roland A. Duerksen (Indianapolis: Bobbs-Merrill, 1970). The acknowledgement to Calderon occurs in footnote 3 in Shelley's preface.
2. Stuart Curran, *Shelley's Cenci: Scorpions Ringed with Fire* (Princeton: Princeton University Press, 1970), pp. 28–29.

since the first reviewers of the play, some critics have claimed
that the extent of the plagiarism from Shakespeare in *The Cenci*
raises serious doubts about its value as a play.[3] Other critics,
coming to Shelley's defense, have discounted the importance of
the Shakespearean echoes in *The Cenci*, claiming that Shelley
did not exceed the ordinary license of a playwright in his borrowing.[4]

The debate over Shelley's debt to Shakespeare in *The Cenci*
shows every sign of swinging back and forth forever, with those
who dislike the play to begin with using Shakespeare as the standard for denigrating it, and those who already admire it invoking
Shakespearean precedents of imagery and structure as evidence
of its value. Perhaps a more fruitful approach to *The Cenci*
would be to consider the role of the Shakespearean echoes in
our understanding of the play's significance, rather than in our
estimation of its artistic worth. Most critics seem to leave the
matter of Shakespeare and *The Cenci* at compiling lists of verbal
parallels and supposed plagiarisms,[5] as if there were nothing
problematic about the way Shelley specifically uses Shakespeare.
But consider, for example, one of the most blatant of Shelley's
"borrowings," Giacomo's meditation on the dying flame of his
father's life:

3. In one of the earliest reviews (*The Literary Gazette*, April 1, 1820),
plagiarism is charged as one of Shelley's lesser sins: "Cenci's impreca-
tion on his daughter, though an imitation of Lear, and one of a multi-
tude of direct plagiarisms, is absolutely too shocking for perusal." Quoted
in Newman I. White, *The Unextinguished Hearth: Shelley and His Contemporary Critics* (Durham: Duke University Press, 1938), p. 170.
Among modern critics, George Steiner, *The Death of Tragedy* (New
York: Hill and Wang, 1961), pp. 147–148, claims that in *The Cenci*
"pastiche is carried to the level of art . . . but even at the best, the fact of
imitation intrudes."
4. See Curran, *Shelley's Cenci*, pp. 35–41; Richard M. Fletcher, *English
Romantic Drama, 1795–1843* (New York: Exposition Press, 1966), p.
102; and Seymour Reiter, *A Study of Shelley's Poetry* (Albuquerque:
University of New Mexico Press, 1967), p. 194.
5. For a few such lists, see Ernest Sutherland Bates, *A Study of Shelley's Drama "The Cenci"* (New York: Columbia University Press, 1908),
pp. 54–55; David Lee Clark, "Shelley and Shakespeare," *PMLA*, LIV
(1939), 278–286; Beach Langston, "Shelley's Use of Shakespeare," *The
Huntington Library Quarterly*, XII (1949), 168; and Curran, *Shelley's
Cenci*, p. 38.

> Thou unreplenished lamp! whose narrow fire
> Is shaken by the wind, and on whose edge
> Devouring darkness hovers! Thou small flame,
> Which, as a dying pulse rises and falls,
> Still flickerest up and down, how very soon,
> Did I not feed thee, wouldst thou fail and be
> As thou hadst never been! So wastes and sinks
> Even now, perhaps, the life that kindled mine:
> But that no power can fill with vital oil
> That broken lamp of flesh.
>
> (III.ii.9–18)

These lines immediately bring to mind Othello's approach to the sleeping Desdemona:

> Put out the light, and then put out the light:
> If I quench thee, thou flaming minister,
> I can again thy former light restore,
> Should I repent me; but once put out thy light,
> Thou cunning'st pattern of excelling nature,
> I know not where is that Promethean heat
> That can thy light relume.
>
> (V.ii.7–13)[6]

As if to leave no doubt as to his source, Shelley repeats the lamp conceit, as Giacomo relights the flame and uses two of the poetically distinctive words from the *Othello* passage:

> And yet once *quenched* I cannot thus *relume*
> My father's life.
>
> (III.ii.51–52; my italics)

An evaluative comparison of these passages could only work to Shelley's disadvantage: Shakespeare is poetically concise, whereas Shelley is wordy; Othello's concern for the light arises naturally out of the dramatic situation of a man about to commit a murder, who wants darkness for the deed, whereas Giacomo,

6. All quotations from Shakespeare are taken from the *Riverside Shakespeare*, ed. G. Blakemore Evans and others (Boston: Houghton Mifflin Co., 1974).

with nothing to do in his scene but wait passively for news, has
no particular reason to be thinking about a lamp.[7] What is truly
problematic about the passage from *The Cenci*, though, is why
Shelley chose to echo or allude to *Othello* at just this point and
in just this way. It would be strange enough for Shelley to be
suggesting a parallel between the weak indecisive Giacomo and
the grand resolute Othello, but if one extends the parallels from
the speakers to the characters they are speaking of, one finds
oneself in the preposterous position of equating Count Cenci
with Desdemona. One might immediately object that since Shelley was not intentionally plagiarizing from Shakespeare, there
can be no possibility of his intending to set up any parallels between Giacomo and Othello, or Count Cenci and Desdemona.
But even if Shelley's plagiarism from *Othello* were entirely
unconscious, one is still left wondering what made him "unconsciously remember" Othello's fifth act speech, even down to the
detail of the unusual word "relume," when he was writing a
third act speech for his Giacomo. What could have set off this
peculiar poetic reverberation in Shelley's creative imagination?
As we shall see, the problem with the "quotations" from Shakespeare in *The Cenci* is that many of them are "misquotations." [8]
Particularly in the case of the more obvious and extended parallels, a comparison with the originals reveals that the contexts of
Shelley's passages seem at odds with those of his "models" in
Shakespeare. What emerges from a study of *The Cenci* in relation to Shakespeare is thus a sense of Shelley not passively imitating his predecessor but actively struggling against a conception of tragedy antithetical to his own.

Some of the Shakespearean echoes in *The Cenci* are of course
reasonably appropriate in their context. We are not surprised,
for example, to hear Beatrice sound like Hamlet when she speculates about suicide and death (III.i.132–134, 148–151; V.iv.
72–73). Other Shakespearean echoes are relatively neutral, in

7. Moody E. Prior, *The Language of Tragedy* (New York: Columbia
University Press, 1947), p. 227.
8. In examining Shelley's "misquotations" from Shakespeare, I believe
I am dealing with something akin to the phenomenon Harold Bloom has
called poetic misprision. See particularly *The Anxiety of Influence* (New
York: Oxford University Press, 1973) and *A Map of Misreading* (New
York: Oxford University Press, 1975).

the sense that when one compares the context in Shelley with the context in Shakespeare one is neither jarred by the incongruity nor struck by the aptness of the parallel. It seems fortuitous, for example, that Othello's phrase, "thrice-driven bed of down" (I.iii.231), should be used word for word by Giacomo ("From thrice-driven beds of down, and delicate food," II.ii. 14). But after leaving aside such passages, one is still left with several Shakespearean reminiscences in *The Cenci* which, like the plagiarism of Othello's "Put out the light" speech, raise doubts about their appropriateness. Two of the Shakespearean echoes most easily recognized in *The Cenci* especially repay careful study, because they are at once the most extensive and the most puzzling of Shelley's uses of Shakespeare.

The first of these passages is Count Cenci's curse upon Beatrice (IV.i.114–159), which clearly derives from Lear's curse upon Goneril (I.iv.275–289), but also draws upon later speeches by the king:

> CENCI. If this most specious mass of flesh,
> Which Thou hast made my daughter, this my blood,
> This particle of my divided being;
> Or rather, this my bane and my disease,
> Whose sight infects and poisons me . . .
>
> (IV.i.115–119)

> LEAR. But yet thou art my flesh, my blood, my daughter—
> Or rather a disease that's in my flesh,
> Which I must needs call mine. Thou art a bile,
> A plague-sore, or embossed carbuncle,
> In my corrupted blood.
>
> (II.iv.221–225)

The second example is a complex of *Macbeth* reminiscences running throughout the murder of Count Cenci and reaching a peak in act IV, scenes iii and iv. Shelley repeatedly uses key words from *Macbeth*, like "deed," "act," "done," "undone," "palterers," "equivocation," and "innocent sleep," and draws upon the resemblance of the man to be murdered with the father of his would-be murderer (IV.iii.16–22), as well as the similarity of sleep and death (IV.iv.57–58), both points familiar to us from *Macbeth*. In itself there is nothing strange about Shel-

ley echoing *Macbeth* in the course of portraying a murder, but in
the process he creates a parallel between Beatrice and both Macbeth and Lady Macbeth, for it is Beatrice's speech which is most
thoroughly saturated with the idiom of *Macbeth*, as two examples will illustrate:

> Ye conscience-stricken cravens, rock to rest
> Your baby hearts. It is the iron gate,
> Which ye left open, swinging to the wind,
> That enters whistling as in scorn. Come, follow!
> And be your steps like mine, light, quick and bold.
>
> (IV.ii.39–43)

> O, fear not
> What may be done, but what is left undone:
> The act seals all.
>
> (IV.iii.5–7)

These debts to *Lear* and *Macbeth* in *The Cenci* have long
been noted by critics; but it is surprising how little has been
made of the apparently puzzling fact that Shelley has his black-
est villain echo one of the noblest figures in Shakespeare and
then portrays his pure heroine echoing two of the most con-
science-stained and guilt-ridden of Shakespeare's characters.[9]

9. G. Wilson Knight, *The Golden Labyrinth* (New York: W. W. Norton, 1962), p. 216, notes the "paradox" of Beatrice resembling Lady Macbeth. Milton Wilson, *Shelley's Later Poetry* (New York: Columbia University Press, 1959), p. 88, approaches the problem when he notes:
"whereas the darker side of Beatrice resembles Lady Macbeth, the
brighter side at moments in the last act reminds us of Desdemona. It is
hard to imagine Lady Macbeth and Desdemona in the same heroine, but
Shelley's unconscious reminiscences of Shakespeare force us to do so."
Reiter, in *Shelley's Poetry*, pp. 194–195, sees nothing problematic about
the Shakespearean echoes: "If the like passages are read with a mind not
clouded by the prejudice of 'imitation,' the continuity of human experiences that those passages reflect can strengthen the scenes, just as the
echoes of the Bible do in *Paradise Lost*." Reiter's "continuity of human
experiences" must embrace quite a wide spectrum, if it runs from Lear's
nobility to Cenci's depravity and from Macbeth's guilt to Beatrice's innocence, and one might legitimately question whether the biblical echoes
in *Paradise Lost* serve the same function as the Shakespearean echoes in
The Cenci. Indeed the question is whether Shelley "believed" in Shakespeare the way Milton believed in the Bible.

This situation is not quite clear-cut enough to be reduced to the straightforward formula: villain in Shelley echoes hero in Shakespeare, while heroine in Shelley echoes villains in Shakespeare. Since Shakespeare's characters, with their tragic mixture of virtues and vices, are fuller and more complex portrayals than the comparatively one-sided and almost melodramatic creations of Shelley, one can find things to say against Lear, just as one can find things to say in favor of Macbeth and his wife. For all his greatness of soul, Lear is obviously flawed by his willfulness and failure to understand himself and those around him. And though Macbeth and Lady Macbeth are driven by a base form of ambition, the fact that we witness the growth of evil in them and its tragic impact on them allows us to sympathize with them as human beings. By contrast, Count Cenci's evil is presented as a given, and one would be hard-pressed to find any redeeming features in his portrayal.[10] Beatrice's characterization is somewhat more complex, and one could trace a progressive degeneration in her soul, as her father's cruelty finally corrupts her innocence, causing her to answer violence with more violence. As several critics have noted, Beatrice takes on some of her father's less attractive features; for one thing, she learns how to outface moral reproaches with outright lies and a pious assurance that God is on her side.[11] Nevertheless, whatever faults emerge in Beatrice (and they are a subject of ongoing critical debate), we never feel that she is an active force of evil, but rather a passive victim, who is compelled to whatever crimes she commits. Thus having made all the qualifications possible concerning the moral status of the characters involved in our Shelley-Shakespeare parallels, we still cannot eliminate our sense of incongruity at

10. But see Knight, *The Golden Labyrinth*, p. 216: "In Cenci evil has become pretty nearly good"; and Curran, in *Shelley's Cenci*, p. 76, who sees Cenci as "one with the other great heroes of Romantic drama, Faust and Manfred."

11. See Bates, *Shelley's Drama*, pp. 70–73; Wilson, *Shelley's Later Poetry*, pp. 83–87; Curran, *Shelley's Cenci*, p. 87; and Terry Otten, *The Deserted Stage* (Athens: Ohio University Press, 1972), pp. 32–33. In Beatrice's last line in Antonin Artaud's reworking of *The Cenci*, she says of her father: "I fear that death may teach me that I have ended by resembling him" (New York: Grove Press, 1970; tr. Simon Watson Taylor, p. 52).

the way the characters pair up. At the very least, one must admit that we can admire Lear in ways we cannot admire Cenci, and we would reproach Macbeth and Lady Macbeth in ways we cannot reproach Beatrice. Thus there is inevitably something jarring about hearing Cenci echo Lear and Beatrice echo Macbeth and Lady Macbeth.[12]

Perhaps the simplest way to grasp the oddness of Shelley's Shakespearean quotations is to ask oneself, "Without the verbal parallels, would I ever have mentioned Count Cenci in the same breath as King Lear, or Beatrice in the same breath as Macbeth and Lady Macbeth?" If the answer to this question is even a qualified "no," then we must consider why Shelley forced us to think of these parallels, or at least why they occurred on some subconscious level of his own imagination. One possibility is that the Shakespearean echoes in *The Cenci* should make us rethink our view of the play, with Cenci's quotations from *Lear* somehow raising him in our esteem and Beatrice's quotations from *Macbeth* somehow lowering her. Although many literary allusions work in this way, suggesting a deeper or ironic level of meaning that qualifies the surface meaning of a work, it does not seem likely that Shelley wished to overturn, or even modify, our initial reactions to his characters on the basis of Shakespearean standards. If the poetic substratum of Shakespearean reminiscences in *The Cenci* is not an oblique comment on the play in the light of Shakespeare, then the other possibility is that, consciously or unconsciously, it has the effect of commenting on Shakespeare in the light of *The Cenci*. What this would involve becomes clear if one pauses to reflect upon the crudest formulation of the parallels we have been working with: "Evil" character in Shelley sounds like "good" character in Shakespeare; "Good" character in Shelley sounds like "evil" character in Shakespeare. Substitute here Blake for Shelley and Milton for Shakespeare and we are back on more familiar territory in Romantic criticism. Perhaps Shelley's "misquotations" from Shakespeare can be understood on the model of the gnostic inversions the Romantics work upon traditional beliefs through such

12. It seems much more natural for Cenci to quote Macbeth and for Beatrice to quote Lear, as does occasionally happen in the play (see I.i.140–144; II.i.123–128, 181–193; III.i.85–86).

literary techniques as allusion and parody.[13] When Blake's Urizen begins to sound like Milton's God, and Blake's Orc begins to take on the features of Milton's Satan, we are not supposed to revise our estimates of Urizen and Orc, but to take a new look at the traditional evaluation of God and Satan and to change our view of the relative merits of the forces they represent in Blake's eyes (reason vs. passion, authority vs. rebellion, and so on). From Shelley's reworking of the Prometheus myth, as well as his comments on Milton's Satan in the preface to *Prometheus Unbound* and the *Defense of Poetry*, we know that he, like Blake, took a gnostic approach to existing myths and beliefs, portraying the sublime guardians of law and morality in traditional religion as petty tyrants, and the tricksters and rebels as the potential saviors of mankind.[14] Thus when Shelley's Jupiter virtually quotes Milton's God in announcing what he thinks to be the begetting of an heir (compare *Prometheus Unbound*, III.i.18 with *Paradise Lost*, V.603–604), the reminiscence works to lower Milton's God in our esteem, not to raise Shelley's Jupiter.

Shakespeare's plays, of course, do not embody traditional mythology in the way *Paradise Lost* does, and without direct archetypal figures of God and the devil they do not lend themselves to the kind of gnostic reversals Blake and Shelley attempted with the characters in Milton's epic. Nevertheless, and however highly Shelley regarded Shakespeare as an artist, one would think something in Shakespeare's plays would have made Shelley at the very least uncomfortable, given the fact that Shakespeare's view of the relation of reason and passion, or of authority and rebellion, is undoubtedly closer to Milton's than to Shelley's. Lear is an authority figure in Shakespeare — perhaps the authority figure par excellence; Macbeth and Lady Macbeth are rebels against the conventional order. Perhaps Shelley's deep-rooted dissatisfaction with Shakespeare's view of authority and rebellion is what surfaces in the peculiar form of the misquotations from *Lear* and *Macbeth* in *The Cenci*, mis-

13. On gnostic treatments of traditional myth, see Hans Jonas, *The Gnostic Religion* (Boston: Beacon Press, 1958), pp. 91–97; on the relation of gnosticism to modern thought, see pp. 320–340.

14. On gnosticism in Shelley, see James Rieger, *The Mutiny Within: The Heresies of Percy Bysshe Shelley* (New York: George Brazillier, 1967), especially the chapter on *The Cenci*, pp. 111–128.

quotations which suggest that Shelley found something repellant in Lear as authority figure and something attractive in Macbeth as rebel. We might, then, think in terms of Shelley's substantive disagreements with Shakespeare when we look more carefully for what might have led him to recall King Lear in connection with the demonic Count Cenci, and Macbeth and his wife in connection with the angelic Beatrice.

The passages Cenci echoes from *Lear* raise the question of the relation of nature and convention, and this issue emerges as one of the focal points of the difference between Shelley and Shakespeare. By having Cenci recall Lear's curse upon Goneril, Shelley focuses attention on the old king in one of his darker moments, for however justified he may be in turning against his daughter, the way he curses her reveals the mistake in his self-conception that underlies all his tragic errors in the play. In calling upon the "dear goddess," Nature, to make Goneril sterile, or to "create her child of spleen" (I.iv.282), Lear assumes that nature will support his decrees, even when he demands something "unnatural," that is, something against the ordinary course of nature. This attitude is already evident in Lear's banishment of Cordelia, when he calls upon the forces of nature to deny his blood tie or natural bond to his youngest daughter:

> For by the sacred radiance of the sun,
> The mysteries of Hecat and the night;
> By all the operation of the orbs,
> From whom we do exist and cease to be;
> Here I disclaim all my paternal care,
> Propinquity and property of blood,
> And as a stranger to my heart and me
> Hold thee from this for ever.
>
> (I.i.109–116)

This blind belief on Lear's part that his orders have the force of laws of nature leads him to overestimate tragically the justness of his personal cause, as well as of his ability to uphold it.

A trait evident only in Lear's most arrogant moments becomes the very essence of Count Cenci's character in Shelley's portrayal. Assured of the parallels between himself and God — "He

does His will, I mine!" (IV.i.139) — Cenci is convinced that
higher powers stand ready to execute his every whim:

> 'Tis plain I have been favoured from above,
> For when I cursed my sons they died.
>
> (IV.i.39–40)

The difference between *Lear* and *The Cenci* is evident in the fact
that Cenci's curses work, whereas Lear's do not. That is, in *Lear*
the putative harmony between nature and human authority is revealed to be a fiction, while in *The Cenci* it becomes the premise
of the tragic action itself. Lear must learn that nature does not
always obey his commands: indeed his inability to direct the elements reveals to him his limitations as a ruler, the disparity between authority by nature and authority by convention:

> When the rain came to wet me once, and the wind to make me
> chatter, when the thunder would not peace at my bidding, there
> I found 'em, there I smelt 'em out. Go to, they are not men o'
> their words: they told me I was every thing. 'Tis a lie, I am not
> ague-proof.
>
> (IV.vi.100–105)

Nature is portrayed as ultimately recalcitrant to the tyrannical
exercise of human authority in *Lear*. The natural convulsions
in the play seem to symbolize a nature rejecting and repulsing
unnatural attempts to exceed human limits. In that sense, nature
in *Lear* provides a standard for setting boundaries to human authority, and in doing so must be independent of human convention.

As in *Lear*, the third act of *The Cenci* is accompanied by
sounds of thunder and a storm. But unlike Lear's storm, which
strips him of his belief in his natural right to rule, Cenci's con-
spires to uphold his power:

> Then wind and thunder,
> Which seemed to howl his knell, is the loud laughter
> With which Heaven mocks our weakness!
>
> (III.ii.37–39)

Whereas Lear's tragedy has its roots in the gap between nature and convention, Beatrice's arises from her inability to appeal from convention to nature,[15] for in her world nature and convention become indistinguishable once nature is seen as just another form of arbitrary law limiting man. As several critics have noted, Beatrice is surrounded by concentric circles of authority (Father-Pope-God) which mutually support each other.[16] The action of the play demonstrates that she cannot escape from the tyranny of her immediate family situation by appealing to any force in nature, for wherever she turns she finds the power of fathers again, and that means the power of convention: "a marble form, / A rite, a law, a custom" (V.iv. 4–5). One of the deepest ironies of the play is that the murder of her father, far from destroying his hold on her, eventually causes her to project his spirit onto the entire universe, transforming him in her eyes into an "omnipotent" and "ever present" force (V.iv.57–72), in fact the ordering principle of a cosmic — and therefore inescapable — tyranny. In *Lear*, nature is arrayed against convention; in *The Cenci*, nature and convention are together arrayed against a pure spirit whose only hope would be to transcend this world entirely.

This is what is most fundamentally gnostic about the view of human existence presented in *The Cenci*: Shelley sees all order in this world, natural and conventional, as imprisoning the human spirit, and therefore avoids the question that is central to *Lear* of how to discriminate between just and unjust uses of authority on the basis of a natural standard.[17] The point of *The Cenci* seems to be that all forms of authority are corrupt and unjust, whereas the course of action in *Lear* works to reestablish a just basis for the exercise of authority once the forces of injustice have revealed and ultimately destroyed themselves. A

15. Ibid., p. 118.
16. See Knight, *The Golden Labyrinth*, pp. 216–217; Rieger, *Mutiny Within*, p. 115; and Northrop Frye, *Fools of Time* (Toronto: University of Toronto Press, 1967), p. 45.
17. On gnostic attitudes towards world order, see Jonas, *Gnostic Religion*, pp. 250–253, especially p. 250: "Order and law is the cosmos too, but rigid and inimical order, tyrannical and evil law, devoid of meaning and goodness, alien to the purposes of man and to his inner essence, no object for his communication and affirmation."

comparison of the judicial proceedings in the fifth acts of *The Cenci* and *Lear* will show how much less radical is Shakespeare's view of authority than Shelley's, for, although *Lear* chronicles many abuses of power, in Edgar's triumph over Edmund it at the same time affirms the need for some principle of order to reassert itself over the uncontrolled force of the passions in evil men and women. One can learn a great deal about the differences between Shakespeare and Shelley by juxtaposing the ways they choose to portray an authority figure: the kingly Lear, for all his flaws and errors, represents the potential for — and at times the actuality of — a positive force of order in the world, necessary to combat the disordering force of human passion; the degenerate Cenci reflects Shelley's distrust of authority as such, embodying a nightmare vision of the warped principle of order behind both nature and convention in this world.

It seems reasonable that Shelley's Romantic, and even gnostic, hatred for all worldly power could transform — on whatever level of his imagination — Shakespeare's balanced portrayal of Lear's virtues and defects into the horrifying caricature of authority in *The Cenci*, thus sparking the verbal reminiscences of Lear's curse of Goneril in Cenci's curse of Beatrice. But by what imaginative process could Macbeth turn into Beatrice in Shelley's mind, at least long enough for Beatrice to pick up Macbeth's habits of speech? The one quality in Macbeth that might be called Romantic, that might link him with the heroine of a Romantic drama, is his yearning for the Absolute, his quest to find the one act that "might be the be-all and the end-all" (I.vii. 5) of his life. To be sure, the form of the Absolute that Macbeth pursues is at first a narrowly conceived one: "the sweet fruition of an earthly crown," to quote another quester for the Absolute in Renaissance drama. But as Macbeth is led from deed to deed in an increasingly fruitless attempt to make secure his dubious achievement, he finds himself involved in an endless quest in which satisfaction continually eludes him, a quest for which his wife provides the motto:

Nought's had, all's spent,
Where our desire is got without content.

(III.ii.4–5)

In his ceaseless striving for the one act that will have no further consequences, and thus relieve him of the necessity to act again, Macbeth begins to take on the character of a Romantic quester, perpetually trying to leave his past behind him, forever dissatisfied with his present, and always looking to the future to yield him the fulfillment the past and present have denied him. Obsessed with security, Macbeth develops an all-or-nothing attitude towards life: he must either have the unchallenged position he dreams of, or he is left in a nightmarish world of doubts that make his crown worthless to him:

> To be thus is nothing,
> But to be safely thus.
>
> (III.i.47–48)

Macbeth alternates between the hope of winning everything with one stroke and the fear of never winning anything at all, as expressed most powerfully in his reaction to the news that Fleance has escaped his ambush plot:

> Then comes my fit again. I had else been perfect,
> Whole as the marble, founded as the rock,
> As broad and general as the casing air;
> But now I am cabin'd, cribb'd, confin'd, bound in
> To saucy doubts and fears.
>
> (III.iv.20–24)

These lines evidently registered in Shelley's mind, for he has Beatrice repeat the first half of Macbeth's thought after she seems to have successfully carried out her plot against her father:

> The deed is done,
> And what may follow now regards not me.
> I am as universal as the light;
> Free as the earth-surrounding air: as firm
> As the world's centre. Consequence, to me,
> Is as the wind which strikes the solid rock
> But shakes it not.
>
> (IV.iv.46–52)

It is remarkable how Shelleyan the idea of this passage is, and yet how suffused it is with the vocabulary and thought-patterns of *Macbeth*. The verbal parallels here suggest how *Macbeth* and *The Cenci* came to meet in Shelley's mind. Beatrice is as much of an absolutist in her innocence as Macbeth is in his guilt, and yet paradoxically both forms of absolutism lead to acts of crime. Beatrice craves perfection, and desires to be free of the limiting factors of human life, but she is hemmed in on all sides by the powers of this world. For her, the corrupting influences of earthly existence are summed up in the domineering figure of her incestuous father, allowing her to strike out against the forces that bind her with one blow. Because her father is so demonized, and appears to be responsible for all the evil in her world, removing him holds out the promise of redeeming human life. Thus, whereas Macbeth can lay claim to the Absolute only in the conditional — "I had else been perfect" — Beatrice is allowed to echo his statement in the simple affirmative: "I am as universal as the light." Temporarily Beatrice seems to achieve the absolute moment when she is freed of any earthly limitations, but soon prison walls close in upon her and she is once again subject to the force of authority, soon to be haunted by the nightmare image of her father pursuing her throughout the universe of life and death. A passage from Shakespeare one is surprised not to see plagiarized in *The Cenci* is Hamlet's outburst:

> O God, I could be bounded in a nutshell, and count myself a king of infinite space—were it not that I have bad dreams.
>
> (II.ii.254–256)

With its characteristically Shelleyan movement from the confinement of a nutshell to the boundless reaches of infinite space, this passage sums up Beatrice Cenci's tragedy, the tragedy of a woman yearning to escape from the limits of the world, but in the end unable to flee the nightmare visions of her own mind.

Comparing Beatrice's tragedy with Macbeth's, we see once again that Shakespeare and Shelley are working with different conceptions of the tragic. In Shakespeare's portrayal, Macbeth's desires are in themselves tragic; what is tragic for Shelley, by contrast, is the inadequacy of the world to satisfying Beatrice's desires. Macbeth, in his yearning for the absolute act, tragically violates both the natural and the conventional orders. Having destroyed the only setting in which his life had meaning and value, he seeks in vain to find something to replace the secure and honored position he once held under Duncan's rule, eventually turning to the illusory support of supernatural agencies to prop up his regime. When Macbeth himself is finally overthrown, we have the feeling that the powers of nature have combined to expel this unnatural tyrant. But in the world of Beatrice Cenci, tyranny cannot be confidently labeled "unnatural"; on the contrary, in Shelley's view it seems to be in the nature of authority in this world to be tyrannical.[18] Shelley does not see Beatrice's desire to transcend the limits of nature and convention as inherently tragic; only her inability to escape these limits successfully turns her story into a tragedy. It is above all her conventional reaction to her father's assault upon her, her acceptance of the idea that anything external could stain the inner purity of her soul, that turns her story in a tragic direction, as Shelley points out in his preface:

> Undoubtedly, no person can be truly dishonoured by the act of another ... If Beatrice had thought in this manner she would have been wiser and better; but she would never have been a tragic character.

18. Several times in the play Cenci is referred to as "unnatural" (I.iii.54; II.i.44), but by the same token he himself is able to charge his sons with being "unnatural" (II.ii.133). Moreover, the Pope, who is the highest authority within the world of the play, evidently rejects the charge that Cenci's conduct was "unnatural" (V.iv.15–27; see also I.ii.75–79). Thus nature does not provide the standard by which Cenci's actions can be unequivocally condemned. Cf. Frye, *Fools of Time*, p. 45: "For Shelley, tyranny and repression are essentially a part of the *data* of existence, the state of things associated with Jupiter in *Prometheus Unbound*." The fact that just after Beatrice murders her father a messenger arrives to reveal the Pope's intention of prosecuting Cenci might be cited to show that authority is at times opposed to tyranny in the world of *The Cenci*. Aside from the fact that in context Savella's embassy serves merely as a kind of cruel joke at Beatrice's expense, the opening lines of the play prepare us to assume that if higher authorities ever were to take action against Cenci's tyranny, it would only be out of tyrannical motives on their part; the Pope covets Cenci's wealth and moreover fears that his wanton abuses of power will undermine papal authority. The fact that Savella, having come to Cenci's castle as Beatrice's liberator, ends up as her jailer shows how easily authority passes over into tyranny in the universe of Shelley's play.

For Shelley, Beatrice's tragedy is that in her efforts to rebel against the oppression of this world, she covertly accepts the world's standards and thus only perpetuates its oppressiveness. Macbeth and Beatrice provide as illuminating a comparison as Lear and Cenci: the yearning for the Absolute which Shakespeare depicts in such dark colors in *Macbeth* is bathed in rays of purest light in *The Cenci*, and the force of boundless desire in the soul which Shakespeare sees as potentially tyrannical (*Macbeth*, IV.iii.66–67) becomes the one source of liberation in Shelley's view.

To sum up the difference between Shakespearean and Shelleyan tragedy: Shakespeare explores the sources of tragic conflict within this world, in particular the tragic conflict of desires within the individual soul, whereas Shelley portrays the conflict between desire as such and the world as such; that is, for Shelley what is fundamentally tragic is the contradiction between the world as presently constituted, which entraps and imprisons the human soul, and the world of ideal beauty and freedom, to which the soul aspires but cannot as yet attain.[19] Thus when Shelley consciously or unconsciously drew upon Shakespeare in writing *The Cenci*, we should not be surprised that some of his Shakespearean quotations strike us as out of context, for indeed the two writers approached tragedy in different contexts. Perhaps we have not sufficiently reflected upon the incongruity of Romantic writers turning to Shakespeare as the model for their dramas. Shakespeare is not a Romantic in his thought; if any relation between content and form in literature exists, then it follows that the form of Shakespearean drama should not serve well for expressing Romantic content.[20] Many of the oddities of *The Cenci* as a play may well be the result of Shelley's working within a dramatic form that is basically unsuited to the vision he wished to embody. His misquotations from Shakespeare are perhaps one sign of his conflict with his models, and suggest that while imitation may be the sincerest form of flattery, in the hands of the Romantic poets it became an extremely subtle form

19. For a similar contrast between Shakespeare and a German Romantic playwright, see Max Lüthi, "Kleist und Shakespeare," *Shakespeare Jahrbuch*, XCV (1959), 141.
20. See Otten, *Deserted Stage*, pp. 7–11.

of criticism as well. In any event, Shelley's boldness in imitating Shakespeare, together with the extremism of the concept of the tragic he evolved, helps make clear the essential moderation, balance, and sanity of Shakespearean tragedy.

ALFRED HARBAGE

Shakespeare and the Early Dickens

Dickens' wistful sketch of himself as a "queer small boy" of nine who knew "all about" Falstaff because he read "all sorts of books" [1] does not mean that the text of *Henry the Fourth* was the primer of his childhood. The ages had not withered Falstaff. His undignified adventures on Gad's Hill now lent dignity to the whole district of Chatham, and one could read all about him in the sort of books which were bringing Shakespearean tales, jollities, lessons, excerpts, and beauties to families whose aspirations were wider than their means, or perhaps span of attention, and to the kind of academies attended by the younger members during affluent intervals. The shelf of cheap reprints in the Dickens home held, besides eighteenth-century novels and periodical essays, Mrs. Inchbald's *Collection of Farces*.[2] If it had held also her *British Theatre*, or any other repository of Shakespeare's plays, we would probably know of it. Neverthe-

1. "Travelling Abroad," *The Uncommercial Traveller*. When Dickens' novels are quoted, the chapter reference is inserted in the text, with chapters numbered continuously as in the most accessible editions: the softcover student texts and the *New Oxford Illustrated Dickens* (New York: Oxford University Press, 1948–1958). When Shakespeare's plays are quoted, the act-scene-line reference approximates the numbering in the Globe and most modern editions.

2. John Forster, *The Life of Charles Dickens*, ed. J. W. T. Ley (London: Cecil Palmer, 1928), p. 8.

less, Mrs. Dickens, who taught Charles the "rudiments" of Latin,[3] is likely to have taught him also the "rudiments" of Shakespeare, which had become the rival token of culture and gentility. It is even more likely that Mr. Dickens was able, and eager, to recite "To be or not to be," "Friends, Romans, countrymen," and "Most potent, grave, and reverend signiors." This, fortunately, is the kind of people they were.

Even before he was nine Charles, at least twice, was treated to Shakespeareana of a more thrilling kind, when he was taken to see rough facsimiles of *Richard the Third* and *Macbeth* staged in Rochester's small Theatre Royal. He may have been precociously aware that Richard "slept in war-time on a sofa much too short for him," and that Duncan "couldn't rest in his grave, but was constantly coming out of it, and calling himself somebody else," [4] but to see such works was distinction for a boy. In the odd caste system then imposed on theatrical offerings, a claim to quality was permitted only to five-act comedies and tragedies, the latter in blank verse, with the oldest plays in the repertory established as the nobility clustered about Shakespeare's royal brood, while the spawning masses of melodramas, burlettas, farces, pantomimes, and "operas" remained docilely inferior as art. Dickens' fondness for the lower orders of drama developed side by side with his respect for Shakespeare. He never became ambitious in his own writing for the stage. The comic opera and the two comic burlettas (brief farces) successfully produced at the St. James Theatre in 1836–1837, while the installments of *Pickwick Papers* and *Oliver Twist* were winning him fame, are almost ostentatiously professional. Unlike the novels they show not a trace either of genius or of Shakespearean influence. As a literary craftsman Dickens was not romantic. Except on one unlucky occasion, to be described at the end of the present discussion, he realized that old masterpieces could be written only by old masters.

After his family had moved to London, and the shadows of the Marshalsea and the blacking warehouse had receded, Dickens improved his acquaintance with Shakespeare at Covent Garden, Drury Lane, and elsewhere. Half the office boys, shop

3. Ibid., pp. 3–4.
4. "Dullborough Town," *The Uncommercial Traveller*.

assistants, and copying clerks of the city were stagestruck, and hence sometimes the prey of the owners of "private" theaters. For as little as half-a-crown one could play the Lord Mayor in *Richard the Third*, and for two pounds (sneaked shilling by shilling from an employer's till?) could have the lead, with a chance to deliver Cibber's immortal line, " 'Orf with his ed' (very quick and loud! — then slow and sneeringly) — 'So much for Bu-u-u-uckingham!' " [5] His backstage knowledge of these vanity playhouses and the surprising bitterness with which he describes them suggest that on some sad occasion Dickens himself was one of the "donkeys" roped. The regular theaters, large and small, he attended regularly, becoming one of the teen-age critics of the rival interpretations of fiery Edmund Kean, sturdy Charles Kemble, and sensitive William Macready. Years later he wrote the latter after his farewell appearance in *Macbeth*: "When I was a mere boy, I was one of your faithful and devoted adherents in the pit . . . As I improved myself and was improved by favoring circumstances in mind and fortune, I only became more earnest (if it were possible) in my study of you. No light portion of my life arose before me when the quiet vision to which I am beholden, in I don't know how great a degree, or for how much — who does? — faded so nobly from my bodily eyes last night." [6] His "study" was of Macready as interpreter of Shakespeare. The actor he studied for practical purposes (when he thought of becoming an actor himself and applied for an audition to Kemble's stage manager) was Charles Mathews, the comic mimic.

Dickens was reticent about his social disadvantages, and rarely spoke of having "improved" himself. A poignant early instance occurs in his last letter to Maria Beadnell, to whose family he still seemed ineligible after he had presented himself

5. "Private Theatres," *Sketches by Boz.*
6. February 27, 1851: *Letters*, ed. Walter Dexter, 3 vols. (Bloomsbury: Nonesuch Press, 1938), II, 274–275. He had written Macready much earlier, April 7, 1839, of the "delightful recollections" of him heaped up "from boyhood": *Letters*, ed. Madeline House, Graham Storey, Kathleen Tillotson, 3 vols. (New York: Oxford University Press, Pilgrim edition, 1965–1974), I, 540. (Hereafter these editions will be cited as *Letters* (Nonesuch) and *Letters* (Pilgrim), the latter used for the years thus far covered by this definitive edition, i.e., to 1843.)

as her suitor from his eighteenth to his twenty-first year: "all that any one can do to raise himself by his own exertions and unceasing assiduity I have done." [7] One of the things he had done was to begin reading at the British Museum on the day after he reached the required age of eighteen. Of his eight "indents" or call-slips which survive,[8] two are for editions of Shakespeare: the first published in eight volumes in 1825, edited by the Reverend William Harness, M.A., of Christ's College, Oxford, and the second published in twelve volumes in 1826, edited by the suggestively named Samuel Weller Singer, with a life by Charles Symmons, D.D. It is ironic that Harness, who would soon be trying to cultivate Dickens' acquaintance,[9] rejects Malone's wicked opinion that Shakespeare's father was a mere retail glover. Perhaps the young reader found a little more comforting Dr. Symmons' remark that "Mary Arden did not come dowerless to her plebeian husband," and that William was not ignorant even though he was prematurely recalled from school because of his father's "straightened circumstances." [10]

The interesting question is why he called for such volumes. With the London book stalls loaded with cheap texts of one kind or another he did not have to go to the British Museum to read Shakespeare. Probably he was curious about their scholarly apparatus and about the distinction between the plays in their original form and that in which they were being acted and often printed. He would have been aware of the current agitation to restore the true texts to the stage. One of the squalid features of the "private theatres" he describes is that *Macbeth* is there studied "in Cumberland's edition." [11] Harness and Singer would have served him well enough. They condensed the apparatus of the twenty-one volume "Variorum" editions, whose compilers they charged with pedantry while they pillaged them. Dickens made amusing capital of the idea of fidelity to the text in the second of his Boz sketches, written while he was still twenty-one. At a home production of *Othello* the actors have to put up with

7. May 19, 1833: *Letters* (Pilgrim), I, 29.
8. Some are reproduced in *The Dickensian*, XLIII (1946–1947), 83–84. All are listed in *Letters* (Pilgrim), I, 9n.
9. "Dickens's Diary," February 5, 1839: *Letters* (Pilgrim), I, 639.
10. Shakespeare, *Works*, ed. S. W. Singer (1826), I, 7, 9.
11. "Private Theatres," *Sketches by Boz*.

the ebullience of a rich uncle in the audience who knows all the principal plays by heart and keeps interrupting with, "that's wrong my boy," or "you've left out something." [12] The young author of the piece was far from naïve. Close to the time when he wrote it, he produced in the Dickens home on Bentinck Street his own "O'Thello," in which his father played the Duke of Venice and sang in a quartette with Cassio, Desdemona, and Iago. The surviving fragments[13] show that the piece was an incongruity joke illustrating the distance to which one might go in "improving" Shakespeare.

If not already schooled, Dickens would have had to become so in sheer self-protection in his early twenties when his rising fame thrust him into the midst of the literary elite, including Shakespearean scholars, critics, actors, and enthusiasts. John Black, his editor in 1834 when he was contributing some of his Sketches by Boz to the *Morning Chronicle*, was the translator of Schlegel's *Vorlesungen*. Black called Schlegel the "first . . . truly enlightened interpreter" of England's "brightest poetical ornament";[14] and Dickens called Black his own "first hearty out-and-out appreciator." [15] Among those who commended him to the proprietors of the *Morning Chronicle* was the most fertile (and flawed) Shakespearean scholar of the era, John Payne Collier, who thought "very well of his abilities" although he was "so young that he had no vestige of beard or whiskers." [16] Soon after, he came to know "true hearted" [17] Charles Knight, whose pictorial edition of Shakespeare, issued in monthly numbers, was designed to offer good texts "to the popular understanding in a spirit of love." [18] Later he was associated with Knight in the

12. "Mrs. Porter 'Over the Way,' " *Monthly Magazine* (January 1834); "Mrs. Joseph Porter," *Sketches by Boz*.
13. Reproduced in *The Dickensian*, XXVI (1929–1930), 9–12, and in *Collected Papers* (Nonesuch), II, 59. See also *Letters* (Pilgrim), I, 31, 38.
14. A. W. Schlegel, *A Course of Lectures on Dramatic Art and Literature*, tr. John Black (London, 1815), p. iv.
15. Forster, *Life*, pp. 65, 72n.
16. *An Old Man's Diary Forty Years Ago*, part 4 (London, 1872), entry for July 27, 1833, pp. 14–15.
17. Forster, *Life*, p. 531.
18. *Passages of a Working Life*, 3 vols. (London, 1864–1865), II, 286; III, 34–38. Knight, like Collier, was informed by John H. Barrow of the latter's "clever young relative," and was on "tolerably familiar terms"

Shakespeare Club (1838–1839)[19] and with both Collier and Knight in the Shakespeare Society (1840–1853)[20] and on the committee for raising funds for the Shakespeare Birthplace.[21] Before he had finished *Pickwick Papers*, he became intimate with John Forster and through him with William Macready, both devoted to restoring the true texts to the stage. After becoming editor of *Bentley's Miscellany* at twenty-four, he began publishing William Maginn's studies of Shakespeare's characters, which appeared in the magazine concurrently with installments of *Oliver Twist*.[22] By the time he had completed *Nicholas Nickleby* and *The Old Curiosity Shop*, he had come to know Thomas Campbell, Walter Savage Landor, and similar devotees of England's "brightest poetical ornament."[23] It follows inevitably that he was conversant with most of the plays before 1842 when he traveled in America with a one volume edition (probably Campbell's) in his greatcoat pocket.

Dickens may never in his life have more than skimmed the lesser plays, but the same may be said of Coleridge — and nearly everyone else except the editors. By the time he had written his early novels, he was familiar with more than twenty, with some of them since boyhood. He may have admired Shakespeare at first because he knew that he should, but his appreciation soon became very real. No one is better qualified to recognize literary genius than a literary genius. To grant to a Dickens (or a Shakespeare) a great imagination but no ideas, or a great capacity to write but little capacity to read, is to say (as an abacus

---

with him when they became fellow-members of the Shakespeare Club. They became firm friends later.

19. Knight, *Passages of a Working Life*, III, 38, describes its last stormy meeting when Dickens, who was in the chair, walked out after Forster had been heckled. Mary Cowden Clarke (*Recollections of Authors*, London, 1878, pp. 295–296) writes of being a guest at a dinner given by the Club in honor of Macready. She listened to Dickens' tribute in starry-eyed admiration of his appearance and eloquence.

20. Organized by Collier, Knight, Dyce, Halliwell, and others to promote scholarly research and publication. Dickens became a member in its first year.

21. Knight, *Passages of a Working Life*, III, 110.

22. The first, on Falstaff, appeared in May 1837; the sixth, on Timon, in March 1838.

23. *Letters* (Pilgrim), I, 34n, 460n; II, 23n, 102–103.

might say of a computer) that the mind of a genius is not so remarkable after all. It is risky to patronize Dickens' critical perception, or to question his sincerity when he called Shakespeare "the great master who knew everything" [24] and his plays "an unspeakable source of delight." [25] He wrote no criticism, but he could distinguish between the good and the bad. A century before it appeared as a satirical title in *Scrutiny*, he knew that "How many children had Lady Macbeth?" is the wrong kind of question to ask. His Mr. Curdle in *Nicholas Nickleby* "had written a pamphlet of sixty-four pages, post octavo, on the character of the Nurse's deceased husband in Romeo and Juliet, with an inquiry whether he really had been a "merry man" in his lifetime, or whether it was merely his widow's affectionate partiality that induced her so to report him" (24). He also ridiculed gush — like Mrs. Wititterly's: "I'm always ill after Shakespeare . . . I scarcely exist the next day; I find the reaction so great after a tragedy, my lord, and Shakespeare is such a delicious creature" (27). It speaks well for his discernment that his favorite volume of criticism was Maurice Morgann's on Falstaff — "a delicate combination of fancy, whim, good heart, good sense, and good taste." [26]

What he looked for in the theater, at least after Macready's memorable seasons at Covent Garden in 1837–1839, was the kind of productions which proved that "Shakespeare was right, after all." [27] He wrote Blanchard that, when the last night of Macready's enlightened management came, Shakespeare would be banished "for years to come . . . I verily believe I shall cry." [28] Years later he saw in Paris an *As You Like It* (as improved by George Sand) which seems to have given him a prophetic vision of the worst the theater of our own day can do — ambush the play in plastic shrubbery, or twist it to the shape of the Theater of the Absurd:

24. "Night Walks," *The Uncommercial Traveller.*
25. To Forster from America, March 22–23, 1842: *Letters* (Pilgrim), III, 165.
26. To John Lord Campbell, January 27, 1859: *Letters* (Nonesuch), III, 90. See also letter to T. J. Serle, January 29, 1844: ibid., I, 565.
27. John Forster, *Examiner*, January 28, 1838; quoted by William J. Carlton, *The Dickensian*, LXI (1965), 133.
28. July 11, 1839: *Letters* (Pilgrim), I, 561.

a kind of Theatrical Representation that I think might be got up, with great completeness, by the Patients in the asylum for Idiots. . . . Nobody has anything to do but to sit upon as many grey stones as he can. When Jacques had sat upon seventy-seven stones and forty-two roots of trees (which was at the end of the second act), we came away. He had by that time been made violent love to by Celia, had shown himself in every phase of his existence to be utterly unknown to Shakespeare, had made the speech about the Seven Ages out of its right place, and apropos of nothing on earth, and had in all respects conducted himself like a brutalized, benighted, and besotted Beast.[29]

(Like Antony in fighting mood Dickens here seems ready to "burst the buckles on his breast.") He said of Macready and later of Fechter that they should be judged not on the basis of "little theatrical prescriptions" but on what appeared in Shakespeare's text.[30]

Dickens did not, as has been charged, despise scholarly research. True he doubted whether audiences at the Mechanics Institute lectures would "be stunned by a weighty inquiry whether there was internal evidence in Shakespeare's works, to prove that his uncle by the mother's side lived for some years at Stoke Newington," [31] and he was happy that the poet had had no Boswell, to induce posterity to have "his skull in the phrenological shop-windows";[32] but he was respectful, even diffident, in his general attitude towards those he called "the knowing-ones." [33] Especially interesting is the maturity of his view of the Shakespeare cult and industry, as compared with the amazing naïveté of Henry James and the tantrums of Mark Twain. No incon-

29. To Wilkie Collins, April 22, 1856: *Letters* (Nonesuch), II, 762.
30. See "Macready As 'Benedick' " (1843) and "On Mr. Fechter's Acting" (1869), *Collected Papers* (Nonesuch), I, 144, 116.
31. "Dullborough Town," *The Uncommercial Traveller*, p. 172.
32. To William Sandys, June 13, 1847: *Letters* (Nonesuch), II, 31.
33. He consented to bring an alleged portrait of the Poet to the attention of the scholars of the Shakespeare Club and asked for its history (*Letters*, Pilgrim, I, 610); he praised Collier's pamphlet proposing a new edition, mentioning that he owned Boswell's twenty-one volume Malone edition (ibid., II, 432–433); he served on the Council of the Shakespeare Society, acquired its publications, and lent them to friends (ibid., III, 455); he forwarded William Sandys' Shakespearean "extracts" to Collier (*Letters*, Nonesuch, II, 31).

gruity ever escaped Dickens' eye, and he was well aware that many of the pilgrims to Stratford-upon-Avon were no more cognizant of what the worship was all about than were the old woman who presided over the "Birthplace" and the Italian "image boys" who sold statuettes of the Bard.[34] However, he could respond with amused tolerance, realizing that the fakeries of the shrine had nothing to do with the authenticity of the one enshrined. He did not even despise relics.[35]

It did not escape the notice of his admirers or himself that his achievement resembled Shakespeare's. Born of plain provincial parents and sketchily educated, he was becoming England's most famous writer and moral force. While *Pickwick Papers* and *Oliver Twist* were in progress, he wrote that he was "tracking out [Shakespeare's] footsteps at the scarcely-worth-mentioning little distance of a few millions of leagues behind." [36] He must have felt that he had lessened the distance somewhat by the time he had finished *Nicholas Nickleby* and *The Old Curiosity Shop*. Shakespearean allusions are rare in *Pickwick Papers* but abundant in *Nicholas Nickleby*, the reason being that he identified with Nicholas to a greater extent than with any of the characters he had created thus far. Nicholas is actually "tracking out" Shakespeare's footsteps by serving as actor-playwright of a theatrical company when his mother, unaware of the fact, speaks of prenatal influences she narrowly escaped while visiting Stratford-upon-Avon:

> "I recollect that all night long I dreamt of nothing but a black gentleman at full length, in plaster-of-Paris, with a lay-down collar tied with two tassels, leaning against a post and thinking . . . I recollect I was in the family way with my son Nicholas at the

34. "Dickens's Diary," *Letters* (Pilgrim), I, 634. His visit was in October 1838; and in the December number of *Nicholas Nickleby* he lets Mrs. Wititterly speak of "that dear little dull house he was born in!" Seeing the place and signing the book "kindles up quite a fire in one" (27). Still, he returned for a visit with his family and was active on behalf of its proper supervision.

35. A plaque in his Gad's Hill home marked it as the site of Falstaff's robbery. He thought that a cup "made from the Bard's mulberry tree" and once owned by Garrick should go to Macready: *Letters* (Pilgrim), II, 229–230. Shakespeare's birthday he and Forster "kept always as a festival" (Forster, *Life*, p. 323).

36. "The Pantomime of Life," *Bentley's Miscellany*, I (1837), 297.

time, and I had been very much frightened by an Italian image boy that very morning. In fact it was quite a mercy, ma'am," added Mrs. Nickleby, in a whisper to Mrs. Wititterly, "that my son didn't turn out to be a Shakspeare, and what a dreadful thing that would have been!" [27].

Since he has chosen to make this character comically addle-pated, he makes her view all prenatal influences as bad; but just as he converted into comedy an actual daydream of his own when he made Nicholas join Crummles' troupe and star in the part of Romeo, so he may here be converting into comedy an actual dream of his mother (far from dreadful) inspired by his cleverness in childhood as an entertainer and the author of *The Dog of Montargis*.[37] He is certainly speaking through Nicholas' mouth when he makes him lecture a theatrical plagiarist on the difference between improving old stories, as Shakespeare had done, and debasing new ones (48) — as the pirates were doing in the case of *Pickwick Papers* and *Oliver Twist*.

Whenever he stated his creed as a writer, he was apt to quote Shakespeare. "All the world's a stage" — sometimes the stage of a pantomime.[38] A novelist like a dramatist holds the "mirror . . . up to nature." [39] A poet should avoid Byronic gloom and

37. This detail weakens rather than strengthens the contention that Mrs. Nickleby represents Mrs. Dickens. The influence of maternal aspirations upon the achievement of sons is often great, a fact which Dickens may have recognized even though he ridiculed the grandiose dreams of Mrs. Nickleby (and Mrs. Micawber). The use to which he put the traits of his parents and friends, too often viewed as an indication of his personal attitudes, is an indication of his remarkable powers of artistic detachment. He virtually admits that certain traits of Leigh Hunt are portrayed in Harold Skimpole at the same time that he indignantly, and truthfully, denies that Skimpole is a caricature of Hunt. See "Leigh Hunt, a Remonstrance," *Collected Papers* (Nonesuch), II, 16–17. An excellent discussion of the issue appears in J. W. T. Ley, *The Dickens Circle* (New York, 1919), pp. 155–160.

38. "The Pantomime of Life," *Bentley's Miscellany*, I (1837), 297. Dickens' point is that in certain actual individuals human nature caricatures itself, and hence certain "caricatures" in literature may be regarded as "true to life." Interestingly, George Santayana makes precisely this point about Dickens' characters in "Dickens" (1921), reprinted in *The Dickens Critics*, ed. George H. Ford and Lauriate Lane (Ithaca: Cornell University Press, 1961).

39. *Speeches*, ed. K. J. Fielding (New York: Oxford University Press, 1960), p. 262.

seek "sermons in stones, and good in everything." [40] He almost adopted as his motto, "There is some soul of goodness in things evil." At the great Edinburgh dinner given in his honor in 1841, the tribute to him by John Wilson ("Christopher North") alluded to this line, and it was this allusion that he chose to pick up in his own speech in reply.[41] Dickens' specific allusions to Shakespeare, in his letters, his fiction, his articles, are usually humorous, often flippant, but there can be no doubt that, in navigating his artistic course, he viewed the man from Stratford as his "bright particular star."

It would have been tactless as well as onerous for his admirers to draw parallels between his and Shakespeare's humble origins and high achievements, but the idea was in the air. Forster said that in writing *Pickwick Papers*, Dickens needed "not the whip but the drag . . . Sufflaminandus erat, as Ben Jonson said of Shakespeare." [42] That he "flowed with that facility, that sometimes it was necessary he should be stopped" came to be understood between them. [43] Others were more explicit in comparing his art with Shakespeare's. After reading *Pickwick Papers*, Mary Russell Mitford said that his was not a Hogarthian but "a Shakespearean view of humanity." [44] Similar remarks were soon made openly by Landor,[45] Lord Jeffrey,[46] and others. A summary article on the early novels in the *Edinburgh Review* seems in some passages to have been influenced by Coleridge's dictum that Shakespeare held to *"the high road of life . . .* he never rendered that amiable which religion and

40. To R. S. Horrell, November 25, 1840: *Letters* (Pilgrim), II, 155.

41. Forster, *Life*, p. 176n. See also *Letters* (Pilgrim), II, 117; III, 17n. He used the line as a running head in chapter 26 of the 1867 edition of *Oliver Twist*.

42. *Life*, p. 124.

43. To Forster, October 3, 1846: *Letters* (Nonesuch), I, 793: "I . . . put on the drag as I wrote [*Dombey and Son*]."

44. *The Life of . . . Told by Herself in Letters to Her Friends*, ed. A. G. K. L'Estrange (Harper, 1870), II, 198.

45. Landor compared him with Shakespeare and said that "his women are superior to Shakespeare's"; see George H. Ford, *Dickens and His Readers* (Princeton: Princeton University Press, 1955), p. 57. See also *Letters* (Pilgrim), II, 310n.

46. Dickens wrote Forster that Jeffrey goes about town declaring that there "has been 'nothing so good as Nell since Cordelia' ": *Letters* (Pilgrim), II, 238, 310n.

reason taught us to detest; he never clothed vice in the garb of virtue." [47] Dickens, said the Edinburgh reviewer, "never endeavours to mislead our sympathies — to pervert plain notions of right and wrong — to make vice interesting in our eyes." [48] One of his correspondents praised him for his mingling of the pathetic and comic — "How well, by the way, that old fellow Shakespeare understood this!" [49] — and for having "too much of old Shakespeare's kidney" about him "to be surprised at the apparent incongruities of human feelings." [50] At the time of the Edinburgh dinner he was called in the *Caledonian Mercury* "the Shakespeare of his day," [51] and later in the same year, in *Parley's Penny Library*, "the living Shakespeare." [52] Such praise, calculated to daunt or overstimulate, to make him too cautious or too reckless, seems to have done neither. Normally he kept his head.

Shakespearean allusions, quotations, and verbal and visual reminiscences are more abundant in the novels of Dickens than in those of any other Victorian, but for reasons which will soon be apparent it would be impossible to supply an inventory. A sampling may suffice to let us hazard a guess about the general nature of his indebtedness, the distinction between what he took and what he learned from Shakespeare, even about the creative process itself. His early writing offers the most fruitful area of inquiry because, like all fine writers, his powers of assimilating and transforming materials increased as he matured, and it is easier to detect what is going on in his earlier than in his later work. Such is the case with Shakespeare himself, in regard to the influence of Seneca, Ovid, Lyly, and others. Lyly no doubt had something to do with the wonderful prose of Hamlet's

47. *Coleridge's Writings on Shakespeare*, ed. T. Hawkes (New York: Putnam, 1959), p. 97. The passage had recently been edited in approximately this form by H. N. Coleridge, *Literary Remains* (1836–1839).

48. H. N. Lister, *Edinburgh Review*, LXVIII (October 1838), 77–78.

49. Basil Hall to Dickens, January 10, 1841: quoted in *Letters* (Pilgrim), II, 185n.

50. Ibid., II, 215n. (February 13, 1841).

51. June 26, 1841: quoted in *Letters* (Pilgrim), II, 315n.

52. Volume I (December 1841): quoted in *Letters* (Pilgrim), III, 410n. (The publisher was pirating his works, and the flattery did not sooth Dickens.)

apostrophe to Man (II.ii.290), but it is the earlier and inferior prose of Portia's complaints to Nerissa (I.ii.12) that provides irrefutable proof of the Poet's debt to the Euphuist. In this connection it should be noted that a minor writer can have a good influence on a great one, and that a great one can (and usually does) have a bad influence on a minor one. Nicholas Rowe might have been mediocre in a more interesting way had he not "Written in Imitation of Shakespear's Style." [53] It seems a safe assumption that the influence of one great writer on another will be good; however, it need not be consistently so.

In the few surviving Dickens letters earlier in date than his first published sketch, "A Dinner at Poplar Walk" (December 1833), an interest in Shakespeare's language is already evident. The youthful correspondent quotes *A Midsummer Night's Dream* (V.i.17) in telling a friend of his efforts to "find a local habitation and a name" in lodgings away from Bentinck Street;[54] and he adapts a line from *As You Like It* (II.vii.166) in telling how he pleads his case to Maria Beadnell, "sans pride, sans reserve, sans anything." [55] We find also a standard misquotation from *Othello* (I.iii.90) in "plain unvarnish'd tale," [56] just as we shall find in *Nicholas Nickleby* (41) "method in his madness," a standard misquotation from *Hamlet* (II.ii.204). Such locutions represent what happens to quotations in passing into general currency, and they provide no evidence that Dickens was familiar with *Othello* and *Hamlet* (although, of course, he was).[57] Neither do such correct quotations as the following, and others like them, which appear in the early novels, prove his familiarity with the texts from which they come: "touch of nature" from *Troilus and Cressida* (III.iii.174), "milk of human kindness" from *Macbeth* (I.v.15), and "there's the rub" from *Hamlet* (III.i.65). These, too, had passed into the public domain. How-

---

53. *The Tragedy of Jane Shore* (1714), title page.
54. To H. W. Kolle, April–May 1832: *Letters* (Pilgrim), I, 5.
55. To H. W. Kolle, May 19, 1833: *Letters* (Pilgrim), I, 29.
56. To H. W. Kolle, January 1833: *Letters* (Pilgrim), I, 14.
57. Sometimes an apparent misquotation actually proves his familiarity with a text. In *Nicholas Nickleby* (19) he levies on *King Lear* (III.iv. 138) in a description: "Rats and mice, and such small gear, had long ago been starved or had emigrated." The "gear" for Shakespeare's "deer" is an emendation by Hanmer ("geer").

ever, "a local habitation and a name" [58] as it appears in his letter is a conscious misapplication of the line as it appears in the
play (he is seeking self-identity away from his family), just as
"sans pride, sans reserve, sans anything" is a conscious para-
phrase.

Putting it briefly, his misapplications, paraphrases, and alter-
ations of Shakespeare's language best illustrate his susceptibility.
He might have said truly (as some of us have been known to say
falsely when caught) that he did not misquote but quoted creatively. Sometimes his exercises in comic incongruity resemble
schoolboy jokes, as when Macbeth's welcome to his guests (III.
iv. 38) appears in *Pickwick Papers* (51) as "to dinner they went
with good digestion waiting on appetite, and health on both, and
a waiter on all three." He has an eye for oddities of expression,
like Balthasar's "all convenient speed" in *The Merchant of
Venice* (III.iv.56), which is duplicated in *Nicholas Nickleby*
(16) and altered in *The Old Curiosity Shop* (23) to "all convenient expedition." His more serious paraphrases are likely to
be of lines which would have had a strong ethical or emotional
appeal to him, such as those in *The Merchant of Venice* (IV.i.
214) and in *Measure for Measure* (II.ii.121) which appear in
Oliver Twist as "to do a great right, you may do a little wrong"
(12) and "within such walls enough fantastic tricks are daily
played to make the angels blind with weeping" (11). Quotation marks occasionally appear, as in *The Old Curiosity Shop*
(56) when Swiveller and Chuckster between them conflate
(with emendations) a line from *Hamlet* (III.ii.373) and one
from *Julius Caesar* (II.ii.18):

> " ' 'Tis now the witching—' "
> " 'Hour of night!' "
> " 'When churchyards yawn,' "
> " 'And graves give up their dead.' "

58. *A Midsummer Night's Dream* is a play which he is not likely to
have seen staged. It provides him with a self-mocking allusion to his efforts while putting on a home production of *Clari, or The Maid of Milan*,
which contains a famous scene lighted by the moon. He and his carpenter
must face the problems of "making moonlight" (as did the carpenter
Peter Quince in staging "Pyramus and Thisby"). See letter to Miss Urquhart: *Letters* (Pilgrim), I, 31. Since Miss Urquhart acted in *Clari*, the
"moonlight" reference suggests that the letter should be dated April 1833.

But usually the borrowing is unmarked, as when Swiveller levies upon *The Merchant of Venice* (III.ii.70) in proposing to Quilp that they "go ring fancy's knell. *I'll* begin it" (21). The little heroine's name may be glanced at in "knell" but not her fatal end.

That a process of absorption is going on is best illustrated by the verbal reminiscences which are barely perceptible, standing so to speak at the waterline of the iceberg, such as the following from *The Old Curiosity Shop*. Quilp's epithet addressed to his wife, "you bird of evil note," (67) probably derives from the "bird of night" in *Julius Caesar* (I.iii.26) and the "deed of dreadful note" in *Macbeth* (III.ii.44). In *Hamlet* (V.ii.89) the prince speaks of Osric (owner of much land) as "spacious in the possession of dirt." Dick Swiveller tells the fickle Miss Chuckster (8) that she is "sorry in the possession of a Cheggs" (who works the land as a market gardener). This may seem far-fetched, but our author had a far-fetching sort of mind. He may even have recalled speech rhythms and echoed them with his own words for his own purposes. In *The Winter's Tale*, which Macready had recently revived, occurs an endearing reference (II.ii.25) to a babe, "lusty and like to live," and in the novel (21) a description of an unendearing summer house, "rotten and bare to see." [59] It is unlikely that the slightly archaic phrase "houseless wretches" would appear in *Oliver Twist* (5) were it not for the "naked wretches" and "houseless heads" in the speech in *King Lear* (III.iv.28), which would have had for Dickens an enormous appeal.

A genius is preternaturally teachable, but still he must be taught. Dickens was taught language by the speakers he heard at home, in the streets, in the comic theater, in the law offices where he ran errands, in Parliament where he reported speeches. He was taught also by such English masters as Addison, Fielding, Sterne, Smollet, Goldsmith, and Shakespeare. Sometimes his

59. Bottom's "Let him roar again" may account for Dickens' fondness for "again" as an intensive after a verb. The blank verse which occasionally intrudes into his prose (at least as late as *A Christmas Carol*, 1843) is too regularly iambic, too chanting, to be good, but Shakespeare may be partially responsible for its presence. However, his examples of how certain Shakespearean lines should be read ("Mrs. Joseph Porter," *Sketches by Boz*) ignore the iambic pattern.

humorous use of Shakespeare's words may seem callow and coarse, but the humor itself is rarely callow and never coarse. He took what he needed where he found it. Some of the things he needed to write as he did were a remarkably large and wide-ranging vocabulary, resourcefulness in the use of imagery, great verbal dexterity — rhetoric. None of his masters were better qualified to help him acquire these things than Shakespeare.

He learned something from Shakespeare in what as well as how to write, and here too he shows himself as far from a docile pupil. A few illustrations must suffice. Before creating Bill Sikes, Dickens had written a news report of an actual London gangster arrested for a lethal attack upon his trull,[60] so that we can say that the character emerged from the author's personal experi-ence. However, when Sikes murders Nancy, recollections of Shakespeare began to work upon Dickens' imagination. Fagin, who certainly had not been conceived with any thought of Iago in mind, steps momentarily into the latter's buskins. When Iago conceives of his plot, leading to Desdemona's death, he says, "I have't! It is engend'red!" (I.iii.397). When Fagin conceives of *his* plot, leading to Nancy's death, he says, "I have it all. The means are ready, and shall be set to work" (44). At the time of the murder, Othello extinguishes the light he has brought to Desdemona's chamber: "Put out the light, and then put out the light" (V.ii.7). At the time of the murder, Sikes tosses under the grate the candle in Nancy's room: "There's light enough for wot I've got to do" (47). When Maria Edgeworth said of the scene, "I certainly never read anything so effective — out of Shake-speare," [61] she was surely thinking of *Othello*. But *Othello* had no binding claim upon Dickens' imagination, and in the sequel another of Shakespeare's murderers enters. Macbeth, haunted by Banquo's maimed body, says, "Avaunt, and quit my sight! Let the earth hide thee!" (III.iv.93). Sikes, haunted by the thought of Nancy's maimed body, says, "with a glance behind him, 'Wot do they keep such ugly things above the ground for? — Who's that knocking?' " (50).

Before creating Daniel Quilp, Dickens had observed in Bath

60. "The Hospital Patient" (1836), *Sketches by Boz.*
61. Basil Hall to Dickens, January 27, 1841: *Letters* (Pilgrim), II, 196n.

" 'a frightful little dwarf named Prior, who let donkeys on hire'
. . . and used a heavy stick impartially on his wife and the donkeys." [62] As introduced in *The Old Curiosity Shop*, Quilp displays physical and temperamental traits common in achondro-
plastic dwarfs, often carnival people like Prior, jolly in public
and vicious in private, but as the story progresses his gleeful
villainy begins to remind certain readers of Shakespeare's Richard
III.[63] Dickens himself began to be so reminded, and he added
incidental touches to his portrait of Quilp which, except for the
first, seem to have escaped notice. When the story begins, it is
the good Master Humphrey and not Quilp who is deformed like
Shakespeare's "bunch-backed toad," but in the fifth chapter of
the novel Mrs. Jiniwin, who is Mrs. Quilp's "lady mother" (see
Madam Capulet), is accused of calling him "a little hunchy
villain." Perhaps "hunchy" may mean only "barrel-chested," but
in the preceding chapter Mrs. Quilp has said, "I know that if I
was to die to-morrow, Quilp could marry anybody he pleased."
There follows this fascinating bit: "Marry whom he pleased! . . .
One lady (a widow) was quite certain she would stab him if he
hinted at it." The episode has figured in speculations about
Quilp's sexual prowess and Dickens' kinship with him, and no
one would wish to deny the novelist the psychological insights
derived from this or any other affinity, but we are bound to
recognize that at this particular moment he is thinking (and not
with a strictly straight face) of the famous scene of the wooing
of the widow Anne, who "offers at" Richard's breast with a
sword (I.ii.178–182) but soon changes her mind. It may be as
risky for the literary analyst as it is for the psychological one
to make assertions about what goes on within an artist's mind,
but in this instance the former is reassured when he reads later
(67) that Quilp had no "perception of the cloud which lowered
upon his house" (*Richard III*, I.i.3). Like Sikes, Quilp can inherit traits from more Shakespearean villains than one. A critical
crux in *Othello* is provided by Iago's mention of his suspicion,
almost as a casual aside, that the Moor has seduced his wife

62. *Letters* (Pilgrim), II, 107n.
63. Thomas Hood was the first, in *The Athenaeum*, no. 680 (November 7, 1840), 887–888; but see also E. Polack, "Humourous Villains,"
The Dickensian, VI (1910), 182–184, and later commentators.

Bianca (I.iii.381) — a detail which inspired Coleridge's famous phrase, "the motive-hunting of a motiveless malignity." Even more surprisingly (and unconvincingly) Quilp couples with one of his intended victims, that "shallow-pated fellow" Swiveller, the latter's friend Mr. Trent, who "once made eyes at Mrs. Quilp, and leered and looked" (21).

It would be frivolous to remark upon the shadows cast by Richard, Iago, Macbeth, and so on which move fleetingly over the surface of these Victorian tales were it not that they make us wonder, To what extent are the little debts the visible token of larger ones? If Dickens had not known *Macbeth*, would the slaying of a gangster's moll have created in a London slum a sense of almost doomsday horror? Why do Sikes's cronies fall away from him leaving him in morose isolation? Where did Sikes acquire the conscience, or at least the imagination, to suffer such anguish after his deed? The murderer in Dickens' news report appeared stolidly unmoved. Or consider Quilp. He and his accomplices, Samson and Sally Brass, are so amusing that we wonder why Dickens did not mete out to them the same kind of comic punishment he did to his other amusing scoundrels, Noah Claypole, Seth Pecksniff, Uriah Heep, Silas Wegg, and so on. Instead they are as harshly dispatched as Fagin and Bill Sikes. Is it not because their persecutions are presumed to be the ultimate cause of Little Nell's death, and, as in Shakespeare, murderers must not be parolled? If the work is to seem sound to its creator, the treatment of certain actions must be as dissuasive as it is sensational. We cannot say that Dickens was drawn by the plays into Shakespeare's moral world — he was born into it — but the plays may have taught him ways of portraying its landscape. To what extent did they teach him? Dickens himself did not know. As he said in his letter to Macready, "Who does?" [64]

We cannot pretend to be more able than the artist to map out precisely the road to his Xanadu, but the study of "influences" may assist in critical analysis. What happens to Quilp and the Brasses, however morally inspired, is one of the things wrong

64. See above, note 6.

with *The Old Curiosity Shop*. That he should be drowned, and condemned to be buried with a stake through his heart, and they doomed to prowl the London streets by night, feeding from dustbins like rats, strikes discriminating readers as poetic injustice. When we come to the end of the story, we remember them as entertaining figures, not as predestined killers like Sikes. The fact that Dickens has desperately considered magnifying their turpitude by making the Marchioness the fruit of an adulterous relationship between Quilp and Sally Brass suggests the seriousness of his problem.[65] It was too late now to daub them with the colors of Edmund and Goneril. The fact is that they were not originally conceived as tragic villains because Nell was not originally conceived as a tragic heroine. She was murdered not by Quilp and the Brasses, but was assassinated (with good intentions) by Forster and Dickens, with Shakespeare, Tate, Lamb, and Macready as their unwitting accomplices. The events leading up to the tragedy are as follows.

In 1681 Nahum Tate gave Shakespeare's *King Lear* a happy ending, and his adaptation was still supplanting the original play on the stage in 1811 when Charles Lamb wrote his splendid denunciation:

A happy ending! — as if the living martyrdom that Lear had gone through, — the flaying of his feelings alive, did not make a fair dismissal from the stage of life the only decorous thing for him. If he is to live and be happy after, if he could sustain this world's burden after, why all this pudder and preparation, — why torment us with all this unnecessary sympathy? As if the childish pleasure of getting his gilt robes and sceptre again could tempt him to act over again his misused station, — as if at his years, and with his experience, anything was left but to die.[66]

---

65. Only a hint of this weird fancy remains in the actual ending. The fact that the Marchioness is so unlike an Edmund may have helped to restrain Dickens, but Oliver, Smike, and later characters demonstrate his refusal to associate baseness with the base-born. Still, a natural sweetness in the by-blow of a Daniel Quilp and Sally Brass over-tests our willingness to suspend disbelief.

66. "On the Tragedies of Shakespeare, Considered with Reference to Their Fitness for Stage Representation," *The Reflector* (1811), reprinted in *Works* (London, 1818), II, 1–36. T. N. Talfourd, close friend of both Forster and Dickens, reedited Lamb's works in 1840.

John Forster, fervent admirer of both Shakespeare and Lamb, had become acquainted with Macready in 1833 and thereafter kept exhorting him to restore the original *King Lear* to the stage, retaining the part of the Fool as well as the tragic ending. In a review of Macready's partial restoration in 1834, he speaks of Tate's rewarding Lear for his suffering "by getting him back again his gilt robes and tinsel sceptre," [67] thus slightly elaborating a phrase in Lamb's condemnation of the happy ending. In 1838 Macready restored "Shakespeare's true *Lear*" to the stage of Covent Garden, and Forster repeated himself (and Lamb) in an ecstatic review. Truly banished at last was Tate, who had repaid Lear "for all his suffering, by giving him back again his gilt robes and tinsel sceptre." [68] Dickens, Forster, and Macready were close friends, in frequent contact at the time of this momentous production, and Forster was justly proud of the part he had played in the rescue of Shakespeare's play. Unfortunately, the event seems to have lodged in his mind the common though fallacious notion that tragic endings are inherently more artistic than happy ones.

In 1840, by which time Forster had fully devoted himself to the guidance of Dickens, *The Old Curiosity Shop* was begun. The wrongness of its ending has hung like an albatross about its author's neck, often biasing conceptions of his artistry and casting suspicion on his scenes of pathos wherever they may occur. The death-of-little-Nell denouement is objectionable less because the treatment is distended and lachrymose (although it is that) than because it is false, and would be so no matter how restrained the treatment. We can forgive excesses, and must do so sometimes in Shakespeare himself, but not when they are also excrescences. The fictions which Dickens was born to create (and did in all instances but this one) belong to a category

67. *The Weekly True Sun* (January 26, 1834), quoted by W. J. Carlton, "Dickens or Forster? Some *King Lear* Criticisms Re-examined," *The Dickensian*, LXI (1965), 137.

68. *The Examiner* (February 4, 1838). This fine review, until Carlton's corrective article appeared, was often attributed to Dickens and included in his works. It appears in vol. I of *Collected Papers* in the Nonesuch Dickens. (Although he went much further than Edmund Kean, Macready's promptbook reveals that he did not quite restore "Shakespeare's true *Lear*.")

familiar to all times and places, embracing as it does the peripatetic romances of the Greeks, Elizabethan "tragicomedies," and most eighteenth-century novels. It is the category designated by Boccaccio as "tales of evil fortune turning to good." [69] Not "good" for all the characters to be sure, but good for the person or persons in the tales who have chiefly engaged our sympathy. Such stories usually end in marriages. Samuel Pickwick is too old for that consummation, and Oliver Twist too young, but the marriages of others occur as the happy fallout of their rescue from distress and danger. The happy marriages at the end of *The Old Curiosity Shop* are more pleasing than the punishments, but they are inappropriately set — "mirth in funeral" so to speak.

In *Oliver Twist* a little boy appears as "the principle of good, surviving through every adverse circumstance, and triumphing at last" [70] (like the stainless Lady in the rout of Comus). The story is sound in conception, all of one piece, in spite of extravagances like Monks and his incomprehensible machinations. It had satisfied its author's inner monitor at the same time that it had done wonders for the circulation of *Bentley's Miscellany*. Dickens would naturally think of it when the circulation of his own miscellany, *Master Humphrey's Clock*, began to falter. Why not a little girl counterpart of Oliver, "surviving through every adverse circumstance, and triumphing at last" — not amidst thieves and murderers, but, since she is lovely as well as young, amidst the old, the ugly, the deformed? It will be a story of renewal, life against death, the fresh flower rising from a bed of dry stalks, brown burrs, twisted husks.[71] Thomas Hood when he reviewed the story at its halfway point saw it in this way. He commented upon the illustration of Nell sleeping in her little bed surrounded by ugly antiques: "How sweet and fresh the youthful figure! how much sweeter and fresher for the rusty,

69. *Decameron*, Novellas of the Second Day.
70. Author's preface to third edition (1841). Oliver's cultivated speech is in harmony with his character and contrasts with the cockney of Noah Claypole although their "education" has been identical. Dickens followed this poetic convention fairly consistently in later works, in the unrealistic fashion of Shakespeare. Compare the speech of Phebe and Audrey in *As You Like It*.
71. That it was planned first as a much shorter story makes it all the more incredible that it was designed to end in the child's death.

musty, fusty atmosphere of such accessories and their associations! How soothing the moral, that Gentleness, Purity, and Truth, sometimes dormant but never dead, have survived." [72] For Hood the later illustration of Nell leading her grandfather toward Codlin and Short, as they sit in a churchyard with their Punch perched on a gravestone, carried no intimations of her death. On the contrary, the scene is "satirical" — surrounding her, like the antique shop itself, with everything which she is not. Dickens was so pleased with Hood's review that he echoed it when he revised his first chapter and made Master Humphrey muse prophetically upon the child's future — living "in a kind of allegory . . . holding her solitary way among a throng of wild grotesque companions: the only pure, fresh, youthful object in the throng." When he makes Master Humphrey add, "I checked myself here . . . I already saw before me a region on which I was little disposed to enter," Dickens is supplying foreshadowing after the fact.[73] The revision was made after he had let his little flower die.

That he had done so in error, and in violation of his initial design, was stated in hostile reviews and hinted at in a friendly one. To Thomas Latimer's comment that the novel was "without much elaborateness of plot, or apparently fixedness of purpose," Dickens replied, "I never had the design and purpose of a story so distinctly marked in my mind, from its commencement. All its quietness arose out of a deliberate purpose; the notion being to stamp upon it from the first, the shadow of that early death. I think I shall always like it better than anything I have done or may do. So much for authorship . . . I know a great many people are of yours [your opinion], or I shouldn't say so much." [74] Dickens always defended himself most vigorously when his cause was weakest, but here he seems to be resorting to downright falsehood. Actually he thought he was telling the truth. He had been thoroughly sold a bill of goods.

Below is a record of the transaction. The first item consists

72. *The Athenaeum*, no. 680 (November 7, 1840), 887.
73. The revision appears in all editions except the first (in *Master Humphrey's Clock*).
74. *Western Times* (March 6, 1841), referred to in Dickens' letter to Latimer, March 13, 1841, and quoted in note 4; *Letters* (Pilgrim), II, 233n.

of three passages brought together from Forster's *Life*, with the most relevant phrases italicized:

> He had not thought of killing her, when, about half-way through, I asked him whether it did not necessarily belong to his *own conception*, after taking so mere a child through such a tragedy of sorrow, to lift her also out of the *commonplace of ordinary happy endings*, so that the gentle pure little figure and form should never change to the fancy. All that I meant he seized at once, and never turned away from it again [p. 151] . . . [*The Old Curiosity Shop* was begun] with less *direct consciousness* of design on his part than I can remember in any other instance throughout his career [p. 146] . . . Its very incidents created a necessity *at first not seen*; and it was carried to a close only contemplated after a full half of it was written. *Yet from the opening of the tale to that undesigned ending . . . the main purpose seems to be always present* [p. 152].   •

The second item is part of a letter from Dickens to Forster written just after the novel was completed, again with significant words italicized:

> The assurance that this little closing of the scene, touches and is felt by you so strongly, is better to me than a thousand most sweet voices out of doors. When I first began (*on your valued suggestion*) *to keep my thoughts* upon this ending of the tale, I resolved to try and do something which might be read by people about whom Death had been, — with a softened feeling, and with consolation.[75]

Two things are clear. Forster, with a laudable belief in Dickens' Shakespearean potential, persuaded him not to let his heroine fade out in a "commonplace" happy ending, as did Tate's Cordelia. She and her old grandfather must not be given back "gilt robes and tinsel sceptre" — regardless of the trifling detail that they had never had any. And second, Dickens, in the flush of his early successes, was susceptible to the idea that the "Shakespearean" ending was his "own conception." He could thank Forster for the "valued suggestion" which made him keep his

75. January 1841: *Letters* (Pilgrim), II, 188.

thoughts on the tragic ending, and at the same time tell Latimer that such thoughts were "distinctly marked" on his mind from the beginning — the more imposing, presumably, for being unconscious until he observed what he had been doing.

It is difficult to mark the exact point in the novel when Nell's false fate was sealed. As noted earlier, variegated Shakespearean shadows flit over the surface of these early novels, and since in this one the solicitude of a young girl for an old man is being treated, it was inevitable that some of the shadows be cast by Cordelia and Lear. It is in the first half of the novel (29) that the old grandfather is called "a harmless fond old man," recalling Lear's "I am a very foolish fond old man" in the scene where he recovers his reason while Cordelia kneels at his side (IV.vii.-60). This same scene is recalled midway in the second half of the novel when Nell rejoices over the old man's mental recovery:

> "Thank heaven!" inwardly exclaimed the child, "for this most happy change!"
> "I will be patient," said the old man, "humble, very thankful, and obedient, if you will let me stay" [54].

and so on, in patches of iambics interspersed with such archaic expressions as "a pleasant jest indeed," "a brave thought," "a kind office," and the like. But later still (57) the image of King Lear provides the occasion for broad humor, in Samson Brass's preposterous statement that Mr. Garland resembles him — "the same good humour, the same white hair and partial baldness, the same liability to be imposed upon." If there are details pointing in a tragic direction at this point, there are others that still do not.

Dickens no doubt had qualms, arising from an "unconscious" more reliable than that which Forster had persuaded him to heed — artistic instincts insistently whispering that he was doing something wrong. He tried to right things by working harder on his tragic ending than he had ever worked on anything before. How he wound himself up to it, avoiding diversions and making his mind dwell again on the death of Mary Hogarth; how he convinced himself that the ending would have a cathartic effect upon friends who had lost children, consoling them in their grief; and how those friends were, or pretended to be, consoled need not be detailed here.[76] Readers in general wanted Nell to live, for the uncomplicated reason that they had grown fond of her, but they seem to have accepted the idea that their tears would do them good. Those who perceived that her death was uncalled for, and its treatment strained, nevertheless recognized that the author's own tears were genuine.

The Old Curiosity Shop has wonderful stuff in it, some of Dickens' best writing thus far, but its ending must be recognized as a contretemps. It must also be recognized as untypical. As a rule Dickens was strong enough to profit from the literature he knew, using it independently and spontaneously, his back unbroken by the "burden of the past." When *Pickwick Papers* was being launched, he told Chapman and Hall that they had better let him go his own way because he would probably do so in any case. Chapman suggested that Pickwick be fat since "good humor and flesh had always gone together since the days of Falstaff." [77] He accepted the fat, but turned a blind eye on any other Falstaffian characteristics. His Pickwick descends from Don Quixote through certain amiable and unworldly country squires and clergymen created by Addison, Fielding, Goldsmith. Literature would have suffered a grievous loss if he had been misshaped in any degree by the Boar's Head wit and handicapped roué. Dickens knew that there could be only one Falstaff.

John Forster, too, should not be misjudged because he mistook Little Nell for Cordelia. Usually he guided Dickens in the direction he truly wished to go. In spite of superficial traits shared in common with Podsnap, Forster had the gift of *caritas*. His life of Dickens, faulty in many ways, still has truth at its center because, like his other biographies, it is written in the spirit of the words of the Canon of Thurgarton in *The Cloud of Unknowing*: "For not what thou art, nor what thou hast been, beholdeth God with his merciful eye — but that thou wouldest be." It might be well to end with some words by this remarkable man. *The Old Curiosity Shop* is not the sole instance in which

76. See Editors' Preface to *Letters* (Pilgrim), II, ix–xii, and references in the letters of 1841, pp. 125, 144, 171–172, 192n, and passim.
77. Arthur Waugh, *A Hundred Years of Publishing, Being the Story of Chapman & Hall, Ltd.* (London, 1930), p. 21.

Dickens acted upon faulty advice. *Dombey and Son*, another
deeply flawed work, was injured by Lord Jeffrey, who protested
against Dickens' evident intention to let Edith Dombey become
the mistress of Carker. The problem was how she might be extri-
cated, since she had already deserted her husband under Carker's auspices in the installment Jeffrey had read. "What do you
think," asked Dickens, "of a kind of inverted Maid's Tragedy,
and a tremendous scene of her undeceiving Carker, and giving
him to know that she never meant that?" [78] It was a bad idea
— even though Edith's earlier tragical posture has reminded us
of Evadne's. Her aggressive gloom over having let herself be
auctioned off as Mr. Dombey's wife makes us think of Thomas
Rymer's rhetorical question to the heroine of *The Maid's Tragedy*: "good Madam, what reason is there for you to complain?
did any force or philter overcome you?" [79] Forster praises
Dickens' willingness to accept advice from friends, and conjectures that Shakespeare was similarly yielding. He cites for
the second time in the *Life* Ben Jonson's opinion that Shakespeare needed supervision, then adds thoughtfully: "Whether he,
as well as the writer of later time, might with more advantage
have been left alone, is the only question." [80]

78. To Forster, December 21, 1847: *Letters* (Nonesuch), II, 63.
79. Thomas Rymer, *The Tragedies of the Last Age* (1678), ed. J. E.
Spingarn, *Critical Essays of the Seventeenth Century*, 3 vols. (Oxford,
1908), II, 196.
80. *Life*, p. 477.

DAVID H. HIRSCH

Hamlet, *Moby-Dick*, and Passional Thinking

The most salient clue to Melville's adaptation of Shakespeare lies, as has oft been noted, in his essay on Hawthorne's *Mosses*.[1] There Melville explicitly revealed his love of "blackness" and his shocking discovery that truth was both ungraspable and thickly interwoven with the cords of human emotions. Partly, the "blackness" that Melville found in his reading of Shakespeare was related to the elusiveness of truth, and partly it was related to the unsettling insight that truth was intertwined with madness.

It is this "blackness" in Hawthorne, Melville declares, that "so fixes and fascinates me," and that "furnishes the infinite

1. The Shakespeare-Melville relationship has been widely commented upon, most notably by F. O. Matthiessen in *American Renaissance* (New York: Oxford University Press, 1941) and Charles Olson in *Call Me Ishmael* (San Francisco: City Lights Books, 1947). Many articles and most book-length studies of Melville recognize the relationship. Two dissertations should be mentioned: Raymond Long, "The Hidden Sun" (University of California, Los Angeles, 1965), and Roma Rosen, "Herman Melville's Use of Shakespeare's Plays" (Northwestern University, 1962). Useful for their attempts to identify specific allusions are Thomas A. Little, "Literary Allusions in the Writings of Herman Melville" (Nebraska, 1950), and *Moby-Dick or The Whale*, ed. Luther S. Mansfield, Howard P. Vincent (New York: Hendricks House, 1952, 1962). See also W. W. Cowen, "Melville's Marginalia," 10 vols. (Harvard, 1965); the *Hamlet* marginalia are in IX, 489–520.

135

obscure of [Shakespeare's] background — that background against which Shakespeare plays his loftiest but most circumscribed renown, as the profoundest of thinkers." Melville goes on to connect this very "blackness" to "those deep far-away things in him [Shakespeare]; those occasional flashings-forth of intuitive Truth" which Shakespeare "craftily says or sometimes insinuates . . . through the mouths of the dark characters of Hamlet, Timon, Lear, and Iago," sayings which "we feel to be so terrifically true that it were all but madness for any good man, in his own proper character, to utter, or even hint of them." Lear he describes as speaking "the same madness of vital truth." [2] Shakespeare gave Melville the voice with which to articulate a truth that was not a benign static entity floating unchanging and eternal in ideal space, but rather a passional experience rooted deep in the human soul. This truth was very far from the Good of the philosophers, and instead of being associated with light and set adrift from human feelings and the flesh, it was, on the contrary, associated with darkness and was never dissociated from human emotions. I shall try to demonstrate this thesis by analyzing two texts, one from *Hamlet*, one from *Moby-Dick*, both of which seem to be deeply rooted in the biblical psalms.[3]

In act II, scene ii, Hamlet utters one of his many powerfully moving speeches. He has just discovered that Rosencrantz and Guildenstern have been sent for by the King and Queen and that their purpose in visiting him is to extract from him information that will, presumably, better enable the royal couple to cope

2. *The Literary World*, VII, nos. 185 and 186 (August 17 and 24, 1850), 125–127, 145–147. This essay has been widely reprinted and anthologized.

3. My choice is not arbitrary. *Hamlet* is generally conceded to be the most problem-ridden of Shakespeare's plays and *Moby-Dick* is probably the most problem-ridden of American masterpieces. Moreover, there seems to be agreement that *Hamlet* is the single Shakespeare play that gripped Melville's imagination most powerfully. Long writes that "the relative influence of *Hamlet* is approached by no other four plays combined. So great is its majority, that it alone accounts for more than forty percent of the allusions from all the plays . . . *Hamlet* also provides the most ubiquitous of the influences" (p. 295). Critics agree also that *Moby-Dick* is the Melville book that is most successfully Shakespearean.

with his errant behavior. And so, as he disingenuously informs them, he will tell them why they were summoned and in so doing disarm them.[4] Whereupon he slides into what seems to be one more description of his melancholy condition, a condition of which his mother and stepfather are only too well aware:

> I have of late, but wherefore I know not,
> lost all my mirth,
> foregone all custom of exercises;
> and indeed it goes so heavily with my disposition, that
> this goodly frame, the earth, seems to me a sterile promontory;
> this most excellent canopy, the air, look you,
> this brave o'erhanging firmament,
> this majestical roof fretted with golden fire,
> why it appeareth nothing to me
> but a foul and pestilent congregation of vapors.
>
> What a piece of work is a man,
> how noble in reason,
> how infinite in faculties, in form and moving,
> how express and admirable in action,
> how like an angel in apprehension,
> how like a god!
> The paragon of animals;
> and yet to me what is this quintessence of dust?
>
> Man delights not me —
> nor women neither,
> though by your smiling you seem to say so.[5]

Brian Vickers feels that the speech conveys "Hamlet's absolute disillusionment, with considerable eloquence . . . used on a negative topic." The "soliloquy," he finds, is "the most misread speech in Shakespeare." I agree with Vickers that the speech

4. I assume that this is Hamlet's initial intention. In terms of dramatic action it makes sense, though it must be conceded that in this problematic play even this is a problem; nevertheless, I am not directly concerned here with the puzzling prologue to the speech.

5. Following the lead of Brian Vickers, *The Artistry of Shakespeare's Prose* (London: Methuen, 1968), pp. 253–255, I have presented this prose passage in verse, though I have not followed Vicker's versing at all points. The punctuation and diction are those of the *Riverside Shakespeare* (Boston: Houghton Mifflin Co., 1974), ed. G. Blakemore Evans, and others.

should not be taken as an unqualified encomium, and that such
"ennobling images" as "this majestical roof fretted with golden
fire" and "how like an angel" are deflated by the resolutions of
the sentences in which they appear, but I would like to consider
the entire speech as something other than an expression of
purely personal melancholy and personal disillusionment. Also,
I want to consider it as something other than a diagnosis of the
malady of an age or of "the ennui of every sentient mind in mid-
career." [6]

Vickers attributes the misreadings of this speech to the tendency to connect it "with Renaissance orations on the dignity of
man." "Robert Burton," he says, "would be a better gloss than
Pico della Mirandola." I shall take the position here that the
Bible would be a better gloss than Burton, and that Hamlet's
speech is neither a "paean to the greatness of humanity" nor an
anatomy of melancholy, but a meditation[7] on the pathos of man,
a pathos inseparable from his dignity.

Theodore Spencer comments on both the conventionality and
the peculiarity of Hamlet's speech. "To understand the force of
[Hamlet's] remarks," he writes, "we should have clearly in our
minds the thousand and one sixteenth century repetitions of the
old teaching, with which every member of Shakespeare's audience must have been familiar, that the surest way to understand
man's place in the world and to realize the magnificence of
God's creation, was to contemplate the glory of the superior
heavens which surrounded the earth. But what Hamlet says is
exactly the opposite." [8] I think that "exactly the opposite" may
be misleading, for it implies that Hamlet is saying that contem-

6. Harry Levin, *The Question of Hamlet* (New York: Oxford University Press, 1959), p. 31.
7. I am speaking, at this point, of a reader's, rather than a theater-
goer's, *Hamlet*. For a theater-goer the speech may arouse admiration for
Hamlet's mental dexterity and further sympathy for him as a brooding
soul. But the theater-goer hears the speech once and then must turn his
attention to the Players, who make their appearance at this juncture. For
the reader, however, who can reread the words again and again and
ponder over them, the speech becomes more of an incitement to thinking.
8. "Hamlet and the Nature of Reality," *ELH*, V (1938), 266. See also
p. 265, where Spencer mentions Spenser's "Hymn of Heavenly Beautie"
and Thomas Digges's "Perfit Description of the Coelestiall Orbes" (1576)
as possible models.

plating the glory of the superior heavens is not the surest way to understand man's place in the world. In fact, what happens is that Hamlet's contemplation of the heavens does provide him with an understanding of man's place in the world, but this understanding does not fit what Spencer describes as the Renaissance stereotype. Hamlet converts the Renaissance cliché into a probing analysis of the human condition that puts man naturally into a biblical, as well as classical Renaissance, context.

This particular speech of Hamlet's seems to reflect his inability to fix on an absolute nonproblematic truth that is wholly separate from his emotional being. He thinks feelingly, to adapt T. S. Eliot's phrase, and his truths, like those of the Bible "are emotive rather than conceptual." [9] Indeed, this speech not only reflects the biblical view of man, but it is biblical in its form and diction as well. Especially remarkable, merely in terms of poetic structure, is Hamlet's use of biblical parallelism and antithesis. The anaphoras set up a syntactic parallelism which reflects parallels in thought and imagery. For example, the lines

> this goodly frame, the earth, seems to me a sterile promontory;
> this most excellent canopy, the air . . . appeareth nothing to me
> but a foul and pestilent congregation of vapors.

constitute an excellent example of

$$a, b, c, d$$
$$a', b', c', d'$$

parallelism.[10] "This goodly frame" is paralleled by "this most excellent canopy," "the earth" by "the air," "seems to me" by "ap-

9. A. C. Partridge, *English Biblical Translation* (London: Academic Press, 1973), p. 57.

10. My primary sources for the workings of biblical poetry have been George Buchanan Gray, *The Forms of Hebrew Poetry* (London: Hadder and Stoughton, 1915), W. O. E. Oesterley, *The Psalms* (London: Macmillan, 1953), Artur Weiser, *The Psalms* (Philadelphia: Westminster Press, 1962), Theodore H. Robinson, *The Poetry of the Old Testament* (London: Duckworth, 1947). The pioneer work on the subject was done by Robert Lowth and appeared in 1753. It is not my purpose to establish Shakespeare's knowledge of the theory of biblical poetry. To so towering a literary genius and so versatile a craftsman the theoretical knowledge would have been superfluous. Shakespeare would not have required theo-

peareth to me," and "sterile promontory" by "congregation of vapors."

Shakespeare further complicates the parallelism by setting up a series of parallels within a parallel in a periodic sentence. Hamlet stretches language and the imagination of the reader or listener to the breaking point. Four times he launches a pronominal clause, each time following the pronoun with a striking image and metaphor.[11] These cumulative images also expand phonemically until the abbreviated adjective-noun phrase "sterile promontory" finds its parallel resolution in the compound-adjective compound-noun prepositional phrase "foul and pestilent congregation of vapors." The accumulation of beautiful metaphors culminates in a waste and a void.

It is as if Hamlet were reversing the account of Creation in Genesis 1. There, a divine Creator started with a watery chaos and shaped it into an orderly universe, dividing darkness from light, day from night, the waters into those above the firmament and those below it, the dry land from the waters, and then "made also the starres, and . . . set them in the firmament of the heaven to shine upon the earth" (Bishops' Bible, 1572). Hamlet, on the other hand, starts his imagery with "this goodly frame, the earth," expands to the thrice ascending imagery of

---

retical knowledge to emulate the biblical style. For an excellent analysis of Hebraic prose and Hebraic poetry, see Harold Fisch, *Jerusalem and Albion: The Hebraic Factor in Seventeenth-Century Literature* (New York: Schocken Books, 1964). See especially pp. 49f for a discussion of the Psalms and meditation. Fisch also attempts to distinguish between classical balances and decorum on the one hand and biblical parallelism and antithesis on the other (pp. 38–62).

11. Jonas A. Barish says of this speech that "These lines display a perfectly crystalline transparency" and are not rich in metaphorical expressions. "Continuities and Discontinuities in Shakespearian Prose," in *Shakespeare 1971: Proceedings of the World Shakespeare Congress, Vancouver, August, 1971*, ed. Clifford Leach and J. M. Margeson (Toronto: University of Toronto Press, 1972), pp. 62–63. I can only say that "majestical roof fretted with golden fire," "most excellent canopy, the air," "goodly frame, the earth," "foul and pestilent, etc." seem to me to be rather spectacular metaphors. It is the power of the metaphors and the effectiveness of the syntax that makes the speech so memorable and thought-provoking. Maurice Charney, *Style in "Hamlet"* (Princeton: Princeton University Press, 1969), p. 151, comments on the imagery as a reference to the immediate surroundings of the Elizabethan audience, but to grant this, I believe, is not necessarily to deny the metaphorical potentialities, but rather to add to the possibilities.

air, firmament, and stars, and then collapses back into the watery chaos, the "foul and pestilent congregation of vapors." The same kind of reversal also takes place in the second sentence of the speech, the "encomium" on man, where Hamlet again starts at a high point (man's dignity) and descends to "this quintessence of dust." In the second creation account (Genesis 2:7) God first shaped man out of the dust of the ground and then exalted him by inspiriting him with the breath of life.

Critics have been generally dismayed by this speech. Either they overlook the negative elements and thus misread it as an encomium (as Vickers notes), or else they see the divisions in the speech as representing a conflict characteristic of Renaissance man. Theodore Spencer, for example, sees these reversals as an indication of the fact "that in *Hamlet* Shakespeare for the first time used to the full the conflict between the two views of man's nature which was so deeply felt in his age. On the one side was the picture of man as he should be — it was bright, orderly and optimistic. On the other was the picture of man as he is — it was full of darkness and chaos. Shakespeare puts an awareness of this contrast into the character of Hamlet, and his having done so is one of the main reasons for *Hamlet's* greatness." [12] I shall not question the presence of this conflict in the Elizabethan age, nor the intensity with which the age felt it. Neither shall I question the assertion that Hamlet's awareness of the conflict is part of *Hamlet's* greatness. What I do wish to argue, however, is that this conflict between "the two views of man's nature" is not necessarily a conflict between what should be (presumably the ideal) and what is (presumably the real). Rather, the conflict in this particular speech is inherent in the biblical view of man, and it is this view that is beguiling Hamlet as he speaks. Having tried to demonstrate that the form of the speech comes close to biblical poetry, I should like, now, to turn to the diction of the speech. Richmond Noble has already suggested that the second sentence of the speech alludes to Psalm 8:4–6; I believe it is a mistake to omit verses one to three of this psalm, which I shall include in the following quotation:

12. *Shakespeare and the Nature of Man* (New York: Macmillan, 1967; first published 1942), p. 94.

O Lorde our governour, howe excellent is thy name in al the
worlde: thou that hast set thy glory above the heavens.

Out of the mouth of very babes and sucklinges has thou ordeyned strength, because of thyne enemies: that thou myghteth
styl the enemie, and the avenger.

For I wyl consyder the heavens, even the woorkes of thy fin-
gers: the Moone and the Starres whiche thou hast ordeyned.

What is man that thou art so myndful of hym: and the sonne
of man that thou visitest hym.

Thou makest hym lower then the angels: to crowne hym with
glory and worshyp.

Thou makest hym to have dominion of the woorkes of thy
handes: and thou hast put althinges in subjection under his feete.[13]

In describing Hamlet's movement from sentence one to
sentence two of the speech, Spencer comments that "from this
consideration of the macrocosm he passes at once to the micro-
cosm: the sequence of thought was, in his time, almost inevitable." [14] Inevitable as the sequence of thought may have been in
Shakespeare's time, it appears to be wholly consonant, also, with
the sequence of thought expressed in the psalm. Contemplating
the heavens, the psalmist is struck by a double awareness: the
majesty of God and the diminutiveness of man. As one modern
commentator puts it: "It is at eventide that the psalmist gazes up
at the illimitable expanse of the heavens with the mysterious
glory of the moon, and studded with stars; and an overpowering
sense of the greatness and might of God takes hold of him. With
holy self-contempt at the thought of the insignificance of humanity in the sight of God, he cries: *What is man that thou
shouldest think of him . . . ?*" [15]

Of course, there is no explicit indication that Hamlet feels a
holy self-contempt. His universe seems to be emptied of holiness
and the poles of opposition are between man's dignity and his
frailty. Commenting on the allusion to Psalm 8:4, Harry Levin

13. Richmond Noble, *Shakespeare's Biblical Knowledge* (London:
Macmillan, 1935). This translation of the psalm is from the Bishops'
Bible (1572). See Noble, chapter 4, "Which Version did Shakespeare
Use?" pp. 58–59; see also pp. 200–209 for a detailed list of biblical allu-
sions in *Hamlet.*

14. *Shakespeare and the Nature of Man*, p. 100.

15. Oesterly, *The Psalms*, p. 140.

concludes that Hamlet echoes "the anxious question of Old Testament ethics, voiced by the Psalmist: 'What is man, that thou art mindful of him?' " and he then puts the question into Renaissance life-setting. There, he finds, the speech represents a dislocation of man's middle position in the great chain of being. "At one extreme," writes Levin, "is the 'Oration on the Dignity of man,' by Pico della Mirandola, with its lofty plea for man's self-liberation through his intellectual and spiritual faculties. At the opposite pole is Montaigne's 'Apology for Ramon Sabunde,' with its devastating critique of the senses and of man's consequent frailties and confusions." [16] Spencer, too, argues for the primacy of reason as a standard of human behavior, but he concedes, also, that "the standard which Hamlet's soliloquy describes is . . . the standard which his own behavior violates." [17]

Whether Hamlet is putting on an antic disposition or whether his reason has been shaken by recent events, the Hamlet of the play is no paradigm of rational man. Ophelia sees him as once having been "the glass of fashion and the mould of form" but now as a "noble mind . . . o'erthrown," with "that noble and most sovereign reason / Like sweet bells jangled, out of time and harsh." It is Claudius who provides an apt description of Hamlet's demeanor: "There's something in his soul / O'er which his melancholy sits on brood." To pinpoint the cause of that "melancholy" and to define that "something" in his soul has been the quest not only of Claudius but of numberless commentators. Without accepting T. S. Eliot's contention that the play is "certainly an artistic failure," we should perhaps reconsider his observation that "Hamlet (the man) is dominated by an emotion which is inexpressible, because it is in excess of the facts as they appear." [18] The facts that Eliot has in mind are those that define "the essential emotion of the play [as] the feeling of a son towards a guilty mother." The emotion is also excessive if it is that of a man who is working out the conflict between dignified rational man and contemptible fleshly man.

But if Hamlet's brooding is viewed in the light of this allusion

16. *The Question of Hamlet,* p. 62.
17. *Shakespeare and the Nature of Man,* p. 101.
18. "Hamlet and His Problems," *Selected Essays of T. S. Eliot* (New York: Harcourt, Brace, 1960), pp. 124, 125.

to the psalms, then it does not seem excessive. And if Hamlet's brooding is seen more as the contemplation of a paradox than as the stress of a conflict, again it does not seem excessive. A commentator says about Psalm 8:4 that "the finite is confronted with the infinite, the transient with the eternal, the perpetual sorrows and anxieties of man, who constantly goes astray, with the peace, steadiness and order manifested by the heavenly bodies which run their prescribed course. All these thoughts are implied in the question, 'What is man?' " [19]

What I want to suggest is that Hamlet's allusion evokes the thoughts and feelings implicit in the biblical question. I believe that in saying so I am not departing from previous commentators who have noted the allusion, but what I want to stress is the passional nature of the question in the psalm and Shakespeare's brilliant success in capturing that passional quality. Partly he captures that quality by emulating the biblical form, the parallelism in which the gloriousness of the universe is stated at length and then undercut in one final phrase, and similarly in which the majesty of man is stated and restated, also only to be undercut in a single phrase, so that the heavy concentration of affirmative utterances is undercut by the syntax, which gives finality to the nullification of the affirmatives.

But partly the passional element enters in through the multiple echoes in Hamlet's words. For example, the biblical question that is conjured by "What a piece of work is a man!" is not simply the question "What is diminutive man in this vast universe?" but "What is man that Thou thinkest of him?" The question does not simply express wonder at man's smallness but wonder that he should occupy a place in the consciousness of a divine being infinitely beyond him in magnitude and infinitely beyond his understanding. The biblical question is relational, not merely inquisitive. As Artur Weiser puts it:

The difference between the Greek and biblical estimates of man is demonstrated by the very fact that in the Old Testament human dignity has no value of its own, but has value only because it is a gift from God. In this connection we must take notice of the fact that in vv. 5 and 6 it is always God who is the subject and that it

19. Weiser, *The Psalms*, p. 143.

is from his hand that man receives the position of a ruler in the world. In these verses, too, the note of wonder is sounded, the wonder which fells the heart of the psalmist as he contemplates the miracle of the divine order of creation. In spite of his insignificance man has been appointed by God to have dominion over the earth.[20]

But while Hamlet seems to yearn for, and at times to embody, the psalmist's passional relation to the universe, he is, nevertheless, out of joint. He can express the glory of the universe and the dignity of man, but only to reject them. Artur Weiser states the relational element in the psalmist's question in terms of grace: "That man who just felt constrained to recognize the total insignificance of his life in the sight of God may nevertheless say 'yes' to that life and accept it with confidence, represents the most profound miracle of divine grace which man is privileged to experience." [21] Hamlet, of course, does not say yes to his insignificance. It is interesting, however, that even his no resounds with biblical echoes.

In a brilliantly searching analysis of the double creation narrative in Genesis, Joseph B. Soloveitchik speculates that taken together the two narratives give us a full picture of "dual man." [22] Adam the First (Genesis 1:26–28) is dignified man, the technician-scientist who was made in the image of God and told to subdue the earth, whereas Adam the Second (Genesis 2:7) is passional man in need of relation, shaped of the dust and into whom was breathed the spirit of life, and whose mission is not to subdue the earth but to overcome his cosmic, existential loneliness. It is almost as if we may say of the Hamlet of the speech under consideration that he is Adam the Second speaking the thoughts of Adam the First.

In the first part of the speech he extols the majesty of the cosmos in terms reminiscent of the psalmist's expressions of wonder. For example, the image of this most excellent canopy, the air, brings to mind Psalm 19:5, where God sets "a tabernacle for the sun" in the heavens, "which cometh forth as a

20. Ibid., p. 144.
21. Ibid., p. 143.
22. "The Lonely Man of Faith," *Tradition,* VII, no. 2 (Summer, 1965), 5–67.

bridegroom out of his chamber." The image also recalls Psalm 104:2: "Thou deckest thyself with light as it were with a garment, and spreadest out the heavens like a curtain." Spencer says that Shakespeare's audience would have understood both his melancholy and his generalizations, but in an age of prolific Bible translating and of avid public and private Bible reading, would not the audience have responded to these echoes of the voice of the psalmist? Yet, having extolled the majesty of the cosmos, Hamlet then resolves it into a foul and pestilent congregation of vapors, just as he had earlier wanted his too sullied flesh to resolve itself into a dew.

The same process takes place in the second part of the speech. Hamlet praises the dignity of man in phrases highly suggestive of the biblical text. Psalm 8 has already been mentioned, but the image of man as "a piece of work" also recalls Isaiah 64:8, "But nowe, O Lorde, thou father of ours, We are thy clay, and thou art our potter, and we al are the woorke of thy handes" (Bishops' Bible). Both this verse and Hamlet's apostrophe remind us, moreover, that in Genesis 2:7 God shaped man out of the dust of the ground.[23] The second sentence of the speech seems to be cognizant of the two creation narratives, the first part setting forth man as *imago dei*: noble in reason, infinite in faculties, admirable in action, like an angel, like a god, the paragon of animals. All these qualities can be attributed to Adam the First of Genesis 1:26: "God saide, Let us make man in our image, after our likenesse, and let them have rule of the fisshe of the sea" (Bishops' Bible). But the resolution of Hamlet's sentence seems to reflect Adam the Second, of Genesis 2:7: "The Lorde God also dyd shape man, [even] dust from of[f] the grounde, and breathed into his nosethrylles the breath of lyfe, and man was a living soule."

In arriving at "this quintessence of dust," Hamlet not only

23. Noble, *Shakespeare's Biblical Knowledge*, pp. 202–203, cites Ecclesiastes 3:18–20, Geneva version: "I considered in mine heart the state of the children of men that God had purged them: yet to see to, they are in themselves as beastes. For the condition of the children of men, and the condition of beastes are even as one condition unto them. As the one dyeth, so dyeth the other: for they have all one breath, and there is no excellencie of man above the beast: for all is vanitie. All goe to one place, and all was of the dust, and all shall returne to the dust."

sets up a powerful parallel to "congregation of vapors," but he also may be referring back to "this goodly frame, the earth." Customarily the phrase is taken as a reference to the terrestrial globe upon which man dwells, but it may also refer to Hamlet's physical frame, his body. The Hebrew root that was translated as "did shape" in Genesis 2:7 of the Bishops' Bible reappears in Psalm 103:14, which early translations render as: "For he knoweth whereof we are made; he remembereth that we are but dust." But the King James version of 1611 rendered the word more literally: "For he knoweth our frame." A word deriving from the same root is translated as "our potter" in the verse from Isaiah referred to above. My point is that the sense of man as both divine image and as shaped, formed, framed, fashioned, molded out of dust ("glass of fashion, mould of form"; cf. Job 33:6, Bishops' Bible: "I am fashioned and made, even of the same molde") would in no way be alien to anyone with a knowledge of the Bible; the concept projected by Hamlet, of man as a compound of divine dignity and inanimate dust is grander, more moving, and more challenging to the imagination than the concept of him as a creature torn between reason and the flesh.

The sixteenth-century translators of the Bible seem to have perceived man's duality in these terms. For example, the Bishops' Bible, whose version of Genesis 2:7 was quoted above, gave the following gloss for that verse: "This base beginning man shoulde remember, lest he waxe proud of the image of God." And the Geneva Bible comments on Psalm 8:4 that "it had bene sufficient for him to have set forthe his glorie by the heavens, thogh he had not come so low as to man, which is but dust." For verse 5 of the same psalm, ("for thou has made him a little lower than God, and crowned him with glorie and worship"), the Geneva gloss is "touching his first creation." Many of the elements of Hamlet's brooding meditation can be found here: the association between man and dust, between the majestic divine image and mound of clay, and the implication in the comment on Psalm 8:5 that the Adam who was made a little lower than God and crowned with glory was the Adam of Genesis 1. In fact, Hamlet almost seems to be carrying out the instructions of the Geneva Bible's comment on Genesis 2:7, "He

sheweth whereof man's bodye was created, to the intent that
man shulde not glorie in the excellencie of his own nature."

Among the elements of this speech that make it so powerful is
Hamlet's ability to describe the splendor of the Creation in glow-
ing metaphors and man in grand abstractions, and yet, at the
same time, to stop short of glorying in the excellency of his own
nature or of man's. That is, Hamlet, Renaissance man though he
may be, refuses to lapse into a naively Humanist position. Hamlet ends his speech on a peculiar note, with the consistent but
seemingly superfluous observation that "man delights not me,"
which immediately provokes the risibilities of Rosencrantz and
Guildenstern.

Although Melville wrote *Moby-Dick* in America in the middle
of the nineteenth century, in an age and locale dominated by
Emersonian Transcendentalism, which did indeed glory in man's
excellency and which tended to project man to a heavenly estate
right here on earth, Melville found a picture of the human condition more congenial to his own needs and temperament in
Shakespeare and the Bible. I shall not be concerned here with
documenting these influences, a task which has been ably done
already. What I do wish to do is to examine Melville's adaptation of a Shakespearean-biblical meditative style. In what follows, I shall not attempt to distinguish between Shakespearean
and biblical "influences," since my point is that these probably
became conflated in Melville's linguistic imagination. Melville
achieved the astonishing grandeur of *Moby-Dick* (unmatched
in English in the nineteenth century) by returning unabashedly
to the Elizabethan language of both Shakespeare and the Bible,
and also to the world-view embodied in that language.

One peculiarity, however, I must mention before turning to
my analysis of the text. Though Melville announced explicitly
his discovery of the link between truth and blackness and between truth and madness, and though it was so dark a play as
Hamlet that totally suffused and saturated his imagination from
1849 on, yet it is remarkable that the most striking stylistic fea-
ture of *Moby-Dick*, the one that critics most often respond to, is
its ability to arouse in the reader a sense of capaciousness and
euphoria. No doubt this sense of openness and euphoria is owing

to what F. O. Matthiessen calls Melville's "liberation in *Moby-Dick* through the agency of Shakespeare," a liberation that put Melville "into possession of the primitive energies latent in words." Matthiessen expands on this point by saying that "the most important effect of Shakespeare's use of language was to give Melville a range of vocabulary for expressing passion far beyond any that he had previously possessed." [24] I would like to add to Matthiessen's observation that the "vocabulary for expressing passion" which Shakespeare released in Melville was in large part a biblical vocabulary that Melville had been accumulating and storing for years without being able to tap its most glittering peaks and most hidden recesses.

The passage I should like to call attention to here is the peroration of Father Mapple's sermon. Having presented his version of Jonah's resistance to the divine will and his subsequent adventures and eventual deliverance from the whale, Father Mapple goes on to extract his two-stranded lesson. The first lesson is "sin not; but if you do, take heed to repent of it like Jonah." The second strand of the lesson, which applies specifically to Father Mapple himself, is "to preach the Truth to the face of Falsehood." After uttering this summary account of the lesson, Mapple continues to enlarge upon it:

"This shipmates, this is that other lesson; and
woe to that pilot of the living God who slights it.
Woe to him whom this world charms from Gospel duty!
Woe to him who seeks to pour oil upon the waters when God has
      brewed them into a gale!
Woe to him who seeks to please rather than to appal!
Woe to him whose good name is more to him than goodness!
Woe to him who, in this world, courts not dishonor!
Woe to him who would not be true, even though to be false were
      salvation! Yea,
woe to him who, as the great Pilot Paul has it,
      while preaching to others is himself a castaway!"

He drooped and fell away from himself for a moment;
Then lifting his face to them again, showed a deep joy in his eyes

24. *American Renaissance,* pp. 423, 425.

As he cried out with a heavenly enthusiasm,
　　"But oh! shipmates!
On the starboard hand of every woe, there is a sure delight;
And higher the top of that delight,
Than the bottom of the woe is deep.
Is not the main-truck higher than the kelson is low?"

"Delight is to him — a far, far upward, and inward delight — who
　　against the proud gods and commodores of this earth, ever stands
　　forth his own inexorable self.
Delight is to him whose strong arms yet support him, when the ship
　　of this base treacherous world has gone down beneath him.
Delight is to him, who gives no quarter in the truth, and kills, burns,
　　and destroys all sin though he pluck it out from under the robes of
　　Senators and Judges.
Delight, — top-gallant delight
　　is to him, who acknowledges no law or lord but the Lord his God,
　　and is only a patriot to heaven.
Delight is to him, who
　　all the waves of the billows of the seas of the boisterous mob can
　　never shake from this sure Keel of the ages. And eternal
Delight and deliciousness will be his, who coming to lay him down,
　　can say with his final breath — O Father! chiefly known to me by
　　Thy rod — mortal or immortal, here I die."

"I have striven to be Thine,
　　more than to be this world's, or mine own.
Yet this is nothing;
I leave eternity to Thee;
For what is man
That he should live out the lifetime of his God?" [25]

　　I apologize for having quoted at length, but the passage con-
stitutes so perfect a symmetrical unit that there is no way to
break it up and still do Melville justice. As in the case of Hamlet's "soliloquy on man," I have set the entire passage in verse so
as to make some of the outstanding stylistic features even more
obvious.
　　To begin with, the anaphoric style, as in Hamlet's speech,
ushers in a hypnotic set of parallels and antitheses, all set within a
stunning overall symmetrical structure. The first "stanza" con-

25. Mansfield and Vincent, eds., *Moby-Dick*, chap. 9, pp. 47–48.

tains eight "woes" and the third eight "delights." Separating stanzas one and three (the woes and the delights) is a short bridging stanza which makes the movement from woe to delight seem more natural by balancing these two opposites three times in two sentences, at the same time associating woe with downward movement (or with the metaphor of "downness" or depth) and delight with upward movement (or with the metaphor of "upness" or elevation). These internal parallels, like those in Hamlet's speech, are redolent of Hebraic poetic forms: for example, the inverted parallelism of woe-delight, delight-woe, and the trailing and reinforcing parallel, "higher . . . than deep," "higher than . . . low," which weaves high, low, delight, woe, and deep into a baffling net of the literal and the metaphorical. "Starboard hand of every woe" mixes the concrete nautical adjective of location with the nonconcrete noun, "woe." The next clause connects two comparatives ("higher" and "than deep") that are made "abstract" by being linked to the previously articulated abstract nouns. And the final sentence repeats one of the comparatives and gives a synonym for the other, but this time connecting each of them to an exotic concrete noun ("maintruck" and "kelson"). Also, the "deep . . . woe" balances the "deep joy" of the earlier sentence with a jarring semantic inversion (or perhaps crossover would be a more descriptive term), in which "deep" shifts from intensifying a positive word to intensifying a negative word.

The movement between high and low (associated with delight and woe respectively) which is launched in this middle section is continued in the catalogue of delights; H. P. Vincent describes this movement in the delight section succinctly as "the upward thrust of these climactic sentences through the relentless repetition of 'delight,' the bold use of alliteration in the stabbing dentals, and the unexpectedness of and perfection of the adjective 'eternal' placed before the final 'delight.' " [26] But there is more than simple "upward" thrust here. The thrust is, in Mapple's own words, "far, far upward and inward." The motif of "deepness" is never lost sight of, and it is the maintenance of this simultaneous movement in two opposed directions (up and

26. *The Trying-out of Moby-Dick* (Carbondale: Southern Illinois University Press, 1967; first published 1949), p. 75.

in, or outward and inward, or expanding and intensifying) that creates so powerful an effect. Continued too, is the mixing of literal and metaphorical: the locational adjectives, "far," "upward," "inward" applied to a relatively nonconcrete noun.[27] Also, in building up his crescendo, Mapple borrows a device that Hamlet uses in his "soliloquy on man," the use of compound adjectives and compound nouns (delight and deliciousness) and of prepositional phrases that create suspense through phonemic extension ("all the waves of the billows of the seas of the boisterous mob"). Like Hamlet, Father Mapple starts out with the intention of moving his audience. But, as is the case with Hamlet, his own words seem to move him as much as they do his intended listeners. By the time Mapple has arrived at the end of his sermon he has become part of his own audience, as is indicated when he says that one of the strands of the two-stranded lesson is intended specifically for him. Mapple's passional words, like Hamlet's, are propelled out at the cosmos and at the same time probe into the recesses of the self.

Finally, the diction of biblical poetry is richly echoed in Mapple's language. What is more, it is echoed with purpose and with some precision. One might expect, for example, that Psalm 103, which expresses the psalmist's humility and gratitude and at the same time his abiding faith in God's love, would make a suitable conclusion to Mapple's sermon. So it is not wholly surprising to find this psalm invoked by Mapple's declaration: "And higher the top of that delight, than the bottom of the woe is deep." Verse 11 of the psalm reads: "For as the heaven is high above the earth, so great is his mercy toward them that fear him," [28] which fits in perfectly with one of the motifs of the sermon — fearing and obeying God and trusting in his love and mercy.

27. Melville reconcretizes (or demetaphorizes) the adjectives later on, when he has Queequeg "deliver" Tashtego from the inside of a whale: "Queequeg . . . had thrust his long arm far inwards and upwards, and so hauled out our poor Tash by the head," chap. 78, p. 342.

28. Authorized Version. For Melville's allusions I shall continue to cite this translation. See Nathalia Wright, *Melville's Use of the Bible* (Durham, N.C.: Duke University Press, 1949), esp. pp. 146–151, where, in a general discussion of the sermon, allusions to Isaiah and to Psalms 8 and 23 are identified.

Whether ironically (as Lawrance Thompson insists) or straightforwardly, Mapple's sermon is preoccupied exactly with this motif of fearing and trusting God. Moreover, the verses following Psalm 103:11 are also consistent with the imagery of Mapple's peroration and of the sermon as a whole:

12 As far as the east is from the west, *so* far hath he removed our transgressions from us.

13 Like as a father pitieth *his* children, *so* the Lord pitieth them that fear him.

14 For he knoweth our frame; he remembreth that we *are* dust.

15 As for man, his days *are* as grass: as a flower of the field, so he flourisheth.

16 For the wind passeth over it, and it is gone; and the place thereof shall know it no more.

17 But the mercy of the Lord *is* from everlasting to everlasting upon them that fear him.

I shall not dwell on the question of parody or of irony here, whether, as Thompson maintains, Melville is bitterly mocking an authoritarian Calvinist God, or a God who promises pity but punishes severely.[29] It is enough, perhaps, to observe that the poetry of Mapple's sermon and the poetry it evokes are too strong and too moving to admit of a parodic or wholly reversalist ironic reading. That is not to say, however, that there are no paradoxes in the sermon and in the psalm.

For example, in both psalm and sermon God is a stern and demanding, but nevertheless pitying, father. In the psalm he pities them that fear him, and in the sermon he grants delight and deliciousness to that man "who . . . can say with his final breath — O Father! chiefly known to me by Thy rod." And as the psalmist grants that "the mercy of the Lord is from everlasting to everlasting," so Father Mapple is content to "leave eternity to Thee." Many of the paradoxes are similar, also, to those found in Hamlet's soliloquy — the fluctuation between taking pride in man's dignity and nobility, on the one hand, and the unflinching recognition that he is dust on the other. Man, in all three instances, is exalted and is, at the same time fragile,

29. *Melville's Quarrel with God* (Princeton: Princeton University Press, 1952), pp. 161–166.

transient, helpless, "as a flower of the field." The controlling paradox (some might call it an irony) in Mapple's peroration is the same one we saw in Hamlet's speech, the contrast between powerful, dignified man who "ever stands forth his own inexorable self" and the submissive childlike creature "who coming to lay him down, can say with his final breath — O Father! chiefly known to me by Thy rod — mortal or immortal, here I die." Man's return to dust is stated delicately and with a sublime sense of resignation and, paradoxically, of hope, as well.

Although this psalm echoes through Mapple's sermon, yet it is not the only biblical text that informs his thought. Like Hamlet, he conflates several passages of biblical poetry in this powerful utterance. As Nathalia Wright points out, Mapple's "woes" echo those of Isaiah 5:8–24. Verses 8, 11, 18, 20, 21, 22 of the chapter begin with the "woe to those" formula, and, as can be seen by the bunching, the emotional intensity of denunciation rises to a crescendo in the last verses. At first glance, one is tempted to make a straight connection between Isaiah 5 and the recital of woes in the first stanza of Mapple's peroration. But, in fact, the echoes are more striking when Isaiah's "woes" are set against Mapple's "delights."

Otto Kaiser, including among the sevenfold woes the first four verses of Isaiah 10, summarizes them as follows:

5:8–10   The first woe: against the great landlords and property owners . . .
5:11–17   The second woe: Against the debauched and godless life of the nobility . . .
5:18–19   The third woe: against frivolity and mockery.
5:20   The fourth woe: against the perversion of truth . . .
5:21   The fifth woe: against those who are wise in their own eyes.
5:22–24   The sixth woe: against impotent judges . . .
10:1–4   The seventh woe: against those who make laws to suit their own purposes.[30]

Mapple's delights seem to be reserved for the man who goes about the business of frustrating those who generate the woes

30. Isaiah 1–12, The Old Testament Library, (Philadelphia: Westminster Press, 1972), pp. 64–71.

described by Isaiah: the "proud gods and commodores of this earth," "senators and judges," "the boisterous mob," and in general those who pervert truth and conceal sin.

As is the case in contemplating Hamlet's speech, the reader is tempted to ask questions that take him outside the dramatic relevance of the peroration. Compared to Hamlet's speech, how-ever, this sermon seems to be more motivated by social outrage and more centered on social justice, and Melville seems to go to the biblical source to ask the question "What is man?" not only as an ontological question but as a societal question as well. The social orientation of the sermon is underlined by another biblical text that is summoned up by Mapple's list of delights. As Mansfield and Vincent have pointed out in their edition of *Moby-Dick,* "*Delight* both as noun and verb was common in the Old Testament and in Milton; in an 1844 edition of the New Testament and Psalms . . . he sidelined all of Psalm xxxvii, where the word appears in verses 4, 11, and 23, and especially marked verse 11: 'But the meek shall inherit the earth, and shall delight themselves in the abundance of peace.' " [31]

The whole of Psalm 37, like Isaiah 5:8–24, is an apology for perceived inequities in the divine schema, a denunciation of the evil-doers, and an assertion of assurance to the righteous that ultimately the score will be evened, and that those who suffer injustice here and now will be rewarded with future delights. In short, the psalm is the contrapuntal mate to Isaiah 5, and its invocation works to intensify the deeply emotional truths spoken by Mapple.

There is still one more psalm that seems relevant here. De-light, in Father Mapple's sermon, is to the man who has striven to be God's and "who acknowledges no law or lord but the Lord his God." Psalm 119, the longest of the psalms, is an extended tribute to God and to God's law. In that Psalm appear the fol-lowing verses:

14 I have rejoiced in the way of thy testimonies as *much as* in all riches.
15 I will meditate in thy precepts, and have respect unto thy ways.

31. Page 619.

16 I will delight myself in thy statutes: I will not forget thy word.

For the psalmist, God's law is a source of pleasure. The last strophe of the third stanza of Mapple's sermon, in a flash of artistic brilliance, plays on the psalmist's delight. Father Mapple's use of the doublet, "delight and deliciousness," modified by "eternal," intensifies the sense of pleasure and also fuses the abstract offshoot of the original root (Latin, *delicere*) with the sensual branch. Moreover, this fusion sets the stage for the submerged allusion which is to follow, an allusion to what is undoubtedly the best known of all the psalms, perhaps the best known of all religious poems, the psalm that "has won for itself a supreme place in the religious literature of the world," [32] Psalm 23.

I shall return to the delight and deliciousness, but first I would like to recall that in this most beautiful and most comforting of psalms the basic metaphor (it is no exaggeration to call it a "metaphysical conceit") is, as everyone knows, the metaphor of the solicitous shepherd: "The Lord is my shepherd; I shall not want. He maketh me to lie down in green pastures." Father Mapple's redeemed man is the man "who coming to lay him down, can say with his final breath — O Father! chiefly known to me by Thy rod — mortal or immortal, here I die." It will be remembered, too, that the psalmist, though he walks "through the valley of the shadow of death," fears "no evil." He is comforted by the Lord/Shepherd's "rod and staff." Similarly, in Mapple's strophe God as Father is known to man by His "rod," and man's one desire, whether, paradoxically, he be "mortal or immortal," is to lay himself down at God's side. The sense of comfort issuing from the contemplation of eternally resting at peace with a stern but solicitous father seems to come directly from the psalm itself. And although Father Mapple does not repeat explicitly the words of the psalm, nevertheless this strophe conveys the same sense of resignation, of humility, and of being comforted.

32. *The Interpreter's Bible*, IV (Nashville: Abingdon Press, 1955), p. 123.

Returning to the "eternal delight and deliciousness" we must remind ourselves that in the psalm the Lord prepares "a table before me." To the psalmist, God is shepherd, guide, host. In general, He is a provider of physical and spiritual sustenance. Or, it may be that the physical description is a metaphor for the spiritual. Mapple's mixing of delight and deliciousness (that is, of spiritual and sensual pleasure) recompresses the metaphor of infinite Creator as intimate Father who sets a feast for the loved one; it is a brilliant metonymy conveying the understanding that from submission to God comes both spiritual and physical pleasure.

But even man's groping for delight may be an act of hubris. How can this quintessence of dust wax so bold as to aspire to eternal delight and deliciousness? Father Mapple catches himself in his penultimate closing words, and does so by echoing the psalmist's eternally haunting question: "What is man that thou art mindful of him?" But Melville, like Shakespeare, is too great an artist to let his character simply repeat the question. It is enough to pluck the string lightly, to set the vibrations in motion, raising responsive echoes in the reader's soul.

Hamlet's echoing of the question resounds with the technological fixation of post-Renaissance man: "What a piece of work is a man?" Father Mapple's rephrasing reasserts the relational element in the question but points the question in a teleological, rather than ontological, direction: "What is man that he should live out the lifetime of his God?" Mapple's question, by its very paradoxical nature, is a gesture accepting man's diminutiveness. How can man, with his three score and ten allotment of years, hope to relate himself to a God who is without beginning and without end? And in its paradoxicality the question echoes its biblical source: How is it that an infinite, all-powerful Creator relates himself intimately, and passionately, to finite man? And yet the clear implication of the question is, He does.

Mapple, in the kind of movement constantly repeated in *Moby-Dick*, has now turned from societal to cosmic consciousness. But in a way he has not "turned" at all, because in the biblical texts he has been kneading, the societal and the cosmic are already mixed. In their notes, Mansfield and Vincent do not mention Psalm 8:4, but they do give as a possible source for

Mapple's question Job 11:7–8,[33] verses that seem to relate not
only to Mapple's paradox, but also to his earlier antithesis between a delight that is higher than woe is deep: "Canst thou by
searching find out God? Canst thou find out the Almighty unto
Perfection? *It is* as high as heaven; what canst thou do? Deeper
than hell; what canst thou know?" If Mapple's words echo these
verses, as it seems to me they do, then they recognize that man's
grandeur, paradoxically, resides in his shabbiness. Mapple has
moved from a denunciation of man's arrogance as a corrupt
societal creature to a recognition of his "dustness," to an acceptance of man's absurdity.

Father Mapple begins his peroration as a denunciation of the
hypocrite and of the man who sets his own comfort above his
moral duty. He then shifts into a paean to the righteous man
who puts nothing before his allegiance to God and to the moral
law. And he ends by having this grandiose figure who revels in
delight recognize himself as this quintessence of dust. Although
Father Mapple does not use the phrase, clearly that is what man
is reduced to. Here, as in Hamlet's speech, man's grandeur
emerges from a combination of dignity and pathos. That same
man who "ever stands forth his own inexorable self," who "kills,
burns, and destroys all sin," that same man bows himself as a
meek child before a commanding figure of the father. And again,
as in Hamlet's speech, the duality is not between reason and the
flesh but between man's claim to divine dignity on the one hand
and his recognition of himself as inanimate dust on the other.

Nineteenth-century American that he is, Melville associates
that dignity of the *imago dei* with the concept of democracy:
"This august dignity I treat of, is not the dignity of kings and
robes, but that abounding dignity which has no robed investi-
ture. Thou shalt see it shining in the arm that wields a pick or
drives a spike; that democratic dignity which, on all hands, radi-
ates without end from God." Thus speaks Ishmael in his own
magnificent voice. But at all points in *Moby-Dick* this abounding
dignity is bounded in by the mystery and inscrutability of the
universe, and also by man's inescapable mortality, which is no-

33. Page 620.

where more clearly set forth than in the chapter entitled "The Deck. Ahab and the Carpenter." [34]

The carpenter is presented "filing the ivory joist" for Ahab's artificial leg. But since "this bone is dust" it sets the carpenter sneezing and grumbling. "Saw a live tree," he soliloquizes, "and you don't get this dust; amputate a live bone, and you don't get it (*sneezes*)." As he contemplates the task before him, the carpenter muses, "Lucky now (*sneezes*) there's no knee-joint to make; that might puzzle a little; but a mere shinbone — why it's easy as making hoppoles; only I should like to put a good finish on." The entire passage seems, at first glance, to be a parody of the thirty-seventh chapter of Ezekiel (itself a variation on Genesis 2:7), but the passage also mocks hubristic man who aspires blasphemously to create a living limb.[35]

Later in the same chapter Ahab enters, whereupon the following conversation ensues:

> Carpenter? why that's — but no; — a very tidy, and, I may say, an extremely gentlemenlike sort of business thou art in here, carpenter; — or would'st thou rather work in clay?
>
> Sir? — Clay? clay, sir? That's mud; we leave clay to the ditchers, sir.
>
> The fellow's impious! What art thou sneezing about?
>
> Bone is rather dusty, sir.

Melville mixes the man-as-dust imagery of Genesis, Ezekiel, and Job with the man-as-clay imagery of Isaiah and Jeremiah, both sets of images projecting the notion of man as matter which is made living by being infused with the breath or spirit of God.[36]

34. Chapter 108, pp. 465–469.
35. We seem to have some Melville word-play here. In the biblical account, God breathes into the dust and it becomes a living soul. In the case of the carpenter, the dust entering the respiratory tract causes a discharge of breath. It may be noted, too, that "In the South Pacific," it is believed that a sneeze is "caused when an absent soul returns to the body." Gertrude Jobes, *Dictionary of Mythology, Folklore, and Symbols* (New York: Scarecrow Press, 1961), II, 1470.
36. Ezekiel 37:5, Authorized Version: "Behold I will cause breath to enter into you and you shall live."

In his oft-quoted exuberant letter of March 3, 1849 to Evert A. Duyckinck, Melville had declared, "The truth is that we are all sons, grandsons, or nephews or great-nephews of those who go before us. No one is his own sire." [37] And later, in the 1850 essay on Hawthorne, he added that "all that has been said but multiplies the avenues to what remains to be said." Clearly, Melville was resisting the tremendous pressure of "originality" exerted by Romantic theories of art current at the time. Romantic though he was, Melville was very far from accepting (or even being able to tolerate) Emerson's demand, in *Nature*, that "we have a poetry and philosophy of insight and not of tradition." Melville recognized that the poet, like Adam, was formed of the dust of the ground, and that his most penetrating insights might be achieved through the pursuit of a traditional wisdom that would not let him glory in the excellency of his own nature. Despite the sometimes exhilarating tone of *Moby-Dick*, Melville did not imagine himself a "liberating god," which is what Emerson, in his essay, "The Poet," asserted the true poet should be.

Although the reader can feel that in *Moby-Dick* Melville is revelling in the newfound power of his imagination, nevertheless the discerning reader must also recognize that Melville's Shakespearean-biblical view of man did not permit him to participate fully in the excesses of Emersonian dionysianism. Far from being a "liberating god" who brought illuminating truth to mankind from a region of eternal light, the artist was, for Melville, the utterer of dark truths. In the *Mosses* essay, as we have seen, Melville associated truth with blackness and madness. In Father Mapple's sermon truth is, again, not a source of illumination, not an eternally valid abstraction. It is, rather, turbulent and demanding. The man who "gives no quarter in truth" is not a tranquil philosopher but a man who "kills, burns, and destroys all sin though he pluck it out from under the robes of Senators and Judges." This truth of Melville's coincides with Scriptural notions of truth. Leon Shestov writes that

within the "limits of reason" one can create a science, a sublime ethic, and even a religion; but to find God one must tear oneself

37. *The Letters of Herman Melville*, ed. Merrel R. Davis and William H. Gilman (New Haven: Yale University Press, 1960), p. 78.

away from the seductions of reason with all its physical and moral constraints, and go to another source of truth. In Scripture this source bears the enigmatic name "faith," which is that dimension of thought where truth abandons itself fearlessly and joyously to the entire disposition of the Creator: "Thy will be done!" [38]

Just so does Father Mapple's man of delight come to lay him down and die at his Father's side, against all the seductions of reason.

It is not my desire, however, to maintain that either Melville or Shakespeare accepted a conventional doctrinal religion. No one will ever be able to support such an assertion successfully about either writer. What I do wish to suggest, though, is that both of them recognized and pondered man's dual nature as a creature crowned with divine dignity and yet shaped out of dust; that Melville from *Moby-Dick* on, and Shakespeare in the late tragedies, felt that truth was dark and disturbing, and they expressed truths that echo the patterns of biblical "wisdom" literature.[39]

Perhaps, as Matthiessen said, Shakespeare put Melville into possession of the primitive energies latent in words, but he also put him into possession of a language that was more than primitive. He inspired Melville to cultivate, at great risk to his popular success, Elizabethan (both biblical and Shakespearean) vocabulary, syntax, and rhythms. In cultivating them, Melville revitalized Elizabethan language and created, for the last time in En-

38. *Athens and Jerusalem*, tr. Bernard Martin (Athens, Ohio: Ohio University Press, 1966), pp. 67–68.

39. Peter Milward, *Shakespeare's Religious Background* (Bloomington: Indiana University Press, 1973), argues that Shakespeare's plays were not "pervasively secular." He asserts that "a careful collation of . . . those speeches which most linger in the memory with pessimistic impression, such as the soliloquies of Hamlet and Macbeth, and certain speeches of Lear and Prospero . . . with parallel passages in the *Psalms* and the *Book of Job* is enough to show how closely the thought of Shakespeare follows the 'wisdom' of the Bible" (p. 102). See also, Harold Fisch, *Hamlet and the Word* (New York: Ungar, Frederick Publishing Co., 1971); R. M. Frye, *Shakespeare and Christian Doctrine* (Princeton: Princeton University Press, 1963); John Vyvyan, *The Shakespearean Ethic* (London, 1959); William Braswell, *Melville's Religious Thought* (Durham, N.C.: Duke University Press, 1943); Lawrance Thompson, *Melville's Quarrel with God* (Princeton: Princeton University Press, 1952).

glish, a style as infinite in its grandeur as it is unfathomable in its depths.[40]

40. I would like to express my gratitude to the Society for Religion in Higher Education for a study grant which enabled me to spend a year in Israel studying the Psalms.

PAUL D'ANDREA

"Thou Starre of Poets": Shakespeare as DNA

Shakespeare is an instance of that rare creature, an adorable
genius. People like being around him, enjoy being involved
with his work. His plays and poetry are alive at this moment,
and have been so any time these last three hundred and eighty
years. His work is more than alive; it is positively active, and it
is this curious activity I would like to explore in this essay.
Shakespeare is helpful. He has helped modern artists cope with
the problems and mysteries important to them. He is by no
means a dead god in a pantheon, the author of a sacred text
reverenced at a distance and therefore useless. The most ap-
proachable of men of genius, he has a habit of turning up here
and there, now in the theater and now in a title, in a glancing
allusion, a snatch of popular song, or in the approach to a
character, a thought, a situation, a plot, a system of ethics, a
history, a political view, or a philosophy of life. Shakespeare
seems to be there when we need him; he is a *matey* genius.

How does he help? How is he used? This essay considers
the uses of Shakespeare by three playwrights representing a
wide range of political, psychological, philosophical, and artistic commitments — Tom Stoppard, the Pole Slawomir Mrozek,
and Eugene O'Neill. I then want to offer, on the basis of this
study, a new, postromantic metaphor for Shakespeare, who has

been variously figured forth as the mirror up to nature, Fancy's child, crow or warbler, comprehensive soul, organism, aeolian harp, Hamlet-surrogate, Spinozistic deity, prophet, and freedom fighter. And once it is offered, I shall allow my new, postromantic metaphor to be superseded by an old, prescientific one from Ben Jonson.

WORLDS IN CONTACT

In *Rosencrantz and Guildenstern Are Dead*, Stoppard presents us with two worlds, that of Shakespeare's *Hamlet* and the world of Rosencrantz and Guildenstern. The second of these is much like our own, and so we have the opportunity to compare our world, or a representation of it, with its mighty opposite. Moreover, since these worlds interact with each other, we can do more than compare. We can contemplate the effects of one world on the other. This is Stoppard's achievement. He has set up a powerful dialectic by setting worlds in contact.

Stoppard achieves at a bound something most modern artists have sought in vain — a complete and satisfactory, generally intelligible representation of a world of significance and value. He does this by a massive synecdoche: he puts parts of Shakespeare's *Hamlet* on his stage, letting the parts stand for the whole — the whole play and the whole meaning of the play. One of the reasons for the sense of standing still in much modern literature is the absence of a reference point with which the modern condition could be compared. Could they achieve that reference point, the artists of good will in collaboration with their audiences could move intelligently and perhaps even wisely toward it or away from it. In fact, a point of reference, useful in Cartesian geometry, is inadequate in the humanities, since one is dealing with exceedingly complicated personal, social, and metaphysical wholes. A reference *world* is what is needed, and that is precisely what Stoppard secures for his investigation of the contemporary condition. Shakespeare's *Hamlet* is not a myth, although it embodies a number of structures of myth. It would be well described as an elaborated fable. Its elaboration — involving its plot, its thoughts, its magical rhythms — is what makes it a whole world, and an adequate reference. The historicist and the dialectically minded will see the *Hamlet*-world as the middle term in a dialectic leading to the transcendence of both the *Hamlet*-world and the modern condition. My task is more basic. I would like to investigate what these two worlds are like and how they affect each other. How has Stoppard used the available Shakespeare?

The *Hamlet*-world is hard on Rosencrantz and Guildenstern. They lived a normal life until Claudius' messenger banged on their shutters at dawn one day. Once they answer the summons to come to Elsinore and serve their King, their normalcy is gone. Overbearing and powerful figures from the intrigues of court come in and out of their lives, shouting orders, hurrying them on, getting their names wrong, pushing them toward their deaths and not seeming to notice. The world after the summons is changed. The elementary verities disappear. A system as well worked out as the laws of probability stops functioning, as a tossed coin comes up heads ninety-nine times in a row. The two men could not have avoided the encounter. When the *Hamlet*-world calls, you come:

> GUIL: He was just a hat and a cloak levitating in the grey plume of his own breath, but when he called, we came.[1]

Over and over again, they repeat or allude to the phrase "We were sent for." Being sent for is fatal. When they admit to Hamlet they were sent for, they set the seal on their deaths. This noncomprehending participation in a fatal world of great significance and intense activity gives something of the Lenten solemnity of *Everyman* to their actions. Abandoned by the good friends logic, probability, self-determination, and normalcy, Rosencrantz and Guildenstern obey their summons to death, die, and stay dead, no good deeds counted or even inquired after.

The *Hamlet*-world terrifies them. After Claudius and Gertrude give Rosencrantz and Guildenstern their commission re-

---

1. Tom Stoppard, *Rosencrantz and Guildenstern Are Dead* (New York: Grove Press, 1968), p. 39. The edition of Shakespeare used is *William Shakespeare: The Complete Works*, ed. Alfred Harbage and others (Baltimore: Penguin Books, 1969).

garding Prince Hamlet, which is "to gather . . . whether aught
to us unknown affects him thus," the strain of a recurrent terror
begins to cause a crazed permutation of the syntactical structures of Rosencrantz:

> ROS (*cracking, high*): — over my step over my head body! —
> I tell you it's all stopping to a death, it's boding to a depth, step-
> ping to a head, it's all heading to a dead stop —
>
> (38)

Calmed, he says with a dying fall: "I want to go home" (39).
A mere appearance by Hamlet throws them into a stichomythic
tizzy lasting seven pages of text (44). The strange, potent,
energetic world has engaged them in an unequal struggle. The
sanguine Guildenstern wants to pick some success out of the
debacle of their interrogation of Hamlet, but Rosencrantz is
frank:

> ROS (*simply*): He murdered us . . . (*roused*): Twenty-seven —
> three, and you think he might have had the edge?! He *murdered*
> us.
>
> (56–57)

Indeed, Hamlet will murder them. This world sends for you,
beats you in a game you do not understand, and then ships you
off to your death.

Rosencrantz and Guildenstern are passive in relation to the
figures from the world of *Hamlet*. Rosencrantz complains that
Hamlet, Claudius, and Gertrude are always catching them "on
the trot. . . . Why can't *we* go by *them*?" (73). He tries to
approach Hamlet and have it out with him but loses his nerve:

> ROS: We're overawed, that's our trouble. When it comes to the
> point we succumb to their personality.
>
> (75)

They are rendered passive by their awe of these regal beings,
who are highly placed both in rank and, interestingly, in genre.
Hamlet is engaged in a tragedy; Rosencrantz and Guildenstern
have been relegated to an inferior genre, an irony, characterized

by inability to perform significant actions and failure to achieve insight into one's condition. This sense of worthlessness exacerbates their passivity, and that in turn makes them even less able to act and to understand what is happening to them. The coming together of these worlds either destroys their sense of themselves as persons, or causes them to realize they never had such a sense. Guildenstern comments on the matter:

> And yet it doesn't seem enough; to have breathed such significance. Can that be all? And why us? — anybody would have done. And we have contributed nothing.
>
> (92)

If anybody would have done, why them and why kill them? One has to sympathize with the two men. These highly placed people call on them, bring them a terror, gain extraordinary significance for themselves and perpetual fame, and casually go off on their own, leaving death as a tip.

If we sympathize with Rosencrantz and Guildenstern, their most significant failure will be of particular interest. They incessantly worry about understanding and they fail to understand.

> GUIL: . . . All your life you live so close to truth, it becomes a permanent blur in the corner of your eye, and when something nudges it into outline it is like being ambushed by a grotesque.
>
> (39)

He had thought that fear itself might lead to understanding, functioning as "the crack that might flood your brain with light!" (15), an idea echoed later by the Player when he says that theater itself leads to understanding, from theater "there escapes a thin beam of light that, seen at the right angle, can crack the shell of mortality" (83). The play abounds with references to understanding,[2] and the principals doggedly fail to understand.

People in Hamlet's world understand. They inhabit a tragedy, and therefore they achieve the recognitions toward which tragic

2. As at pp. 17, 20, 28, 40, 42–50, 56–58, 61, 66, 69, 74, 92, 111, 122, and 125.

actions tend. Rosencrantz and Guildenstern live in an irony, a difficult and man-defeating way of life in which one can do nothing that makes a difference or creates significance. This is the world of Gregor Samsa.

The most striking manifestation of this occurs as the players rehearse "The Murder of Gonzago," the play Hamlet amended and is using as the thing with which to catch the conscience of the King. Stoppard adds to the dumb show, which slowly evolves beyond the Shakespearean text into a recapitulation of *Hamlet*, with Lucianus substituted for the Prince. The Player explains the mime to Rosencrantz and Guildenstern:

> The King . . . tormented by guilt — haunted by fear — decides to despatch his nephew to England — and entrusts this undertaking to two smiling accomplices — friends — courtiers — to two spies.
>
> (81)

He then reveals that the two spies are killed, by "a letter that seals their deaths" (82).

The irony is that "Gonzago" is the classical instrument of recognition. This is the work that makes the King start up, recognizing his deed and signaling his guilt to Hamlet. Yet Rosencrantz and Guildenstern can see nothing in it, no matter how explicitly the Player hints. They fail to realize that the actors miming the spies are wearing coats identical to their own. Looking at the player playing him, Rosencrantz murmurs "I know you, don't I? I never forget a face" (82) and fails to grasp what is going on, as does his fellow:

> PLAYER (*to* GUIL): Are you familiar with this play?
> GUIL: No.

That was the wrong answer, although true. The "Mousetrap," used successfully as an instrument of discovery by Hamlet, brings about recognition, *anagnorisis*, for Claudius and for Hamlet (84–85), but the play which caught the conscience of the King is utterly lost on Rosencrantz and Guildenstern. In this episode all the elements of the play come together vividly — the two worlds with the players as the mediators between them, one world active, manipulative, aware, charged with significance and comprehension, the other passive and noncomprehending.

Coleridge, who thought *Hamlet* taught that "action is the chief end of existence," and Goethe, who saw Hamlet as a costly jar shivered by the growth within it of something too mighty for its delicacy, would be surprised were they to compare Hamlet's power of action with that of the modern heroes. In this play, text is definitive. When Guildenstern asks who gets to decide who dies in plays, the Player switches off his smile to intone "*Decides*? It is *written*" (80). Rosencrantz and Guildenstern are helpless in the face of the written text. Hamlet, however, can alter text to bring about recognition and find a regicide:

> [To the Player] You could for a need study a speech of some dozen or sixteen lines which I would set down and insert in't, could you not?
>
> (62)

and he alters his own death warrant, turning it into the instrument of the deaths of Rosencrantz and Guildenstern (111). Since the coming of these two worlds into contact is the main action of the play, how they interact is important. The interpenetration of the two worlds is entirely in the control of Claudius and Hamlet. When Rosencrantz and Guildenstern set a trap for Hamlet by linking their belts, the Prince simply refuses to enter it, and "ROS's *trousers slide slowly down*" (89). This is quite different from the power the *Hamlet*-world has over the two men, signaled by that deadly phrase "We were sent for."

Guildenstern begins to realize, moments from the end, that their world is contained in and carried along by an irresistible movement from a larger world:

> Where we went wrong was getting on a boat. We can move, of course, change direction, rattle about, but our movement is contained within a larger one that carries us along as inexorably as the wind and current.
>
> (122)

Hamlet seizes symbiotically on pirates and escapes from that contained, smaller movement toward death. Commentary has made the point that the Hamlet of act V, the Hamlet of "The readiness is all," is transcendent. In *Rosencrantz and Guildenstern Are Dead* he is transcendent in the etymological sense. He literally climbs out of a world and goes about his business. Although the players are a source of menace to the two figures of the irony, they are merely tools to hand for the denizen of tragedy. Hamlet on board ship, beneath a "gaudy striped umbrella," "reclining in a deck-chair, wrapped in a rug, reading a book, possibly smoking," is an effortlessly effective, well-bred and well-spoken daemon. Finally, gratuitously, he kills Rosencrantz and Guildenstern.

Stoppard has set up *Hamlet* as a symbol for *Hamlet*, *feliciter audax*, and pleases, as a poet should, by a fine excess. We are given a world to compare with our own, and ours does not fare so very well in the comparison. Rosencrantz and Guildenstern die badly; they see nothing with blinding sight. They just "fail to reappear" (84). In "Lapis Lazuli" Yeats speaks or sings about tragic gaiety, and asserts that "Hamlet and Lear are gay; / Gaiety transfiguring all that dread." Part of what he means seems to be that these figures participated in actions which were terrible and significant. However painful they may have been to live through, the events conferred high dignity upon all those who "perform their tragic play." Such events — the defeat, wandering, and extraordinary death of Oedipus, the deaths of Cordelia and Lear, the Passion of Christ — are permanent and imperishable events in the spiritual (but not in the positivist) history of the human world. The deaths of Rosencrantz and Guildenstern merely happen. From the worlds in contact we may retrieve an exemplum which chastens us.

However, these worlds were in living, that is to say, artistic contact, and one affected the other. The *Hamlet*-world was cruel to Rosencrantz and Guildenstern; how would it treat us? What is the meaning of this cruelty? I think the implication is that if we were to get a summons from Claudius' dawn messenger, a call to full war, a hello and a handshake from Godot, we might not enjoy what would ensue. "But no matter how loudly we clamor for magic in our lives, we are really afraid

of pursuing an existence entirely under its influence and sign."
This is a warning from Artaud about getting caught up in truly
serious theater. Artaud spoke of cruelty in the theater. He did
not mean gratuitous slashings and gougings on stage, but was
trying to adumbrate the fatal, necessary, and life-changing access of events characteristic of true theater, the "much more
terrible and necessary cruelty which things can exercise against
us. We are not free. And the sky can still fall on our heads." [3]
Cruelty causes suffering, confers meaning, and is fatal. You
learn from it and die of it. Meaning is expensive, and cannot
be had for the cost of a mere exemplum. It requires the ex-
penditure of resources of energy, brain power, and feeling. If
that is the necessary relation between Hamlet's tragedy and
our irony, are we willing to pay? If you inhabit an irony, would
you like to get in touch with a tragedy or have it get in touch
with you?

Were we to be so involved, so caught up, sent for, we might
fare better than Rosencrantz and Guildenstern, for we have had
the benefit of witnessing the play, and can achieve an awareness
denied Rosencrantz and Guildenstern. Mark Van Doren once
offered the following as the proverb most significant to him:

God said, "Take what you want, and pay for it."

Experiencing this cruelty seems to be the price you have to pay
for such knowledge. The final irony of the lives of Rosencrantz
and Guildenstern is that they pay the price and take away none
of the understanding. That does seem thoroughly modern.

AN EAST EUROPEAN USE OF SHAKESPEAREAN FORM

The 1965 Warsaw opening of Slawomir Mrozek's *Tango* has
been described as "the most explosive event in the theatrical
history of Poland for half a century." [4] It is of particular interest

3. Antonin Artaud, *The Theater and Its Double*, tr. Mary Caroline
Richards (New York: Grove Press, 1958), pp. 9, 79.
4. Martin Esslin, *The Theatre of the Absurd*, 2nd ed. rev. (Harmonds-
worth, 1968), p. 309. For accounts of modern Polish thought and theater,
see Maria Kuncewicz[owa], ed., *The Modern Polish Mind* (Boston:
Little, Brown & Co., 1962); Zbigniew Folejewski, "The Theater of Ruth-

for a study of the uses of Shakespeare. Shakespeare has been
an important cultural force in Poland since 1607. "Our greatest
debt to Britain," Zbigniew Raszewski wrote a decade after the
second World War, "is through William Shakespeare . . . our
nation is among those which have incorporated his work most
intimately into their national heritage." [5] On the occasion of the
Shakespeare Quatercentenary, R. Szydlowski stated in the Party
journal *Nowe Drogi* that "every educated man in Poland is familiar with Shakespeare . . . children learn about him at schools,
students study him at the universities . . . grown-up people go to
see his plays on the stage . . . plays which lie as near the heart
of every Pole as the masterpieces of our national literature;
poetry and drama of Mickiewicz, Slowacki and Wyspiański." [6]

Mrozek comes from a country which has had an unusually
profound relation with Shakespeare ever since Fortinbras moved
"against some part of Poland," [7] and possesses a political sophistication simply unavailable in the West. Caught between
East and West, Poland has proved on its pulses partition and
loss of nationhood, extreme romanticism, reunification, Nazi
occupation, and Soviet domination. Mrozek was nine when the
Nazis invaded Poland and Witkiewicz slit his wrists. He has a
special vantage point, and his play *Tango* is built on *Hamlet*.

In this play Mrozek uses the *Hamlet*-fable to portray and
simultaneously to investigate the modern condition. The sensitive young intellectual Arthur returns from the university, to
find his mother Eleanor an adulteress, his father Stomil an
impostor, a usurper in his home, and the time out of joint. He
tries to set it right by staging two plays within the play. His

---

less Metaphor: Polish Theater between Marxism and Existentialism,"
Comparative Drama, III (Fall 1969), 176–182; and Krystyna Przybylska, "The Modern Polish Theater," in Thomas E. Bird, ed., *Queens
Slavic Papers* (Flushing, New York: Queens College Press, 1973), I, 68–
79.

5. "Against Some Part of Poland," *Drama*, XL (Spring 1956), 24–28.
6. Quoted in Maria Kwapień, "Shakespeare's Anniversary in Poland,"
The Polish Review, X, no. 1 (Winter 1965), 65.
7. The subject of Shakespeare in Poland may be reviewed by consulting Raszewski; Kwapień (and in particular the essay by Helsztyński cited
therein); Jan Kott, *Shakespeare Our Contemporary* (Garden City, N.Y.:
Doubleday, 1964); and Oswald LeWinter, "Poland," in *The Reader's
Encyclopedia of Shakespeare*, ed. Oscar James Campbell and Edward G.
Quinn (New York: Crowell, 1966).

betrayal by Ala, the young woman he begs to help him, leads to his death. Eddie, a man *fort en bras*, "packing a wicked punch," kills Arthur and takes over the society.

Arthur faces an unusual problem. Eddie, the incarnation of unreflecting animal force, enjoys regular access to Eleanor's enseamèd bed, while Stomil pretends not to notice and goes on about his work, a series of trivial avant-garde experiments in art. Eleanor and Stomil are twentieth-century revolutionaries grown older. The result of their innovations in politics, social organization, and art is empty nonsense and an unstable equilibrium with Eddie. Arthur expostulates on what is rotten in Eastern Europe:

> I come home and what do I find? Laxity, chaos, shady characters, ambiguous relationships[8] . . . What's going on in this house? Chaos, anarchy, entropy!
>
> (21)

and states his response to it: "I just can't live in a world like this!" (15).

Stomil's "march to the future," with Man as God, has eventuated in muddle — a debile experimental art, casual adultery, endless poker games with Eddie, and "the right to wear short pants."

> STOMIL: Why, it wasn't until after 1900 that the boldest, the most advanced spirits stopped giving up their seats to elderly people . . . if you today can push your grandmother around, it's to us your thanks are due.
>
> (25)

Arthur realizes he is trapped in an ironic mode:

> No order, no sense of reality, no decency, no initiative. You can't move in this place, you can't breathe, you can't live!
>
> (22)

8. Sławomir Mrożek, *Tango*, tr. Ralph Manheim and Teresa Dzieduscycka (New York: Grove Press, 1968), p. 16. *Tango* may be found in Polish in the Warsaw monthly *Dialog*, IX, no. 11 (November 1964), 5–44. His other plays are also published in *Dialog*.

The ugly and normless chaos born of successful revolution moves Arthur a step further along a Dostoevskyan line of thought: "Because everything is possible, nothing is possible anymore." He decides to bring about a renaissance: "If I want a world, I've got to make one" (27). He discovers the necessity of genesis.

Arthur's problem in genesis is more complicated than Adam's. Adam had to name the animals and obey God. Arthur has to create values, because, unlike the plants and the fishes, they do not exist in nature. He tries three solutions to the problem. The first two fail, and the third leads to his death. His first attempt is a play within the play. He tries to get his father to enact a tragedy. Inverting elements of the scene between Hamlet and the Ghost, Arthur upbraids his father for not being angered at Eleanor's adultery, and urges him to sweep to his revenge. Stomil's resolve to avenge his honor is short-lived. Revolver in hand, he approaches his adversary only to falter, sit down, and join in the interminable game of cards. Arthur was trying to create meaning by creating a tragedy, since "tragedy is a form so vast and powerful that reality can never escape its grip" (60). Stomil had realized this:

> How fiendishly clever! So you need a tragedy! Tragedy has always been the most perfect expression of a society with established values.[9]

>   (59)

Tragedy, however, is one of the forms that Stomil's revolution had destroyed. Farce alone of the genres remains (61), and it is farce Arthur gets in his bid for significance as the projected fateful, value-creating denouement ends in a tawdry shuffle.

His attempt at resurrection of a genre a failure, Arthur goes back to the origins of the drama in ritual. His second "Mouse-trap," designed to retrieve values, is a wedding ceremony. One of the results of successful revolution is Ala's willingness to climb into bed with any man who wants her to and is willing

9. Professor George Kliger of the University of Minnesota has pointed out to me that the phrase "established values" might be better rendered "rigid concepts." "Rigid concepts" would seem to be Stomil's view of "established values."

to push a little. Arthur convinces Ala to marry him, just as people did in the old days, with a full-scale ceremony complete with bridal gown, bridesmaids, a procession (an important element in ritual), and Mendelssohn. He wants to create value by enacting an abandoned ritual. Through a species of sympathetic magic the values which used to attach to the ceremony should reappear. The strained logic reveals Arthur's growing desperation:

> I've got to rebuild a world, and for that I must have a wedding.
> (54)

His campaign, with its password "New life" and countersign "Rebirth," is intended "to create meanings, because they don't exist in nature" (42).

Arthur's second approach fails, as it had to. His project was a loveless and over-intellectualized venture, in which Ala was merely a weapon, and treated as such. Arthur had no idea of the complex human response Ala intuitively desired. When he gives Ala her instructions, the gist of her invitation — "There's really nothing else you want to tell me?" (54) — is lost on him. He has tried to force sexuality and its concomitants, good and bad, out of his scheme of things. His over-estimation of the power of pure convention, his lack of self-knowledge, and his suppression of emotion cause and are caused by his spiritual emptiness. Into that vacuum rushes the enthusiasm of fascism, with mortal consequences.

On his wedding morning he drinks himself into what he feels is sanity and abandons the ceremony, because "conventions always spring from an idea" and therefore "form can never save the world" (89). Ignoring Ala's protests that she be taken into account, Arthur has Eddie guard the door while they find a suitable idea. God, sport, experiment, and progress — the last a contribution from Eddie — are reviewed and rejected in order. Arthur adopts the fascist belief that power to kill is a great idea. In a burst of vulgar Nietzscheism, he fulminates his new law for "the herd," and drafts Eddie to kill granduncle Eugene, an Enlightenment figure manqué who had volunteered to serve as Arthur's lieutenant.

Ala prevents the execution by asserting that she has been unfaithful to Arthur with Eddie:

ALA: I didn't think you'd mind. After all, you only wanted to marry me out of principle.

(101)

This drives Arthur into a jealous frenzy. As he searches for the revolver, Eddie kills him. Arthur dies with a fragment of a recognition: "I loved you, Ala," reminiscent of Hamlet's "I loved Ophelia." Eddie takes over the society.

In search of value, Arthur realized an idea was needed to vivify a convention, but chose the wrong idea, fascist power. Eddies are better at that than Hamlets. He was also trapped by the dialectic he allowed to take over his mind. He thought he had to have an idea, and chose a bad one, when his real emptiness was spiritual and emotional. Ala was offering him part of what he really needed — a bond which might be recognized by the intellect but which was informed by emotion. Arthur's lack of self-knowledge and his repression of his sexuality first made him unable to animate convention with the real source of its former power and then vulnerable to desperate passion, easy prey for Eddie. Stomil had thought that Eddie was the simple, real stuff of humanity. With his son's death he realizes that both his own formless experimentation and Eddie's brutishness fail to catch between them what is elusively human:

STOMIL: I've always thought we were slaves of abstractions,[10] but that someday humanity would take its revenge. Now I see that it's only Eddie.

(106)

The tango is a dance so sensual that back in the heady days of revolutionary ferment only the most daring perdu of the human spirit would dance it. *Tango* ends as Eddie, his powerful arms bulging in Arthur's jacket, leads the defeated granduncle in a tango around Arthur's body. A society that did away with

10. Professor Kliger has indicated that the phrase rendered "slaves of abstractions" literally means "ruled by the interhuman." This seems to imply a subjection to mere conventions set up by men and women in society as a means to survival.

its values through revolutions in art and politics now dances to the tune of the totalitarian, its inadequate hero dead, his plans only "words, words, words" (99).

Mrozek has used *Hamlet* as an instrument to explore certain matters of great contemporary concern. These matters are too complex to be exhaustively treated by logic, or even to be set forth in propositions. A work of art, a play, is the thing complex enough to catch the human subtleties. A play is a complex structure of ethically significant events, all interacting with each other in a system of meaning of inexhaustible richness. Propositions have the useful property of being verifiable, but they are simply inadequate to the task of describing and investigating the subtle knot that makes us man.

The densely elaborated fable of *Hamlet* provides Mrozek with a means of studying a young man's attempts to deal with a diminished thing. Mrozek does not follow Shakespeare's scenario event for event, nor does he try to reproduce in, say, Arthur, all the traits of Hamlet. He does use the structure of "a young man in some marvelous relation to a young woman, betrayed by a parent, caught in confusion, trying to catch conscience with a mousetrap" to bring the chaos of elements always faced by an artist or a thinker into some kind of a shape. As the elements of the drama — the characters, thought, rhythms, diction, spectacle — are woven into a signifying whole with a power to move, each element becomes unique, defining the others and being defined by them, taking its color from the creator's mind, and modifying that mind, showing it meanings and harmonies of which it was unaware when it first set the creative process into motion. The author investigates his subject, guided by the unbreakable gossamer of Shakespeare's elaborated fable. His own life's experiences modify parts of that fable. Hamlet's "Mousetrap" was intended to arouse certain emotions in Claudius and expose his guilt. Arthur's play is more ambitious by orders of magnitude. It is intended to be a species of what modern philosophy calls a "performative utterance," [11] something like "Let there be light." He wants to

11. Arthur's play, treated as a kind of locution, would be a rewarding subject for an analysis in the terms of J. L. Austin (*How to Do Things with Words*, Cambridge: Harvard University Press, 1962), since the wedding has both illocutionary and perlocutionary force.

have his play performed and have, not a caught mouse, but value itself appear. Shakespeare's fable gave Mrozek the opportunity to *think* that.

There is no assertion more frequently made in the commentary on Mrozek and other East European playwrights than the declaration that the grotesque situations and blunt illogic of the plays allow the artist and the work to escape the censor and his police arm.[12] By letting Shakespeare's fable replicate itself in his mind, Mrozek escapes not the Soviet censor, but a much more competent and forbidding censor. This censor is human imaginative limitedness, and it has been effectively and faithfully in Eddie's service for millennia. Matey Shakespeare helps out in a pinch.

The range of the artist is increased by his use of the fable. Theodore Spencer and E. M. W. Tillyard pointed out that Shakespeare addressed himself to a large view of man, exploring three dimensions simultaneously — the personal, the social and political, and the religious and metaphysical.[13] Instead of sinking into the murky and hence unsharable depths of one's subconscious or the uncommunicable formlessness of Pure Form[14] — both literarily antisocial activities — Mrozek deals with a man and a woman in a society and a family where ideas

12. As, for example, in Esslin, pp. 306–307; Mardi Valgemae, "Socialist Allegory of the Absurd: An Examination of Four East European Plays," *Comparative Drama*, V (Spring 1971), 44–52; and Przybylska, 71.

13. Theodore Spencer, *Shakespeare and the Nature of Man*, 2nd ed. (New York: Macmillan, 1949); E. M. W. Tillyard, *The Elizabethan World Picture* (New York: Macmillan, 1944).

14. Jan Kott sees *Tango* as a successor to Witkiewicz' *The Water Hen*, a work of "Pure Form" ("La famille de Mrozek," *Preuves*, XVI, no. 183, May 1966, 31–35). For Witkiewicz, if an artifact possessed Pure Form its meaning could be defined only by its purely scenic internal construction ("An Introduction to the Theory of Pure Form in the Theater," excerpted in *The Madman and the Nun*, ed. and tr. Daniel C. Gerould and C. S. Durer, Seattle and London: University of Washington Press, 1968, pp. 291–297). However, Witkiewicz was aware of the necessarily ethical quality of the theater, which by its nature does not allow pure abstractions; *Hamlet* is quoted, in English, in the Polish original of *The Water Hen*. Mrozek's play is ethical and tragic; it is far from Pure Form. Witkiewicz' last sentence in "An Introduction" is chilling when read with the historical facts and *Tango* in mind: "We must unleash the slumbering beast and see what it can do. And if it runs mad, there will always be time enough to shoot it before it is too late" (p. 297).

and actions count and something is at stake. If we make an algebraic move learned from Arnold, and let the poetic stand for the religious and the metaphysical dimension, we see that all three dimensions are explored in *Tango*. Avant-garde art, experimentalism, the issue of the existence of genres, unity of action and perception are the topics which allow for the inclusion of the religious and the metaphysical in *Tango*. The modern play becomes spacious and gains in importance; scope has been conferred. The work of art becomes accountable not to Witkiewicz or Freud but to *us*, concerned and increasingly demanding mankind.

The fable also confers the gift of genre. We lament the loss of the valuable; this is the surd cause of tragedy. We live in a time which has received in close succession bulletins announcing the deaths of God and of tragedy and have pretty much believed all we have read. Yet Arthur or Blanche struggling with limited resources to deal with a *Geist* move us. It is like a human hand put up to stop a bullet. The bullet penetrates the hand and the throat; the person dies. But there was meaning there. The person did not die like an insect. Arthur by indirections found directions out. He did not create a tragedy with Stomil, but he did with us, that special kind of tragedy in which the *anagnorisis* occurs in the souls of the audience. This opportunity for tragedy comes from the structure of the play, and the structure of the play comes from a great living tragedy, *Hamlet*. Tragedy is a communicable, a catching form, like a virus or genetic coding. Mrozek caught it from Shakespeare. And so we see that we were wrong about the death of tragedy. It cannot die if there are human concerns and these catching forms about.

THE USE OF SHAKESPEARE: FROM DEAD GOD TO DNA

The Blessed Virgin, worshipped for sixteen centuries as the mediatrix between our world of nature and the divine, is one of the two icons of *Long Day's Journey into Night*. The other is William Shakespeare. Both of these figures are involved in the mysterious process of the creation and expression of the valuable. Both, after seeming inaccessible and remote, become informing spirits.

In *Long Day's Journey into Night*, one of the great plays of his extraordinary last eight years of writing,[15] Eugene O'Neill explores the life of his family. The four characters of the play — Mary, James, Jamie, and Edmund Tyrone — are, in a sense, portraits of his mother, Mary Ellen ("Ella") Quinlan O'Neill, his father James, his brother Jamie, and himself. Although the play is the masterpiece of American realism, it is not reportage; its elements have undergone transmutation into art. Shakespeare participates in this transmutation.

O'Neill frequently complained that he, like Larry Slade of *The Iceman Cometh*, was cursed with the power to see many sides of something. He had an inescapable multiple vision, and could not be content with the reductive and highly effective either/or. In 1939–1941, the closing years of his creative life, he "made his peace" with his family — Mary, James, and Jamie by then dead — through writing *Long Day's Journey*, and presenting an unanalyzably complex vision of their lives. The play depicts Mary Tyrone's reduction from wife and mother to addict in sixteen hours of a day in August, 1912. The day begins in sunshine, with Mary and James embracing affectionately, and the family in a mood of relieved happiness after her return from a cure for addiction to morphine. Mary's anxiety concerning the possibility of Edmund's being ill with tuberculosis pushes her back toward dependency on the drug, and this is immediately sensed by Jamie, himself a confirmed alcoholic and cynic because of his boyhood discovery of his mother's addiction. Mary begins to take the drug; her beautiful eyes become bright with it and the family begins its day's journey into night. They learn that Edmund is tubercular and will have to go to a sanatorium in an attempt to save his life. All four Tyrones, in different ways, come to understandings of the complex web in

15. O'Neill began his cycle, "A Tale of Possessors Self-Dispossessed," in 1935. A familial tremor terminated his productive career in 1943, after he had completed his last play, *A Moon for the Misbegotten*. Of the cycle — at one time projected to eleven plays — two were completed, *A Touch of the Poet* and *More Stately Mansions*. O'Neill wrote *The Iceman Cometh* in 1939 and *Hughie* in 1939–1941. See Arthur and Barbara Gelb, *O'Neill*, 2nd ed. enl. (New York: Harper & Row, 1973), and the two volumes by Louis Shaeffer, *O'Neill: Son and Playwright* (Boston: Little, Brown & Co., 1968·), and *O'Neill: Son and Artist* (Boston: Little, Brown & Co., 1973).

which they struggle. As they do, the action of the play reveals both the causes of entrapment and the sources of the valuable.

The journey is not toward doom, nor is it gloomy, deterministic, and morbid. Something of value is at stake, and the humanity of the "four haunted Tyrones" burns the brighter for each wisp of fog that comes rolling in from the Sound, through the windows, and into Mary's mind. These are ghost-ridden people caught up in economic, sociological, psychological, and biological determinism and chemical dependency through drugs and liquor, lost in a spiritual fog, victims of a *Geist* in times that are out of joint, and yet they transcend all this and achieve something of permanent value. *Long Day's Journey into Night* is a terrific conflict on a modern spiritual battlefield. Out of it comes a sense of value, a value created by the heroic struggle of the Tyrones against odds greater than flesh and blood should have to encounter in the course of things. O'Neill wrote of his efforts "to see the transfiguring nobility of tragedy, in as near the Greek sense as one can grasp it, in seemingly the most ignoble, debased lives." He was "acutely conscious of the Force behind — Fate, God, our biological past creating our present, whatever one calls it — Mystery certainly — and of the one eternal tragedy of Man in his glorious, self-destructive struggle to make the Force express him instead of being, as an animal is, an infinitesimal incident in its expression." [16] The *valuable* must appear in the journey. The Forces must express the Tyrones.

The centers of the valuable are Mary the mother and wife; Ireland as the source of a touch of the poet, guts, charm, and comradely laughter; the recovery of one's true self; the sea; the creation of a home; faith, beauty, and art; the loving, potent, forgiving, and human divinity of the Blessed Virgin, *gratia plena* — and Shakespeare.

Shakespeare's significance as an icon is, appropriately enough, second to that of the Blessed Virgin, whose association with Mary is crucial to the creation of Mary's full character. Mary was to have entered a convent and devoted herself to the Blessed Virgin, but

16. Oscar Cargill, N. Bryllion Fagin, and William J. Fisher, eds., *O'Neill and His Plays* (New York: New York University Press, 1961), pp. 125–126.

Then in the spring something happened to me. Yes, I remember.
I fell in love with James Tyrone and was so happy for a time.[17]

When she was married she had the shyness of a convent girl
and yet "she was never made to renounce the world. She was
bursting with health and high spirits and the love of loving"
(138). An Irish lilt sings in her voice when she is merry. Her
eyes are dark and lustrous, full of dreams and mystery, and her
beautiful hands were the hands of an artist, until rheumatism
accompanying the birth of Edmund destroyed them. Mary
Tyrone was once the radiant, loving, vital and sexual, musical,
spiritual, protecting, mystical, home-creating, hope-bearing female, virgin, goddess, nun, artist, wife, lover, and mother,
sought by O'Neill all his creative life, and achieved in *Long
Day's Journey* and again in Josie of the *Pietà* in *A Moon for
the Misbegotten*, his last play.[18]

Mary is intimately associated with the Blessed Virgin, the
Theotokos, the bearer of god. She knows that one day she will
find her soul, and be freed from the drug:

Some day when the Blessed Virgin Mary forgives me and gives
me back the faith in Her love and pity I used to have in my convent days, and I can pray to Her again — when She sees no one
in the world can believe in me even for a moment any more, then
She will believe in me, and with Her help it will be so easy. I will
hear myself scream with agony, and at the same time I will laugh
because I will be so sure of myself.

(94)

This is not irony, since Mary Ellen Quinlan O'Neill was "mirac-
ulously cured of narcotics addiction" through prayer in a convent, at the age of sixty-three.[19] Mary begins to recite the "Hail
Mary," stops, and rebukes herself:

17. Eugene O'Neill, *Long Day's Journey into Night* (New Haven:
Yale University Press, 1956), p. 176.
18. Josie is a titaness, virgin, and mother. *Dynamo* ought to be read
with Henry Adams' essay, "The Virgin and the Dynamo," in *The Education of Henry Adams: An Autobiography* (Boston: Houghton Mifflin
Co., 1918), in mind. See one of the earliest notes for *Days without End*,
cited in Shaeffer, *Artist*, p. 413.
19. Gelb and Gelb, *O'Neill*, p. 407.

You expect the Blessed Virgin to be fooled by a lying dope fiend reciting words! You can't hide from her!

(107)

She rejects suicide, for she knows "the Blessed Virgin would never forgive me, then" (121). In the last scene of the play, considered by O'Neill "the greatest scene I have ever written," [20] Mary appears wearing the Virgin's color — "She wears a sky-blue dressing gown" (170) — and in a trance/vision says she is going to be a nun and knows that Sister Martha will "tell me to pray to the Blessed Virgin." She then regresses to the girl she was in her senior year, and speaks of the vision she had: "The Blessed Virgin had smiled and blessed me with her consent" (175).

It is as an icon and center of value second in importance only to this kind of overwhelming display that Shakespeare appears in *Long Day's Journey*. Eleven of the twelve occurrences of the words "Shakespeare" or "Shakespearean" in the published O'Neill canon occur in this play, as do all eight explicit references to the Blessed Virgin.[21] Shakespeare, presiding as secular icon, appears immediately in the opening stage directions:

A small bookcase, with a picture of Shakespeare above it, containing novels by Balzac, Zola, Stendhal, philosophical and sociological works by Schopenhauer, Nietzsche, Marx, Engels, Kropotkin.

(11)

Here Shakespeare appears as captain of the excellent in James Tyrone's battle with what he considers the decadent reading of Edmund. A large bookcase contains James's books, "three sets of Shakespeare" along with works by Dumas and Hugo and histories by Hume and Smollett, and "*the astonishing thing*

20. Shaeffer, *Artist*, p. 517.
21. J. Russell Reaver, comp., *An O'Neill Concordance*, 3 vols. (Detroit: Gale Research Co., 1969). Underscoring the importance of the concept of The Virgin in these two final plays dealing with O'Neill's family, twenty-four of the twenty-eight uses of the word "virgin" in the canon occur in *Long Day's Journey* and in *A Moon for the Misbegotten*.

about these sets is that all the volumes have the look of having been read and reread" (11). James uses Shakespeare as an ally in a running battle with his sons:

> TYRONE *Scathingly.* If it takes my snoring to make you remember Shakespeare instead of the dope sheet on the ponies, I hope I'll keep on with it.
>
> (21)
>
> Why can't you remember your Shakespeare and forget the third-raters.
>
> (131)
>
> Pah! It's morbid nonsense! What little truth is in it you'll find nobly said in Shakespeare.
>
> (133)
>
> Whoremongers and degenerates! Pah! When I've three good sets of Shakespeare . . .
>
> (135)

This hortatory use of Shakespeare is easily countered by Jamie and Edmund. The sons know the father's quotations, and can finish them for him, brushing them aside (89), or use them as barbs (21).

Shakespeare then begins to stir, and does not remain merely the greatest of a pantheon of dead, glassed-in literary heroes, associated with an inert past. Irishness is a value throughout the O'Neill canon. The Shaughnessy episode, based on the exploits of John ("Dirty") Dolan,[22] attests to the hold upon O'Neill's imagination of the indomitable Irishry — the vivacious bearers of mysticism, spirit, laughter, lyricism, and grace. James asserts that Shakespeare was an Irish Catholic: "So he was. The proof is in his plays" (127). Shakespeare's manifest Irishness, James avers, appears in his hard-drinking healthy good fellowship:

> I don't doubt he liked his glass — it's a good man's failing — but he knew how to drink so it didn't poison his brain with morbidness and filth.
>
> (135)

22. Gelb and Gelb, *O'Neill*, pp. 91–92, and Shaeffer, *Playwright*, pp. 259–261.

Shakespeare's Irish rehabilitation is an intimation of his spiritual significance and his vitality, and he starts to come alive as Edmund and James begin to understand each other, late in the action of the play. When James quotes Prospero's "We are such stuff as dreams are made on, and our little life is rounded with a sleep," Edmund replies:

> *Ironically*. Fine! That's beautiful. But I wasn't trying to say that. We are such stuff as manure is made on, so let's drink up and forget it. That's more my idea.
>
> (131)

This can serve as a paradigm for the encounter between the romantic and the ironic. Edmund's reply reflects the ironic mode, in which the human spirit is mutilated, here, by addiction — "drink up" — and in which effective action is impossible — "forget it." The ironic is the world as we do not want it.[23] Its imagery is the set of things undesirable, and the fecal, "manure," is one of the most frequently recurring images in this mode.[24] The importance of "such stuff as dreams are made on" is clear from the action of the play, as Mary, James, and Edmund evoke the stuff of their dreams in personal revelations.

The sententious Shakespeare, Captain Shakespeare of the Battery of the Ancients, is rejected by Edmund, but the mystery at which Prospero's words hint is not. What might be called the increasing immanence of Shakespeare continues as James reveals his genuine passion for the poet. This is structurally important in the play, since it is one of the revelations of value by Mary, James, and Edmund. They are authentic, and what the action of the play tends toward. Although James had always been haunted by the specter of poverty, he had, as a young man, left a good job because he "loved the theater":

> I studied Shakespeare as you'd study the Bible. I educated myself. I got rid of an Irish brogue you could cut with a knife. I

23. Cf. Northrop Frye, *The Educated Imagination* (Bloomington: Indiana University Press, 1964), pp. 55–57, 96–103.

24. The only other use of this word in a metaphorical sense in O'Neill's plays occurs in *Iceman*, when Slade talks of the essential composition of mankind (*The Plays of Eugene O'Neill*, 3 vols., New York: Random House, 1967, III, 590).

loved Shakespeare. I would have acted in any of his plays for
nothing, for the joy of being alive in his great poetry.

(150)

Shakespeare now appears as a living and life-giving power; one
can be "alive in his great poetry" just as Edmund, in his account of his epiphany, was "dissolved in the sea, became white
sails and flying spray, became beauty and rhythm, became
moonlight and the ship and the high dim-starred sea," and felt
he belonged "to God, if you want to put it that way" (153).[25]
This is such stuff as dreams are made on. Shakespeare is a spirit
in whom one can find life, as Mary found redemption in the
Blessed Virgin and Edmund found a "wild joy" in a huge
moonlit vision of a high romance.

Shakespeare comes down out of the portrait, and begins to
penetrate the characters' lives. Fragments of his characters-in-
action begin to participate in the structure of the lives of the
Tyrones. A vivid example of this occurs immediately after
James revealed his passion for Shakespeare and his genuine
moments of triumph as an actor. Edwin Booth, "the greatest
actor of his day or any other," said of the young James Tyrone
in 1874, "That young man is playing Othello better than I ever
did!" (150).[26] We have learned that James's fear of poverty
made Mary an addict, because he would use cheap doctors and
would not go to the expense necessary to create a home for her.
Without wanting to, he had contributed to Mary's destruction.
The main action of his life was Othello's: he was killing the
thing he loved. He then narrates how greed made him abandon
his genuine art, and make money in a box-office success that
kept him from growth. Having made the money, lost his art,
destroyed his wife, he proceeds to save money:

> *He clicks out one bulb . . .*
> *He clicks out another bulb . . .*
> *He clicks out the third bulb.*

(151)

25. For O'Neill's opinion of this passage, see Gelb and Gelb, *O'Neill*,
pp. 872–873.
26. Again, the center of value comes from an event from the lives of
the O'Neills. See Gelb and Gelb, *O'Neill*, pp. 25–30.

Othello is permeating James Tyrone. As Othello went to kill Desdemona, he murmured:

Put out the light, and then put out the light.

O'Neill's stage directions recapitulate Othello's words in banal quotidian actions embodying the fear of poverty which wrought such havoc with James's whole life. Jamie, who "wanted to believe every man was a knave with his soul for sale, and every woman who wasn't a whore was a fool" (34) and whose motto was "Everything is in the bag" (76), tried to teach this inverted gospel to Edmund, in an effort to destroy him. Jamie quotes Iago twice in the play (21, 165), the second time just before confessing to Edmund his Iagoan efforts to stab him in the back, to make him fail. A part of Jamie is Iago, who hates the Moor who took Mary off to his Cyprus tours, and who hates Edmund, who has "a daily beauty in his life," and gets him drunk. Iago has invaded Jamie.

When Mary appears in the last scene, Jamie ironizes:

The Mad Scene. Enter Ophelia!

(170)

and Mary does have some of the qualities of Ophelia, just as she possesses qualities of the Blessed Virgin and of Mary Ellen Quinlan O'Neill. She had once attempted suicide by drowning (86, 118), and here, in her madness, she is once again going to get herself to a nunnery:

I'm going to be a nun.

(172)

"Get thee to a nunnery. Why wouldst thou be a breeder of sinners?" cries Hamlet to Ophelia, and it is echoed here in the action. Why should Mary have bred the whoremaster alcoholics, Jamie and acolyte-Edmund? She carries her wedding gown, and one might have thought to have decked her bride-bed, and not to have strewn her grave, had her romance succeeded. As Ophelia-in-her-actions permeates Mary, Hamlet permeates Edmund, a young man haunted by ghosts in times that are out of joint, who, through the composition of some seventy plays, must set it right. Edmund, an isolated, sensitive figure, "*enters . . . a book in one hand*" (42), "*sits . . . reading a book*" (51). In a closet scene with his impure mother he turns her eyes into her soul (42–49) in an ambiance of spying. When he learned of his mother's falling-off, "God, it made everything in life seem rotten!" (118). The house is a prison (75).

When we realize Mary's association with the Virgin, her representation of Catholicism, motherhood, pure love, creativity, dreams, art, bursting vitality, her declension becomes so terrible that it would convince even T. S. Eliot, if Gertrude's did not, that here is a loss of the valuable sufficient to generate tremendous correlative emotion, emotion which as a matter of fact drove Eugene O'Neill all his creative life.

DNA AS A METAPHOR

A proper metaphor would have to account for the essential attributes of Shakespeare's works. We need something that is living and also immortal. It should possess a recognizable form, and that form should live on, even when certain elements in its composition are suppressed, just as the fable of *Hamlet* lives even when its dictional excellence is suppressed by the process of translation. It is the shape, after all, of *Oedipus the King* that causes that work to affect Greekless readers powerfully. The entity used as metaphor should be able to reproduce itself as a whole or in parts. This mirrors and aeolian harps do not do. The whole rough plot of *Hamlet* may appear, as in *Tango*, or parts of it perfectly, as in *Rosencrantz*, or elements of it, as when James Tyrone says "Why do you say, seems?" in *Long Day's Journey*. It should be a kind of soul, in that it ought to animate otherwise inert matter. This requirement would please Aristotle, who thought that the plot of a play was its soul. Its reproductive power should embrace a whole species, since a species is defined by the ability of its members to reproduce with each other. The metaphorical substance should be able to affect persons across national boundaries and be, not of an age, but for all time. It should be capable of sexual reproduction as well as replication. That is, the metaphorical substance should be able to mate up with information, ideas, passions, visions, events from someone other than Shakespeare, and make a new thing, a new work of art, which will be a unique individual, although, of course, the father's face will live in his issue. It should be able to help make things outside its own species, but in its genus, such as paintings and the opera *Otello*. It should be elaborated, and fabulously complex, and not merely a simple-minded myth, such as the basic idea of the Oedipus complex. Rather, it should be unanalyzably complex, like the play *Oedipus the King*. Because of our human intellectual weakness, it should be coded for automatic replication through the instincts. It should be restlessly active, and should be, as a molecule is, invisible, beyond our intellectual resolving power, since if it were simple, like a theme or a myth, we would be thigh-high with Shakespeares. It should be able to permeate living ethical and spiritual structures, as happened in *Long Day's Journey*. It ought not to be metabolizable; that is, the metaphorical substance should not be used up in any process, but should dwell apart something like a star, beyond change. This is quite important. Lastly, it should account for everything observed in this essay.

There is only one substance with these attributes, and that is the nucleic acid DNA, which carries in code, immortal, all the genetic information necessary for making thinking and feeling human beings.[27] It is a living form, that never dies and does not metabolize, which is capable automatically of replicating itself so there may be growth and sexual reproduction. It is like a long molecular zipper, which unzips itself. When ambient molecules bump into it in the right fashion, they link up with it, and, after a while, it has replicated itself by virtue of Pure Form. Its Pure Form is able, through messenger RNA and transfer RNA, to make crucial proteins, such as hemoglobin. Therefore it meets the condition of reproducing itself in whole or in parts, and can serve as a template for making things apparently quite unlike itself. It is precisely the kind of *psychē*

27. A good description of the nature, transmission, and function of the genetic material may be found in R. P. Levine, *Genetics* (New York: Holt, Rinehart and Winston, 1965).

or soul Aristotle was talking about when in the *Poetics* he spoke of a *mythos* organizing the elements of a play. Sexual reproduction is one of its subspecialties, and it is complex, restlessly active, and lives anew whenever it encounters the right ambiance of molecules.

The immortal soul encoded in the DNA of the plot of *Hamlet* replicated for Stoppard's use a whole living world, which bonded to the Rosencrantz and Guildenstern world and helped shape it and thereby helped understand it. That plot made a living form available to Mrozek as an instrument of investigation, and the instrument then helped organize the elements of the Pole's experience into a tragedy beyond politics.

Shakespeare's plays replicate themselves in our minds and then create new works in the minds of artists because of their form. They are able to do this because they move in an ambiance of human frustrations, fears, aspirations, and laughter. They organize this chaos into significance, and that organization is usable. Their complexity enables us to do justice to the "four haunted Tyrones," true justice, which Pater said was "in its essence a finer knowledge through love." Justice requires knowledge, and knowledge in turn depends on a suitable richness of understanding. *Hamlet* and other Shakespearean works have offered such a self-reproducing and curiously adequate complexity to the artists considered in this essay.

Ben Jonson's poem in praise of Shakespeare in the 1623 First Folio was acutely titled "To the memory of my beloved, The Author Mr. William Shakespeare: And what he hath left us." Jonson is definitive on Shakespeare's influence, and ought by rights to have the last word in this discussion of modern plays. In his poem he sees Shakespeare made into a constellation in the heavens and cries:

> Shine forth, thou Starre of Poets, and with rage,
>   Or influence, chide, or cheere the drooping Stage;
> Which, since thy flight from hence, hath mourn'd like night,
>   And despaires day, but for thy Volumes light.

This metaphor and that of DNA are not far apart, since "influence" refers to the astrological conception of an ethereal fluid flowing from the stars, "acting on the character and destiny of men, and affecting sublunary things generally." [28] Shakespeare's influence cheers the drooping stage. He helped Eugene O'Neill, who, when dedicating *Long Day's Journey into Night* to Carlotta, spoke of the "deep pity and understanding and forgiveness for *all* the four haunted Tyrones" he was able to achieve through writing the play and how, with her help, he had achieved by 1941 "a Journey into Light." Shakespeare's work helped O'Neill understand and forgive real persons, as Othello, Iago, Hamlet, and Ophelia permeated their representations. Otherwise the stage might have mourned like night, and despaired of day, but for this volume's light.

28. *The Oxford English Dictionary*, s.v. "influence."

MURRAY KRIEGER

Shakespeare and the Critic's Idolatry of the Word

Even in a volume centering on Shakespeare's influence, where exaggerated claims are part of the ritual, it may appear excessive to suggest that he be treated as a shaping force in modern literary criticism. Yet this is the suggestion I shall make and try to justify here.[1] Of course, I shall speak only for one variety of modern critical theory and practice, one with which I associate myself and which I therefore cannot help but see as a dominant variety: it attributes marvelous (I shall later say "miraculous") powers to poetry and centers these powers in its dislocations of normal language. Critics of this sort accord Shakespeare his special and unchallenged place as first without peers in the poet's pantheon by virtue of his capacity for the manipulation of language. Other poets — all substantially lesser poets — are to be subjected to the same measuring instruments, as the verbal analysis found uniquely appropriate to Shakespeare is extended into a general critical method. For these critics Shakespeare functions as a sacred book, the enabling text for their commitment to the special magic of poetic dis-

1. I must at once confess that I have already written a book organized around this suggestion, as can be seen from the two rather oddly conjoined parts of its subtitle: *A Window to Criticism: Shakespeare's* Sonnets *and Modern Poetics* (Princeton: Princeton University Press, 1964).

193

course. Thus, in its most recent version, bardolatry is collapsed into wordolatry.

This is hardly the first time that Shakespeare's works have served as models that are seen to justify a critical movement. Indeed, the history of criticism in English seems again and again to reveal Shakespeare as the supervising spirit of its several major moments. One might claim that the abiding liberalism of the English critical tradition was largely the consequence of Shakespeare's having been the special gift to English critics, the greatest writer given into the charge of any critics. Certainly a succession of critics credited their need to resist dogma to their need to include Shakespeare as chief among those for whom their theories had to account. For here was a writer obviously at odds with many of the conventions critics had too often invented to guide them — and, *ex post facto*, to guide the writer they treated, lest he be subject to the critics' wrath. So the critics could not retain an uncritical allegiance to those conventional "rules" and to Shakespeare too. Surely by at least the late seventeenth century — say, with Dryden — it had become clear that critical practice had to find a shape that reflected in some measure the stubborn and uncooperative fact of Shakespeare's lasting presence among us. Since that time, I would suggest, the best English criticism has continually yielded under his incomparable pressure.

One might argue that we cannot know whether, as I have indicated, it was Shakespeare whose presence breathed a special liberal spirit into the English critical tradition that had to accommodate him, or whether he himself was a product of that same liberal spirit, which we can see at work, for example, much earlier in the grand independence of Chaucer. In other words, we can ask — uncertain of ever finding a satisfactory answer — whether Dryden confronted his French antagonists with a tolerance for dramatic and poetic flexibility because he had to respond sensitively to Shakespeare or whether Dryden and Shakespeare were both moved in that freer direction we associate with English literature and criticism by a similar characteristic deep in the English literary consciousness. Is it, then, that Shakespeare is responsible for the openly empirical bent of English criticism or that he has been shaped by that English bent himself, and Dryden and others later shaped with him, though he serves as so excellent an excuse or precedent for them?

Very likely it does not finally matter which of the two is the case, so long as we note that, in "An Essay of Dramatic Poesy," for example, Dryden resists the extremes of French neoclassical dogma in the name of moderate liberality and that he uses the example of Shakespeare as the special justification for the more open attitude appropriate to the English critic. Dryden, of course, hardly goes all the way, confessing that he must temper his love for the imperfect Shakespeare with his unsurpassed admiration for the "correct" Ben Jonson; but he has set the pattern which later critics can expand as they follow it. The gap between Shakespeare and his more correct rivals widens as later neoclassical critics seek to balance artful regularity with the sublimity of original genius and use Shakespeare to authorize their heterodoxy. As the Renaissance–Enlightenment pseudo-Aristotle gives way to Longinus, the critic justifies the change by waving Shakespeare's works before him as he goes. Addison treats Shakespeare as one of "these great natural geniuses," "nobly wild and extravagant"; Pope sees him as the archetypal "original," producing "Nature herself" rather than mere "copies of her"; and Dr. Johnson extends this notion of Shakespeare as "the poet of nature" to the point where he justifies the confluence of the genres and the explosion of the unities by making "an appeal . . . from criticism to nature," in the interest of opening poetry from the rigidity of convention to the variety of life.[2]

The polarization between Shakespeare and the rule-bound alternative increases as we move through the eighteenth century. Thus, in comparisons between the two, the balance between Shakespeare and Jonson is gradually shifted until all the weight seems on Shakespeare's side. Early in the century Addison is anxious to defend the restrained genius "formed . . . by rules" as a kind separate but equal, in comparison to the natural genius. In his Preface, Pope seems disturbed even by

2. See Addison's *Spectator* no. 160 and Pope's and Johnson's Prefaces to Shakespeare. My later reference to Young is to "Conjectures on Original Composition."

the suggestion of polarity in Dryden's opposition between the poet of wit and the poet of correctness, between his love for Shakespeare and his admiration of Jonson. So Pope denies that there need be a mutually exclusive relation between the two: he prefers to find neither of the two to be without wit on the one side or without art and learning on the other, while his regret over Shakespeare's flaws leaves the neoclassical canon unthreatened.[3] But it is just this mutually exclusive opposition which Edward Young insists upon, in order to praise Shakespeare as the unlearned original and to denigrate Jonson as the imitative slave of his learning. By the time we get to Johnson's Preface, the either/or becomes absolute; and, by referring to the outrageous comparison by Voltaire, Johnson allows the Addison of *Cato* to take the place usually reserved for Ben Jonson as the learned author who is dwarfed by Shakespeare's genius, thus making the disjunction the more obvious.

By now we have come a long way toward the exaltation of Shakespeare for those characteristics most at odds with the neoclassical ideal. That other country to which Pope consigned him is surely cut off from the safe neoclassical domain securely held under what Pope saw as the laws of Aristotle. It often seemed to have no laws, this wilderness produced by genius — no country for old men, or sane ones either. The youthful Edmund Burke only emphasized the irrationalist nature of this alternative to trim aesthetic propriety when he tried to institutionalize the dualism that distinguished the awesome sublime from the merely beautiful, the unclear vastness from the lucidity of finitude. In his treatise he exaggerated the association of the sublime with the limitless — and hence with our sense of mystery. This association is one we have observed to be growing since Dryden first began putting Shakespeare beyond rational criticism. The eighteenth-century notion of Shakespeare as *lusus naturae*, outside the natural order and thus beyond natural law, accentuates his inaccessibility to the critic's normal measur-

3. It is also true that, in allowing Shakespeare his own bailiwick, he is not without condescension. Though it sounds generous to decline to judge Shakespeare "by Aristotle's rules" ("like trying a man by the laws of one country, who acted under those of another"), Pope is keeping his own legalistic country secure and unchallenged — and superior to the popular realm (of actors and audiences) granted to Shakespeare.

ing instruments. The unmatched and often unexplained (or even confessedly inexplicable) depths of response to him by such critics would seem to be testimony supporting the magical character of his work and, by extrapolation, of all the work of Pegasus-poets who, with "brave disorder," "snatch a grace beyond the reach of art," though such graces are "nameless" and teachable by "no methods." [4] This *je-ne-sais-quoi* mysticism pervades the exemptions accorded Shakespeare's work and, through the accompanying cult of original genius, prepares the way for the idolatry that not only makes him our one exceptional poet but enshrines him as the prototypical poet, the Platonic idea of the poet on whom all other poets must try — however in vain — to pattern themselves, with romantic critics using their instincts to judge them accordingly.[5]

If the critic uses Shakespeare to represent the intrusion of "disorder" into the natural order, and a disorder worthy of the highest praise as furnishing the deepest insight, then he seems to be positing an unaccountable mystery at the heart of the universe, which poets like Shakespeare alone can touch. But no matter how "brave," the disorder introduces an element of chaos which imperils any unmodified rational hypothesis that would account for the real or the literary universe.[6] It is this utter polarity, fully developed by the late eighteenth century, between chaos and order or the sublime and the beautiful or the instinctive and the learned — oppositions in nature as in art — that organic theorists like A. W. Schlegel and his adapter-translator Coleridge tried to bridge, to the advantage of Shakespeare.

Their work on Shakespeare — with results they made applicable to poetry and drama generally — was intended in large part to claim, in Coleridge's words, "Shakespeare's Judgment equal to his Genius." What was being denied was that original genius precludes judgment, and vice versa. Quite the contrary:

4. Pope, "An Essay on Criticism," lines 141–155.
5. May I remind the reader that what I mean to offer here is not a thumbnail sketch of directions in the history of Shakespearean criticism so much as the history of Shakespeare's influence on the shape taken by general poetics itself.
6. See my essay on just this consequence in Johnson's work: "Fiction, Nature, and Literary Kinds in Johnson's Criticism of Shakespeare," *Eighteenth-Century Studies*, IV (1970–71), 184–198.

it is in the brilliant display of form-making judgment that genius is to manifest itself. As the argument runs, the neoclassical critic had to associate genius with wild irregularity because his definitions of order and judgment were narrowly circumscribed by mechanical, inflexible, externally imposed rules inherited from earlier poetic practice. Either the poet conformed or he was wild and — unless rescued by genius as in the rare case of Shakespeare — to be rejected. But the disjunctive is overwhelmed if, as with Shakespeare, a more subtle notion of form joined originality to a newly created order. "Are the plays of Shakespeare works of rude and uncultivated genius, in which the splendor of the parts compensates, if aught can compensate, for the barbarous shapelessness and irregularity of the whole? — Or is the form equally admirable with the matter, and the judgment of the great poet, not less deserving our wonder than his genius?" This passage, from Coleridge's "Shakespeare, a Poet Generally" (from the portion headed "Shakespeare's Judgment equal to his Genius"), goes on to claim that Shakespeare's greatness is as much the result of his differences from the ancients as of those elements he shares with them. For while the similarities can arise out of "servile imitation," a "lifeless mechanism," his "free and rival originality" is evidence "of living power."

This is the contrast that leads to the distinction between mechanical and organic form which Coleridge draws in the well known passage that is little more than a translation from Schlegel. Mechanical form, the indifferent imposition of a universal formula on whatever the materials at hand, is apparently what Coleridge sees as the only kind of form the neoclassical critic could recognize. If Shakespeare did not display form of that kind, then he was put down as being wildly formless. Coleridge is arguing that Shakespeare has a far more profound kind of form, however unrecognized earlier, a form that "shapes, as it develops, itself from within; and the fulness of its development is one and the same with the perfection of its outward form. Such as the life is, such is the form." So Shakespeare is to be seen as reshaping whatever materials have been given him from outside until they are forced to grow into the very entity they are forming in the act of becoming it. Such is the organic interrelationship he creates between part and whole. And of course the organic doctrine carries with it a mystique of its own in its attack upon the rationalistic notion of order as a mechanistic one.

This notion — the transformation of generic, borrowed materials, by way of a creativity that is at work in both a unique act and a unique product — marks that variety of recent criticism which draws much of its spirit from Coleridge. But since this criticism begins in our time as the so-called New Criticism, it tends to be language-centered, so that it usually limits the borrowed elements, whose transformation it must trace, to verbal ones. It is the manipulation of words, their conversion from the empty and transparent signs they are for most of us (and were for the poet when he picked them up) into the dense opacity of symbol, that for this criticism enables Shakespeare to work his magic. Later modifications by such critics, still being pressed by Shakespeare, will extend verbal insights (by then seen as inadequate) back into the realms of genre and dramatic structure, though they will not deny that the word retains its primary function in their analysis however it grows into elements with which it has dynamic relations of conflict and resolution.

It is surely ironic that Shakespeare enters the New-Critical dialogue not only as a minor figure but as anything but a model poet. Indeed, if any one poet was the model for the shape of verbal criticism from T. S. Eliot to John Crowe Ransom, Allen Tate, and Cleanth Brooks, he would be Donne and not Shakespeare. This undisputed fact of poetic influence on modern theory would appear to make the opening paragraph of this essay, and my major claim in it, untenable. Certainly, when Ransom wrote his regrettable essay, "Shakespeare at Sonnets," his readers would hardly have predicted that — almost four decades later — one could claim (as I am claiming here) that Shakespeare was both source and model for a verbal criticism further down the line in the same critical tradition.[7] Since he was using the metaphysical strategy as the universal strategy for poets and had selected Donne as the exemplary practitioner of that strategy, it was not difficult for Ransom, measuring Shakespeare by this single gauge, to find him failing precisely where Donne succeeded.

7. *The World's Body* (New York: Scribner, 1938), pp. 270–303.

Ransom defined the metaphysical strategy as the rigorous logical extension of the selected conceit, carried out by the poet who had "the courage of [his] metaphors." The critic's verbal analysis, then, was to concentrate on the ways in which words carried forward this lean line of metaphorical development. Firmly committed to the antiromanticism that moved the early New Criticism, Ransom was careful to encourage clarity, logic, and denotation in language as an alternative to romantic vagueness, the willingness to indulge connotation and its blurred effects. His devotion to logicality in poetry led him to distrust even New Critics like Empson or Brooks whose cultivation of verbal ambiguity and irony in poetry would make them less inimical to some romantic practices. But, more certainly, it led Ransom to underrate seriously — and to misapprehend — the strategy of Shakespeare's language, forced as he was by his theory to see Shakespeare as trying to do poorly what Donne was to do so well. He observed correctly that Shakespeare did not pursue the single line of logical development which we find in the typical extension of the metaphysical conceit, that in Shakespeare there are detours and false starts and multiple paths and surprises. But, of course, if the logical line is weak, the words which — from Ransom's point of view — seem to weaken it may be doing so in order to create a heretofore hidden strength in themselves.[8] So the critic's problem is to determine and account for what it is that Shakespeare *is* doing, and doing inimitably well.

In an essay responding to Ransom's, Arthur Mizener undertook just this task, thus setting in motion a verbal analysis of Shakespeare's Sonnets that focused on a strategy different from the metaphysical and yet brilliantly effective.[9] After Mizener's essay, instead of this criticism shaping Shakespeare, it would come to be shaped by him. It no longer had to reduce Shake-

8. One might well argue that this latter possibility is more in accord with the Coleridgean notion of organic development within the poem, while Ransom's view of the metaphysical strategy, limited as it is to the logical argument within the conceit, would appear to Coleridge as a rather mechanical, universal, externally applied criterion, one which did not submit the poem wholly to the control of the developing elements themselves.

9. "The Structure of Figurative Language in Shakespeare's Sonnets," *Southern Review*, V (1940), 730–747.

speare to its method; rather it could claim a method which, derived from his works themselves, not only could account for them but — using them as its supreme examples — could account for many other works as well. This was still to indulge in methodological imperialism (the application of a method beyond its native grounds, the works that originally nourished it), but Shakespeare was now claimed as its author and beneficiary.

Mizener argues that, just as Ransom charged, Shakespeare's language in a sonnet is not totally responsive to the narrow demands of an extended conceit, but that its seeming waywardness has a method of its own. Using as his example Sonnet 124 ("If my dear love were but the child of state"), he shows the many levels on which the poem's key words operate, from private to public life and the great world, and from the merely political to the cosmic realm. He finds this broad range of simultaneous meanings spreading from the first line, with that endlessly polysemous word, "state." Its echoes in subsequent words and phrases which also have multiple possibilities persuade him that the reader is to press ahead on all levels, eliminating none of the meanings, indeed rather exploiting all of them at once. Unlike the logical delineations of the metaphysical conceit whose effect may amaze us with its far-fetched lucidity but whose lucidity domesticates that amazement, the effect here is one of "soft focus," each of the meanings crowding in with the others without being sufficiently developed to prevent us from holding the others simultaneously with it. Mizener's phrase "soft focus" emphasizes a lack of developed precision in the individual images — almost, indeed, as if they formed a group of simultaneous associations. His own description suggests as much: the meanings in the sonnet are "very like the pattern of the mind when it contemplates, with full attention but for no immediately practical purpose, an object in nature." The pattern "is built for all the kinds of relations known to the mind," so that the figurative language "approaches, in its own verbal terms, the richness, the density, the logical incompleteness of the mind."

My own feeling is that, while many of Mizener's observations about words and lines are striking and important because they force us to reorient ourselves as we address the language of the Sonnets, he reveals the weakness which Ransom would expect of Shakespeare and his defenders: that of resorting to romantic vagueness as the characteristic of Shakespeare's strategy which makes it worth justifying. Mizener's notion of "soft focus" seeks to justify Shakespeare's use of companion elements which, if presented clearly, might be mutually incompatible; it is thus a defense of imprecision that suggests the blurred diction of the romantic who could not totally make up his mind about what he meant. What rather is the case and what, indeed, we see (despite Mizener) to be the case even in his most valuable obseravtions, is that in Shakespeare the effect of an extravagant structure of puns is anything but imprecise.

I have written a much later essay which also takes off from Ransom's and from the dichotomy between the metaphysical and the Shakespearean strategy of wit.[10] In that essay, although many of my observations may seem similar in intention to Mizener's, I use them to support a claim to a multiple precision of meaning in Shakespeare's remarkable choice of just the word to contain that multiplicity. Although I see his strategy as an alternative to the metaphysical, I would not concede any more wit to the metaphysical than to his. The issue between them, I argue, is whether the wit is apparent, like the metaphysical, or whether it is hidden behind a disguise of innocence, as often in Shakespeare, where — as Ransom charges — little more than random association seems to prevail. But, in contrast to Mizener, I insist that Shakespeare's poems neither should be nor are like the incompleteness and randomness of the contemplating mind, though they may initially fool us with the illusion of such a resemblance. So I see "the innocent insinuations of wit" resulting from devices like "association as dialectic" and "pun as argument." All that seems no more than casual turns out, through the expanding possibilities of the right word or phrase, to have been inevitable.

Mizener may have freed this critical tradition for a verbal criticism modeled on Shakespeare and having its source in him, but just as Coleridge had rescued Shakespeare from the charge of formlessness by redefining form, it was now necessary to re-

10. "The Innocent Insinuations of Wit: The Strategy of Language in Shakespeare's *Sonnets*," *The Play and Place of Criticism* (Baltimore: Johns Hopkins Press, 1967), pp. 19–36.

define precision and artfulness in order to find their sources outside the obvious precision and artfulness of metaphysical wit.
The focus must be seen as sharp rather than "soft," even as a
word's meanings multiply. In dealing with Sonnet 64 ("When I
have seen by Time's fell hand defaced"), I treated that same
polysemous word "state" (in the key unifying phrase, "inter-
change of state," line 9), but in a way that emphasized that
sharpness: "As if to prove the claim that the human political
state is a microcosmic reflection of the universal state under
time, the antagonists of the second quatrain, the ocean and the
shore, are rendered totally in human terms, as they act in ac-
cordance with political motives . . . All the realms of 'state' have
been identified and reduced to the extreme consequences of its
narrowest meaning, that of human politics. The word 'state,'
despite its range of meanings, from narrow to broad, from politics to the general condition of being (or rather of becoming),
is shown to be a single reductive entity that can contain and
unite them all even within its narrowest confines. For these
confines can be extended unlimitedly without losing their more
precise limitations." [11]

   This view sees the word as sending forth several diverse
meanings (and yet not so diverse after all) and yet as collaps-
ing them into itself as their single containing element. It is a
view which was first stated systematically for these critics in
Sigurd Burckhardt's essay, "The Poet as Fool and Priest," [12] an
essay which uses a Shakespearean sonnet as the source and the
model of its theory. Burckhardt describes this containing and
unifying element in the word as its "corporeality." The mere
sensuous existence of the word, this constellation of sounds and

   11. Or see my comments on "state" as it functions in Sonnet 124 (in
contrast to Mizener's), in *A Window to Criticism*, p. 141. It is an earlier
statement, but made in the same spirit: "The word 'state' permits us to
join the narrowest political notions in the poem to the broadest sense
of worldly life as the politic enterprise: state as majesty and as political
entity, state as rank or status, state as condition of being . . . In effect,
Shakespeare is demonstrating the sweep of the word's semantic history.
He proves the justness of his political metaphor by allowing his language
to establish the essential oneness of the several political levels of living.
Once again the metaphor is earned totally by moving from similarity to
substantive identity: the human condition *is* the political condition."
   12. *ELH*, XXIII (1956), 279–298; rptd. in *Shakespearean Meanings*
(Princeton: Princeton University Press, 1968).

meanings, allows it to take on a substance in which these elements are fused. The word can be forced by the poet to contain
within itself a world of elements otherwise incompatible with
each other. Hence, Burckhardt argues, verbal ambiguity is at the
heart of poetic possibility not because a word can have many
meanings (as Empson would have it), but because "many
meanings can have *one word*." "Ambiguity, then, becomes a test
case for the poet; insofar as he can vanquish it — not by split-
ting the word, but by fusing its meanings — he has succeeded in
making language into a true medium." That is to say, it is made
a medium like the physical realities of the plastic arts instead of
the transparent, referential sign, without substance, which words
are until the poet goes to work on them. The pun is the ideal example of how he forces the word to take on "corporeality,"
then, in that it is a single identity which, through a phonetic
coincidence, overwhelms other discrete entities and, by enfold-
ing them within itself, makes them an inevitable part of one another. The casual etymological accidents that produce a pun are
forced by the poet to take on the teleological pattern of necessity — surface takes on substance — but only *in* this word.
Other phonetic and metaphorical elements of words are shown
by Burckhardt to take on similarly substantive, corporeal functions, in defiance of the way language is supposed to function
normally. No wonder the poem is untranslatable into other
words than itself.

For Burckhardt, corporeality obviously serves as another
term for incarnation, the making of the word into flesh, in this
case the sensory medium becoming physical container of otherwise incompatible worlds, unifying them because the word is a
unit and they are *in it*. The overwhelming of discrete entities by
way of verbal aggrandizement is a violation of verbal property
and propriety, a subversion of the way language is to work. As
such, and as the word made flesh, this principle of verbal tele-
ology is the aesthetic equivalent of "miracle," though one li-
censed by what Shakespeare's strategy of language has revealed to us. In *A Window to Criticism* I freely call this opera-
tion of words "miraculous," borrowing the notion — ironically
— from Ransom, who was hardly intending to refer to Shakespeare when he used "miraculism" to describe the remarkable

workings of the metaphysical conceit.[13] He was trying to describe the way in which words as sensory and metaphorical elements overcome the limitations of words as concepts by achieving an identity in the poem that transforms the differential nature of words and concepts. And, as we have seen with other claims of Ransom, what was intended as favorable description of the metaphysicals (even if to the detriment of Shakespeare) was extended by others to Shakespeare, who was then shown to be preeminently deserving of the characterization. When George Steiner (whom one would think of as a critic of a very different sort) sought, in a quadricentennial essay, to account for Shakespeare's special magic, he had to point — in much the same spirit and even a similar language — to Shakespeare's power to create one "obvious miracle" after another.[14] "More than any other human intellect of which we have adequate record, Shakespeare used language in a condition of total possibility . . . To Shakespeare, more than to any other poet, the individual word was a nucleus surrounded by a field of complex energies." He goes on to speak of how "a word will shade, by pun or suggestion of sound, into an area of new definitions," or to speak of words that "derive their power to rouse and control our attention from the fact that Shakespeare has made explicit the buried strength of their etymologies."

These critics, with their several ways of claiming a secular miracle — a metaphorical equivalent of the religious one — in Shakespeare's handling of his language, are making more explicit the tendency we have noted, in its varying degrees, since Dryden to resort to irrationalist and magical terminology in dealing with Shakespeare's hold on us. They assume normal habits of semantics and logic to operate in our language, and (Ransom to the contrary notwithstanding) see Shakespeare as forcing upon language an illogic that opens for us, and yet controls, an untold pattern of semantic possibilities. Echoing earlier critics, modern critics since Mizener see Shakespeare as projecting a verbal power that makes mystics of us all. Rather than demythologizing this idolatry of the Shakespearean word, they

13. "Poetry: a Note in Ontology," *The World's Body*, pp. 139–140.
14. "Why, Man, He Doth Bestride the Narrow World Like a Colossus," *New York Times Book Review*, April 19, 1964, pp. 4–6, 43.

have reified it into a general critical system — a rare and daring enough undertaking in these demythologizing days.

But we must see this resort to miracle in its recent forms as a significantly qualified one. I qualified it earlier by speaking of "the aesthetic equivalent of miracle," by which I meant that it was confined to appearance only — as an illusion. Thus the claim to miracle is accompanied by considerable skepticism about the power of any language — even Shakespeare's — to be more than illusively substantive. His magic arises from his power to impose this illusion upon us while his words are doing their work, but of course such magic confesses its own limitations by accepting the aesthetic context within which it assumes those powers. Shakespeare himself, even while he displays his verbal mastery, uses that mastery to express his doubts about the ultimate power of words. His language everywhere reveals its awareness of the incapacity of words to contain their objects — its awareness of their emptiness. Yet, as Shakespeare maneuvers them, words find their unique power in the web they weave in awareness of this incapacity. They play violently and arrogantly with the normal workings of language, achieving a structure of their own that defies the lack to which they testify. Thus does verbal power derive from self-conscious verbal skepticism.

It is obvious, from my comments on recent word-centered criticism, that the Sonnets have played a central role in its development. Whether in Mizener's, in Burckhardt's, or in my own work, these poems permitted a concentration on purely verbal and figurative matters without the additional and complicating variables introduced in his dramatic poetry.[15] When Burckhardt moved to the plays in the balance of *Shakespearean Meanings*, he did so largely by way of the theoretical lessons learned in that key early essay which was enmeshed in his analysis of Sonnet 116 ("Let me not to the marriage of true minds"). Indeed, earlier New-Critical analysis of the plays had already established the practice of reading them more as poems than as dramas for the theater, so that once the words and fig-

15. According this central role to the Sonnets and to the words in them may seem especially revolutionary when we think of how commonplace it was for eighteenth-century critics to reject Shakespeare's language, finding unique value in him despite what they saw as either precious or clumsy—especially in the Sonnets.

ures were sufficiently probed, the problems of dramatic as well as poetic meanings were resolved. The procedures were similar to those we have been observing, more in keeping with the permissive attitude of Mizener than the no-nonsense attitude of Ransom. Thus the treatment of *Macbeth* by Cleanth Brooks, like the treatment of *1 Henry IV* by Brooks and Robert Heilman, is essentially that of a lengthy poem powered by Shakespearean verbal and metaphorical wit, with the dramatic elements falling into place within the poetic structure.[16] Indeed, as Brooks is establishing his method at the outset of *The Well Wrought Urn*, he calls upon his reading of "The Phoenix and the Turtle" to support a commitment to a use of language that, paradoxically, proclaims the destruction of reason in order to affirm the uniqueness of its own order. These are the claims — as this is the primacy of lyric over dramatic, of lyric as absorbing the dramatic—which we have observed in his recent fellow-critics.

So this theory, tailor-made for poetry, was also — as theory so often had been — tailor-made for Shakespeare, though in this case for the Shakespeare of the poems or of the poetry in the plays, if not the plays as poems. The theory is committed to the power of a verbal structure that undermines the capacity of words in order to create the possibility of its own equivocal existence. Hence, in the work of most of these writers we find an accompanying critical theme, similar to what we have just seen Brooks claim, about the subversion of reason by the poem — as by love — so that the poem, like love, can create its own more-than-logical order. Such an accompanying theme would seem inevitable, given the nature of the theory. It is the meta-poetic theme: that each poem must finally turn out to have been about the possibility of its own verbal creation. In effect, then, each poem is an implicit work of poetics as well as whatever else it explicitly may be. Such a development, we should note, is consistent with the historical claim with which I began: that, rather than being a history of Shakespearean criticism, the last three centuries of English criticism have been a series of literary

16. In Cleanth Brooks, *The Well Wrought Urn* (New York: Reynal and Hitchcock, 1947) and Cleanth Brooks and Robert B. Heilman, eds., *Understanding Drama* (New York: Holt, 1945).

theories developed in large part in response to Shakespearean texts which have been seen as licensing certain theoretical directions. So his poems, dramatic and otherwise, have long been permitted to function in the realm of poetics.

The metapoetic theme has permitted recent critics to adapt the principles of word-centered analysis to other centers of critical interest that are less reductive and more respectful of the other-than-verbal elements in the plays. I see no more promising example of such expansion of critical focus than in the work of the Renaissance comparatist, Rosalie Colie, who in the years preceding her death had turned increasingly to Shakespeare and had permitted her methods to be increasingly influenced by what she found in him and in those who have treated him in ways I have been describing here.[17] She modified the study of his language with the study of the genres and topoi of the Renaissance and the earlier periods that influenced their evolution. What made this study excitingly productive — and unique — was the way she showed the literary work to be the product of the mixing and mastering of these genres and topoi, showed it in the act of producing itself as a transformation of its informing elements, becoming at once a repository and a consummation of the literary past that nourished it. The problem of understanding the work becomes a reflection of the problem of the work finding itself in its elements, making itself out of those elements. Here is the metapoetic theme once more, though it is now functioning to trace the poet's remaking of the commonplace elements of genre and topos and not just his remaking of the commonplace words which have occupied our other critics.

17. In her encyclopedic work on Renaissance paradox, *Paradoxia Epidemica* (Princeton: Princeton University Press, 1966), she found in Shakespeare's work the moving force for several of her chapters (especially chapters 7, 12, and 15), and her concern with paradox naturally led her to mix verbal matters with ideational ones. Besides several other later essays on Shakespeare, the final work she saw through to completion was the lengthy study, *Shakespeare's Living Art* (Princeton: Princeton University Press, 1974). In addition there was the series of lectures, assembled for publication posthumously — *The Resources of Kind: Genre-Theory in the Renaissance*, ed. Barbara Lewalski (Berkeley and Los Angeles: University of California Press, 1973)—in which she culminates her argument by using as model her special favorite, *King Lear*, to which she refers as "an ultimate."

We should note also the criticism of James Calderwood as one which moves beyond purely verbal elements to dramatic ones, turning metapoetry into metadrama in order to preserve Shakespeare's theatrical along with his poetic brilliance.[18] Calderwood puts the word as spoken onstage into a dynamic relation to the action onstage, seeing the two as both partners and antagonists through which the Shakespearean drama works to solve the problem of its reality. We may feel the presence of Burckhardt's method at the starting point of Calderwood's work, but he has advanced the method by incorporating nonverbal elements as he makes the metapoem into drama. With recent work like Colie's and Calderwood's, we have the right to look for continuing developments in this line of criticism as, making use of its word-centered heritage, it yet escapes the limitations from which a devotion to the lyrics can suffer when applied to drama.[19]

Still, whatever we may say in defense of the continuing energies being displayed by this kind of criticism or in defense of its broadening directions, we must admit it to be partial and unbalanced — like all criticism. But any criticism so dominated by the experiencing of Shakespeare — and by the need to rationalize that incomparable experience — is perhaps fated to be especially unbalanced. We have noted that Burckhardt's "The Poet as Fool and Priest" found its way into a volume on Shakespeare's plays, and that my own recent contribution to modern poetics is joined to, and grows out of, my study of Shakespeare's Sonnets. There seems to be a hidden assumption in such critical works that a theory of poetry must begin by being adequate to Shakespeare, if it is to be adequate at all. I

18. *Shakespearean Metadrama: The Argument of the Play in* Titus Andronicus, Love's Labour's Lost, Romeo and Juliet, A Midsummer Night's Dream, *and* Richard II (Minneapolis: University of Minnesota Press, 1971). He presses this method further in *Metadrama in Shakespeare's Histories:* Richard II *to* Henry V, a volume to be published shortly.

19. This promise of further development is justified by other recent work in this line. See, just as a single example, Marjorie B. Garber, *Dream in Shakespeare: From Metaphor to Metamorphosis* (New Haven: Yale University Press, 1974). The subtitle alone would delight most of the critics I have been treating.

have been suggesting some such assumption as haunting the
long, unbalanced succession of the best English critics since
Dryden, with George Steiner's tribute to Shakespeare's verbal
power perhaps the epigraph to this historical consensus.

This is to make Shakespeare the test of a literary theory, to
define and measure poetry by its most splendid and incomparable examples — as was sometimes regretted, alas, when the
measuring instruments were applied to lesser poets. But so be
it. I began this essay, after all, by calling it a study of bardolatry
in its most recent form. So how can Shakespeare not be treated
as the model poet? And it should do more good than harm: in
an anti-verbal day Shakespearean criticism of this sort can give
the embattled humanist new courage. I said earlier that idolatry
must be either demythologized or reified into a critical system,
and that the new bardolaters had done the latter. When we hear
all around us of the need to "decenter" discourse, the need to
decenter the word's sense of the world, it is heartening to be
instructed in finding Shakespeare's capacious verbal center as
the center of order. Perhaps recent demythologizing critics have
suffered from not having Shakespeare to influence *their* theory.
When we hear such critics speak of the absence and the emptiness of language, surely the claim that the word can be made
utterly present — a claim supported by a poet whose works
everywhere invite reverence for the potentiality locked in language — must constitute one of the few healthy signs for the
future of criticism.

Contributors

MORTON W. BLOOMFIELD
Department of English
Harvard University

CYRUS HOY
Department of English
The University of Rochester

HALLETT SMITH
Huntington Library

ARTHUR SHERBO
Department of English
Michigan State University

DOUGLAS BUSH, Professor Emeritus
Department of English
Harvard University

PAUL A. CANTOR
Department of English
Harvard University

ALFRED HARBAGE, Professor Emeritus †
Department of English
Harvard University

DAVID H. HIRSCH
Department of English
Brown University

PAUL D'ANDREA
Humanities Program
University of Minnesota

MURRAY KRIEGER
Department of English and Comparative Literature
University of California, Irvine and Los Angeles

211

The eighth volume in this series, *Studies in Biography*, will be edited by Daniel Aaron; the ninth volume, *Literature in Ireland*, will be edited by John V. Kelleher.

Morton W. Bloomfield
Jerome H. Buckley
Harry Levin

— *Editorial Board*